Virginia Woolf and the Lives, Works, and Afterlives of the Brontës

Virginia Woolf and the Lives, Works, and Afterlives of the Brontës

Hilary Newman

LEXINGTON BOOKS
Lanham • Boulder • New York • London

Published by Lexington Books
An imprint of The Rowman & Littlefield Publishing Group, Inc.
4501 Forbes Boulevard, Suite 200, Lanham, Maryland 20706
www.rowman.com

86-90 Paul Street, London EC2A 4NE

Copyright © 2024 by The Rowman & Littlefield Publishing Group, Inc.

British Library Cataloguing in Publication Information Available

Library of Congress Cataloging-in-Publication Data

Names: Newman, Hilary, author.
Title: Virginia Woolf and the lives, works, and afterlives of the Brontës
/ Hilary Newman.
Description: Lanham: Lexington Books, 2024. | Includes bibliographical
references and index.
Identifiers: LCCN 2024004579 (print) | LCCN 2024004580 (ebook) | ISBN
9781666940220 (cloth) | ISBN 9781666940237 (epub)
Subjects: LCSH: Woolf, Virginia, 1882–1941—Criticism and interpretation. |
Brontë, Charlotte, 1816–1855—Influence. | Brontë, Emily,
1818-1848—Influence. | LCGFT: Literary criticism.
Classification: LCC PR6045.O72 Z8276 2024 (print) | LCC PR6045.O72
(ebook) | DDC 823/.912—dc23/eng/20240208
LC record available at https://lccn.loc.gov/2024004579
LC ebook record available at https://lccn.loc.gov/2024004580

For David Still (7 May 1946–23 August 2021)
I wish I could have shared the writing of this book with you, Davy.
Yet never has it been more truly said:
'I couldn't have written this book without you.'

Contents

Acknowledgments

I am indebted to many for help and moral support in the writing of this book. At an institutional level, I am pleased to acknowledge the Society of Authors for permission to quote from the Virginia Woolf writings, for which they own the rights.

On a more individual level, I wish to thank the former editor of *Brontë Studies,* Amber Adams, for reading through various drafts of the manuscript and making helpful and constructive suggestions to improve the book. I also thank my aunt, Dr Anne Crockford, and my friend Sarah Woods for constant support and encouragement. Also, thanks to Sue Larkin. And to Margaret Robson for her unfaltering belief in my critical skills. These people have been with me every step of the way.

Additionally, I am grateful to Dr V. Thiagamoorthy and Donna Douglas.

I am also indebted in more minor ways to Stuart N. Clarke and Sarah M. Hall of the Virginia Society of Great Britain.

List of Abbreviations

THE BRONTËS

Agnes Grey (Oxford: OUP, 1991)	*AG*
The Brotherton Collection	Brotherton
Brontë Society Transactions (1895–2001)	*BST*
Brontë Studies (from 2002)	*BS*
J.A.V. Chapple & Arthur Pollard (eds.),	
The Letters of Mrs Gaskell (Manchester:	
Manchester University Press, 1966)	*LMG*
Charlotte Brontë, 'Biographical Notices of	
Christine Alexander', *An Edition of the*	
Early Writings of Charlotte Brontë	
(Oxford: OUP, 1987–1991)	CAEW
Clement Shorter, *The Brontës; Life and Letters*	
(2 vols) (London: Hodder & Stoughton, 1908)	*L&L*
Elizabeth Gaskell, *The Life of Charlotte Brontë*	
(London: Smith, Elder, & Co, 1909)	*Life*
Ian Jack (ed.), Ellis and Acton Bell in	
Wuthering Heights (Oxford: OUP, 1981)	*CBBN*
Helen Glen (ed.), *Charlotte Brontë: Tales of*	
Angria (London: Penguin Books, 2006)	*Glen*
Jane Eyre (Oxford: OUP, 2000)	JE
Juliet Barker (ed.), *Charlotte Brontë's Juvenilia:*	
1829–35 (London: Penguin Books, 1996)	*JBCB*
Margaret Smith (ed.), *The Letters of Charlotte Brontë*	
(Oxford: Clarendon Press 1995–2004), 3 vols	*LCB*
Derek Roper & Edward Chitham (eds.),	
The Poems of Emily Brontë (Oxford: OUP, 1995)	R&C
The Professor (Oxford: OUP, 2008)	TP
Shirley (Oxford: OUP, 1998)	S

The Tenant of Wildfell Hall (Oxford: OUP, 2008)	TWH
Villette (Ontario, Canada: Broadview Editions, 2006)	V
Wuthering Heights (Oxford: OUP, 2009)	WH

VIRGINIA WOOLF

A Room of One's Own	*AROOO*
A Room of One's Own/ Three Guineas	
(London: Penguin Books, 1993)	*TG*
Between the Acts	*BTA*
Mark Hussey (ed.), *Between the Acts,*	
The Cambridge Edition	
(Cambridge: CUP, 2011)	*BTACE*
Susan Dick (ed.), *The Complete Shorter Fiction*	
(London: The Hogarth Press, 1985)	*CSF*
Anne Olivier Bell (ed.), The Diary of Virginia Woolf	
(5 vols.) (London: Hogarth Press, 1977–1984)	*D1–5*
Andrew McNeillie (ed.), *The Essays of Virginia Woolf*	
(vols 1–4) and Stuart N. Clarke (vols. 5 and 6)	
(London: Hogarth Press, 1986–2011)	*E1–5*
Flush (Oxford: OUP, 2000)	*Flush*
Jacob's Room (London: Penguin Books, 1992)	*JR*
Stuart N. Clarke (ed.), *Jacob's Room*, The	
Cambridge Edition (Cambridge: CUP, 2020)	*JRCE*
The Hyde Park Gate News (London: Hesperus	
Press Limited, 2005)	*HPGN*
Nigel Nicolson & Joanne Trautmann (eds.),	
The Letters of Virginia Woolf (6 vols.)	
(London: The Hogarth Press, 1975–1980)	*L1–6*
Mrs Dalloway (Oxford: OUP, 2000)	*MD*
Anne E. Fernald (ed.), *Mrs Dalloway*, The	
Cambridge Edition (Cambridge: CUP, 2015)	*MDCE*
Jeanne Schulkind (ed.), *Moments of Being*	
(London: Hogarth Press, 1985)	*MOB*
Night and Day (London: Penguin Books, 1992)	*ND*
Michael H. Whitworth (ed.), *Night and Day*,	
The Cambridge Edition (Cambridge: CUP, 2018)	*NDCE*
Orlando: A Biography (Oxford: OUP, 1992)	*O*
Mitchell A. Leaska (ed.), *The Pargiters*	
(London: Hogarth Press)	*P*

Mitchell A. Leaska (ed.), *A Passionate Apprentice*
   (London: Hogarth Press, 1990)   *PA*
Roger Fry: A Biography (London: Peregrine
   Books, 1979)   *RF*
To the Lighthouse (Oxford: OUP, 2000)   *TTL*
The Waves (Oxford: OUP, 2000)   *TW*
Herbert and Susan Sellers (eds.), *The Waves*,
   The Cambridge Edition (Cambridge: CUP, 2011)   *TWCE*
The Years (Oxford: OUP, 2000)   *TY*
The Years, The Cambridge Edition
   (Cambridge: CUP, 2012)   *TYCE*
The Voyage Out (Oxford: OUP, 2000)   *VO*

NOTE

I have chosen to use Clement Shorter's *The Brontës; Life and Letters* (2 vols) (London: Hodder & Stoughton, 1908) in preference to Margaret Smith's more extensive and accurate edition of Charlotte Brontë's letters, since we have evidence that Virginia Woolf was familiar with the 1908 edition. By using this, we know the extent of Woolf's knowledge of the Brontës' letters. If omissions corrected by Margaret Smith seem particularly significant to Woolf's understanding of the famous family, they will be drawn to my readers' attention. The only caution is that we cannot always know whether the extra letters presented by Margaret Smith were unknown to Shorter, or whether he suppressed them. Shorter, as much as Elizabeth Gaskell, wanted his own view of Charlotte Brontë to prevail.

Introduction

OUTLINE OF THIS BOOK

The thesis of this book is that while Virginia Woolf was intellectually a twentieth-century modernist writer, her emotional life had been at its most profound, and largely remained, in the intense Victorian period in which she had passed her childhood and early adulthood. Two of the most important relationships in her Victorian life had been terminated by deaths which shaped her as a person and determined many of her responses in later life. She returned to the Victorian period again and again, both in her criticism and in her novels. In many of the latter, her characters are reared in the Victorian era, and their experiences shape their lives, as they had hers. To a large extent she accepted the same literary canon that her father had, and among the novelists she continued to promote were the Brontë sisters. (It is important to note that when I write of the 'Brontë sisters' in connection with Woolf, I am referring only to Charlotte and Emily Brontë. Woolf, like the Victorians, and indeed among critics until well on in the twentieth century, were entirely dismissive of the claims of Anne Brontë. It is perhaps ironic that the feminists who would promote Woolf from the 1970s onwards, also resurrected Anne Brontë's novels, particularly *The Tenant of Wildfell Hall*, under the same broad banner of feminism.) This intellectual/emotional split frequently created an ambivalence in Woolf's attitude towards the Victorians and the Brontës.

In this book I look at Virginia Woolf and the Brontës from several angles. It will trace the Brontës' influence on Woolf personally, creatively, and professionally. This wide remit dictates the subject matter of each chapter.

Chapters 1 and 2 focus on the personal: it will be approached biographically, by looking at the common elements in the lives of the Brontës and Woolf. Each family's multiple bereavements and their consequences will dominate this opening chapter. It will include the resulting tight sibling bonding between the Brontë and the Stephen children. Both Charlotte Brontë and Woolf followed the pattern of seeking mother-surrogates. The Brontës and Woolf all suffered from a complex tangle of physical and mental ill health,

1

some of which we might classify as psychosomatic. Contemporary medical texts will be examined. These will include Thomas John Graham's *Modern Domestic Medicine* (the family Bible at the Parsonage); and for Virginia Woolf, the American S. Weir Mitchell (who devised the 'rest cures' that Woolf so detested and which her specialist inflicted upon her several times), and her regular practitioner throughout her youth, Sir George Savage, whose attitudes can be deduced from his book, *Insanity and Allied Neuroses: Practical and Clinical*. (This last book, perhaps surprisingly, illuminates the Brontë sisters' experiences of governessing.) I approach these medical texts from the same amateur perspective as that of the Brontës and Woolf themselves.

The importance of literary work to the Brontës (particularly Charlotte) and to Woolf will be explored. It is noteworthy that Charlotte Brontë and Woolf experience profound ambivalence to their literary work at times. When life was difficult, writing could be therapeutic, but writer's block could also cause acute anguish. The critics' responses could cause further pain to the authors; so much so, that they both refer to it (metaphorically) as a physical assault. The Brontës' anonymity as authors was of crucial importance to them. While Woolf published her novels under her own name, her early journalism was anonymously published. Later in life, she increasingly comes to value anonymity as a creative writer. A glance at the history of writers' anonymity, male and female, yields some surprising discoveries concerning the Brontës.

The Brontë and the Stephen children produced juvenilia. It is something of a mystery how this type of writing evolves into their mature writing. I examine the relevance of these juvenile writings to them as adult authors.

Chapter 3, continuing the personal influence of the Brontës on Woolf, examines Woolf's more private or personal comments on the Brontës, particularly stray comments in her letters and diaries which were not intended for publication. These range from observations on Charlotte Brontë's childlessness, through speculation as to what the Brontës would have done had they been Woolf's contemporaries, to the personality of Charlotte Brontë, which appealed to her more than Jane Austen's, and whom she would rather have met.

The latter part of chapter 3 I look at the occurrence and significance of Brontë allusions or references in Woolf's novels. The earliest reference to Charlotte Brontë occurs in *The Hyde Park Gate News*, when Woolf was thirteen years old. It is further evidence of the bookish household in which she was reared. It recurs in two of her early short stories: 'Memoirs of a Novelist' and 'A Society'. In Woolf's first novel, *The Voyage Out* (1915), it is Emily Brontë's *Wuthering Heights* which is in the possession of Rachel Vinrace when she sails for the New World. There are only two references to nineteenth-century women writers in *The Voyage Out* which is bristling with literary allusions to male writers. In *Night and Day*, though neither the

Brontës nor their novels are mentioned, it is entirely possible that the shrine to the great dead Victorian poet, Richard Alardyce, is based on Woolf's memories of the Brontë relics of which she gives details in her 1904 article on Haworth. In Woolf's first full-length experimental work, *Jacob's Room*, she comments on the absence of any mention of a Brontë, or other Victorian female writer, in the British Museum Library. In *Mrs Dalloway*, it is again Emily Brontë's *Wuthering Heights* which is possessed by Sally Seton, to whom Peter Walsh presents it. There follows a long omission of any Brontë reference after 1925, when Woolf herself was moving away from the Brontës as writers. In part of *The Years*, which was subsequently deleted, there is a surprising (though probably ironic) reference to *Jane Eyre*.

Chapter 4 turns to Woolf's professional life, and the presence of the Brontës therein. This chapter explores the influence of Woolf's eminent literary critic father, Sir Leslie Stephen, on his youngest daughter's perspectives on the Brontës as they presented themselves in her later reviews and essays. Stephen wrote on only two literary women at any length: Charlotte Brontë and George Eliot. He devotes an essay to Charlotte Brontë in his three-volume collection, *Hours in a Library,* and he wrote the *DNB* entry for her.

More generally, Leslie Stephen wrote four essays which had been largely neglected by critics. They are crucial to understanding Stephen as a literary critic and reveal a definite influence on Woolf's essays and reviews. These essays are: 'The Study of English Literature', 'The Essayists', 'Biography', and 'Thoughts on Criticism, by a Critic'. They are collected by S.O.A. Ullmann in *Men, Books, and Mountains*. There is a marked tradition of viewing Stephen as a typical male critic, but this series of essays suggest that this is a caricature. Examining these essays produces some very surprising results, as to the similarities between some of their aims and attitudes.

Chapter 5 continues to look at Woolf's relationship with the Brontës' biographies and works as they manifest themselves in her essays and articles. An account of recent interest in literary pilgrimages is scrutinised, particularly in relation to Woolf's 1904 visit to Haworth Parsonage. Woolf wrote a cluster of reviews about books concerned with literary pilgrimages and these will be related to Woolf's ideas. It may be significant that the Stephen siblings made a pilgrimage to St Ives in 1905: it was an extremely emotional return to her own Victorian past. Woolf also engages with Charlotte Brontë as a novelist, particularly her character creation and rejection of didacticism.

Chapter 6 devotes itself to two feminist polemics in which the Brontës, primarily Charlotte, feature. In *A Room of One's Own*, Woolf looks at Charlotte Brontë's *Jane Eyre*, about which she writes ambivalently. She argues that Charlotte Brontë obtruded her own anger at the limitations imposed upon women by a patriarchal society, and thus distorted what would have been a great work of art. This current debate about women's anger will be tapped into. Woolf also mediates between the competing status of Charlotte and Emily Brontë. They feature less prominently in *Three Guineas*, Anne Besnault helpfully suggests that Woolf uses the word 'tradition' in a particular and idiosyncratic way: in *A Room of One's Own* and *Three Guineas* 'it is not based on the expected opposition between old and new trends of thought'. In *A Room of One's Own* 'a "tradition" of their own is what women writers lack and urgently need to forge.' By contrast, Besnault sees in *Three Guineas* that 'tradition' is synonymous with patriarchal ideology; it is 'that ancestral memory which lies behind the present moment' (*TG*, 207) and in which 'the exclusion of women has remained the traditional attitude' (*TG*, 308).

Chapter 7 focuses on Woolf's role as a promoter of certain views of Charlotte Brontë through her professional life as a publisher. Between 1926 and 1936, the Hogarth Press published three important books on *Wuthering Heights*. These books will be analysed and placed within the context of Brontë criticism among Woolf's contemporaries. The 1930s Hogarth publications concerned the authorship of *Wuthering Heights* (for which no manuscript was extant) and which had been disputed since soon after Charlotte Brontë's death. It appears that during the 1930s Woolf ceased to write about the Brontës' novels but was keen to support scholarship which aimed to refute Branwell Brontë's putative authorship of *Wuthering Heights*. It was a subject which made Woolf emotional and even abusive!

A tentative conclusion will attempt to pull together all of the diverse matter of the chapters on Woolf's personal, professional, and creative interactions with the Brontës.

METHOD

This book represents an attempt to approach Woolf's writings on the Brontës in a Woolfian way. Of course, we should never forget that, unlike many commentators on the Brontës, she is approaching them from her own particular angle as a creative writer herself. Although we should expect such a conscious artist as Woolf to have special insights into the novels of other people, in an epigraph to *The Common Reader: Second Series* (1932), she actually allies herself with Samuel Johnson's ordinary or 'common reader' rather than with professional critics. Woolf stresses that this was her approach to literary criticism in a letter to her American publisher, when she describes this book as 'an unprofessional book of criticism'. She denies following any systematic study of literature; but claims she had simply written about books which she came across by chance. She claims that these books she had read in her role of novelist; but instead of suggesting this gave her any special insights, she stresses the reverse. She further dilutes her credentials when she insists that she had just as often read simply for amusement and without any desire to construct a literary theory (this letter is quoted in *E5*, 333).

Woolf several times analysed the best method for reading a book in the genre of what she called 'imaginative literature' (*E4*, 389). In her famous essay, 'How Should One Read a Book?', she draws attention to the question mark. She is adamant that she is not dictating a particular and/or definitely formulaic way of reading. Instead, she intimates that she will outline to her audience some of the reflections which have occurred to her when reading fiction. She stresses that reading techniques for imaginative literature cannot be taught, and anyhow, she wishes to avoid establishing any laws about it. Her task is also negative; she will suggest things that she has found best to avoid in her approach to reading. Her aim is to stimulate her audience into discovering 'better methods' of conducting their reading (*E4*, 389–90).

This method is particularly evident in *A Room of One's Own*: Woolf ironically comments she would never reach a conclusion, thus failing to fulfil the lecturer's chief task (*AROOO*, 3). She also, with equal irony, says at the end of the lecture that convention demands a peroration from her. She leaves that to men (who presumably developed these rules for lecturers; 99). She instead offers an active role to the audience: she suggests that throughout the talk her listeners have been summing up her character and the influence it has had on her opinions. She tells them, they have rightly been rejecting or accepting her ideas and developing their own independent opinions. She considers that truth is elusive and can only be reached 'by laying together many varieties of error' (*AROOO*, 95).

Woolf's success in conveying her method is highlighted by a reader's response to *AROOO*:

> You are not one of those mannish steady & stolidly, sometimes jolly Bank holiday, scribes, who for all their good writing make it clear that their word is law. "I know all about this. You don't. You <u>must</u> take my word for it. Take it or leave it." You have always, it seemed to me, had a game with your reader, have played—& fair. You may even on occasion have him, as they say, on a piece of string, & pull the leg. Conversation is like a game of tennis—there are 2 sides to the game—& each must keep its end up. . . . To read your work is to indulge in the most stimulating intellectual exercise (this is not to say that you can't get our sympathies). (*Woolf Studies Annual,* volume 12, 2006. Letter no. 24, October 23, 1928, 50)

Three Guineas is commonly regarded as a much angrier book than *A Room of One's Own*, but even in this polemic Woolf aims to stimulate people to reach their own conclusions and not to dictate: it was 'meant to stir, not charm;

to suggest; not to conclude' (Joanne Trautmann Banks, 'Some New Woolf Letters', *Modern Fiction Studies*, 199).

That this method was very likely to be misunderstood can be seen in how Arnold Bennett responded to *A Room of One's Own*. What Bennett intended as criticism, I would argue is a merit of Woolf's approach to essay-writing: 'And I have said that you never know where you are in a book of hers. *A Room of One's Own* is a further demonstration of this truth' (*Virginia Woolf: Critical Assessments*, volume 2. Ed. Eleanor McNees, 147). He added to his crass and patronising attitude when he further commented that Woolf's 'thesis is not apparently important to her, since she talks about everything but the thesis. If her mind was not what it is I should accuse her of wholesale padding. This would be unjust. She is not consciously guilty of padding' (148).

This book does not seek to 'convert' its reader to any particular view of Woolf's opinions about the Brontës. My thesis is, as stated, that Virginia Woolf was intellectually a Modernist novelist, but emotionally a Victorian, and that she repeatedly turned to experiences she had had in the nineteenth century in which she had passed her most formative years. Following a Woolfian approach, I present the material on which my opinion rests and suggest you consider the tentative suggestions I offer. Woolf repeatedly refuses to shut down differing perspectives, especially in her longer feminist polemics, *A Room of One's Own* and *Three Guineas*. How Woolf achieves this open-mindedness will be highlighted in the chapter which contains my discussion of these two books.

Arguably, this is equally true about her most successful fiction. For example, in *Between the Acts*, the reader is presented with a dichotomy or even a contradiction: is its vision of continuity or destruction? How effectively does Woolf balance the two ideas? How she leaves the final judgment to the reader is best illustrated by readers' responses. Mitchell A. Leaska describes *Between the Acts* as possibly 'the longest suicide note in the English language' (*Virginia Woolf: Pointz Hall*, 451). An equally well-respected academic, Gillian Beer, while recognising it has a darker side, calls it 'Woolf's most mischievous and playful work' (Introduction to *Between the Acts*, 1992, ix). I will be well-satisfied if this book causes you to reconsider the open-endedness of Woolf's vision in both her essays and in her fiction.

SOME GENERAL REMARKS

In her polemic about women writers, *A Room of One's Own* (1929), Virginia Woolf famously wrote, 'we think back through our mothers if we are women' (*A Room of One's Own/Three Guineas*, 69). Primary among these literary mothers were Charlotte and Emily Brontë. Woolf read and reread their novels throughout her life. At the time of Leonard Woolf's death in 1969, the Woolfs' joint library included an impressive number of various editions of the Brontë novels. There were Anne Brontë's *The Tenant of Wildfell Hall*; Emily Brontë's *Wuthering Heights*; and Charlotte Brontë's *The Professor, Shirley*, and two copies of *Villette* and *Twelve Adventurers and Other Stories*. There was also a complete seven-volume set of *The Life and Works of Charlotte Brontë and Her Sisters, with Introduction by Mrs Humphry Ward and Annotations to Mrs Gaskell's Life of Charlotte Brontë by Clement K. Shorter* (1924). There was also an incomplete twelve-volume edition of *The Works of Charlotte, Emily, and Anne Brontë* (1893). Surviving in the Woolfs' library were 1, 3–7, and 9–11 (*The Library of Leonard and Virginia Woolf A Short-title Catalog*, compiled and edited by Julia King and Laila Miletic-Vejzovic, 30). All these volumes were not solely purchased by the Woolfs. Some came to them through inheritance. It is likely that the 1893 edition came to Virginia Woolf from her father, Leslie Stephen. He also wrote literary criticism, most relevantly on Charlotte Brontë. One of the copies of *Villette* was dated 1853 and had the signature of Julia Stephen's first husband, Herbert Duckworth.

There were also several books about the Brontës remaining in the Woolfs' library. These were often books published by the Woolfs' Hogarth Press, several of which were published during the 1920s and 1930s. These included C. P. Sanger's *The Structure of Wuthering Heights* (1926); E. M. Delafield's *The Brontës, Their Lives Recorded by Their Contemporaries* (1935); and Irene Cooper Willis's *The Authorship of 'Wuthering Heights'* (1936). There are other books on the Brontës that we know Woolf read, but which were not in the library. One was Clement King Shorter's long-titled two-volume *The Brontës; Life and Letters, Being an Attempt to Present a Full and Final Record of the Lives of the Three Sisters, Charlotte, Emily and Anne Brontë from the Biographies of Mrs Gaskell and Others, and From Numerous Hitherto Unpublished MSS. and Letters* (1908). (Ironically, this proved not to be a 'full and final' record, as Charlotte Brontë's letters to her teacher in Brussels, hitherto unpublished in full, appeared in *The Times* in 1913.) Another book Woolf left a record of having read was Alice Law's *Emily Jane Brontë and the Authorship of 'Wuthering Heights'* (1928). Woolf was not sympathetic to this argument and did not retain the presentation copy that Law sent her. Neither did Woolf admire E. F. Benson's *Charlotte Brontë* (1932). Some of these will be discussed in due course.

The difficulties of negotiating a past literary epoch are well illustrated in an amusing fashion in *Orlando*. As a writer and woman in the Victorian period, Orlando wants to read the important novels of her era, so she instructs a bookseller to send them to her (*O*, 271). When she returns to her London home, she discovers that it is 'crammed' with the bookseller's delivery, for he has sent 'the whole of Victorian literature done up in grey paper and neatly tied with string' (*O*, 276). The narrator explains that 'of course, to the Victorians themselves Victorian literature meant not merely four great names separate and distinct but four great names sunk and embedded in a mass' of ephemeral authors' productions (276–77). By the time Woolf was writing, critics had decided on the literary canon for their age. This included Charlotte and Emily Brontë, the subjects, together with Virginia Woolf, of this book. Anne Brontë as a novelist was completely disregarded at this time. Later generations have been more appreciative of her work.

For Virginia Woolf, understanding the past and a person's place in history was essential. This is best expressed in *The Pargiters*: 'we cannot understand the present if we isolate it from the past. We must become the people that we were two or three generations ago. Let us be our grandmothers' (*The Pargiters*, 8). The reference to 'grandmothers' here stresses how important female predecessors were to Woolf. Yet, in *Between the Acts*, Mrs Swithin seems to deny history and historical change: 'The Victorians . . . I don't believe that there ever were such people. Only you and me and William dressed differently' (*BA*, 156). Lest this should be interpreted merely as the idiosyncratic view of a particular character, the impersonal, third-person narrator makes a similar comment: 'They were neither one thing nor the other; neither Victorians nor themselves' (*BA*, 159). These juxtaposed comments express the ambivalence that underlay many of Woolf's attitudes, and, more specifically, her perspective on the—and her—Victorian past.

Several of her friends and acquaintances observed how much of the Victorian age Woolf carried with her through life. Clive Bell wrote that he perceived in Woolf 'a sort, a very odd sort of Victorianism'. Bell believed that she had not only inherited her beauty and intelligence from her Victorian forebears; he also saw in her an inheritance of their moral code: 'Every good Victorian knew that a young man should have a sensible profession, something solid and secure, which would lead naturally to a comfortable old age and a fair provision for the children' (Noble, 71–72). Bell added that although Woolf knew intellectually that it was absurd, she could not refrain from suggesting this course of action to Lytton Strachey or Duncan Grant.

William Plomer also traced Woolf's and other Bloomsbury members' 'self-assurance' to the positions of their families in the Victorian world into which they had been born (Noble, 101). Another outsider, T. S. Eliot, believed that Woolf's position in society 'was due to a concurrence of qualities and circumstances which never happened before and which I do not think will ever happen again. It maintained the dignified and admirable tradition of Victorian upper middle-class culture' (Noble, 122).

Sir Osbert Sitwell, who was not intimate with Woolf, nevertheless observed that 'something of the Victorian past' hung 'about the Bloomsbury women'. He suggested that Woolf's appearance showed that 'in spite of the modernity that was also clearly hers', she also had the quality of 'a Victorian distinction' (Stape, 50–51). A similar comment was made by Hugh Walpole when he wrote that though she was a modernist in her feminism, she 'could not help but be courteous in the Victorian tradition even had she wished to.' He adds: 'And she did not so wish' (Stape, 188)

Like T. S. Eliot, Woolf firmly believed in a literary tradition, in her case both among male writers, and, more particularly among authoresses. She took a general position on older classics when she expressed her belief in the symbiotic relationship between past and present literature. (This was also central to T. S. Eliot's criticism.) It is perhaps relevant that she offers this opinion in an essay whose title of which she took from her Victorian literary father's three-volume collection of essays: *Hours in a Library*.

This symbiotic relationship between past and present literature was expressed in Woolf's 'How It Strikes a Contemporary', in which she appeals to contemporary writers to judge their own work by comparing them with the classics. But the latter should also be continually referred to check that they really deserve their high reputations. She advocates that some of the great nineteenth-century critic John Gibson Lockhart's irreverence for his own contemporaries should be applied by the present age to the works of dead writers (*E5*, 245). A distinction drawn by Leslie Stephen is illuminating: 'Contemporaries are interested by the accidents, and posterity by the essence' ('Art and Morality', 97).

It is noticeable that after 1918 there is a marked decrease in the number of essays Woolf devoted to the Brontës' novels. In volume 4 (1925–1928) of her essays there is only one, and this is on *Jane Eyre* and *Wuthering Heights*. Further, like Leslie Stephen, Woolf never devoted an entire essay to Emily Brontë. In volumes 3 (1919–1924), 5 (1929–1932), and 6 (1933–1941) there is no entire essay on the Brontës' novels, either in the form of one on a single sister or on them collectively. However, frequently in essays not specifically about the Brontës, references to some aspect of their lives or works crept in. By contrast, volumes 1 (1904–1912) and 2 (1919–1924) provide a rich crop of essays on Charlotte Brontë.

Some of Woolf's contemporaries linked the Brontës' novels with those of Virginia Woolf, while others wrote to her and made this connection. In a letter dated 22 November 1939, Elizabeth Jenkins wrote that when she heard of the Victorians excitedly awaiting the next great novel, it reminded her of how eagerly she anticipated Woolf's next work. Jenkins felt this connected her with the literary past, with such writers as Charlotte Brontë, and brought that period nearer to the present. She added that Woolf's works were 'in the same category as what we had understood to be great literature' (*WSA*, volume 12, 2006, 66–67). Leonard Woolf also compares two of Virginia's novels to the Brontës' novels: he thought that *The Waves* and *To the Lighthouse* are 'great' novels, by which he means they are on the same level as, say, a book by Charlotte Brontë or even George Eliot or probably *Wuthering Heights* (Stape, 150).

Another imaginative reader says she is paying Woolf the highest compliment which she can offer: that 'the egotistical adorable Charlotte Brontë would have loved' *The Waves*, 'not thinking of it as "literature," but poring over it over the fire as she sat lonely at Haworth, learning from it, adding from it to her pitiful store of the world—& people—knowledge, & with it oiling of her own stiff puppets' (*WSA*, volume 12, 2006, 120–21). Another letter, whilst connecting Woolf and the Brontës, does so by suggesting their difference: while she enjoys Woolf's novels, which she seems to link with the Russian novelists, from whom she rushes 'to the passionate, but safe, bosom of Charlotte Brontë or Jane Austen' (*WSA*, volume 12, 2006, 121).

Actually, Charlotte Brontë's novels—and certainly her sister Emily's *Wuthering Heights*—do not offer a 'safe bosom'; neither do Woolf's. As will emerge, the Brontë sisters' novels deal with the extremities of passion. Less noticeably, so do Woolf's. The latter thought that imaginative literature succeeded when it roused strong emotion in the reader. A brief look at *Mrs Dalloway* may be instanced. The characters in that book are at the extremes of emotional lability. Peter Walsh ruminates on 'these astonishing accesses of emotion' (68) and tells Sally at the party that in maturity 'one does not lose the power of feeling' (164). Many of the characters, major and minor, either cry or have tears in their eyes or wish to weep. Of the minor characters, Mr Bowlby, at the sight of widows and orphans, has 'tears in his eyes' (17) and Maisie Johnson 'positively felt she must cry' when witnessing the behaviour of Septimus and Rezia (23). It is perhaps not surprising that Rezia should shed tears over her husband's condition: 'Slightly waved by tears' her surroundings 'rose and fell before her eyes' (56). Later we are told that she 'cried for the first time since they were married' (76) and soon after Septimus hears her 'sobbing' (77). Septimus too weeps: 'Tears ran down his cheeks' (19) and perceiving beauty in music, he exclaimed 'Lovely' and 'the tears would run down his cheeks' (119). Miss Kilman is also lachrymose: treated badly in the war she 'had wept copiously' (105). And when she feels that Clarissa has mocked her, Miss Kilman 'very nearly burst into tears' (109). Both Clarissa and Peter weep at their morning reunion. Of Clarissa we are told: 'Quite simply she wiped her eyes' (37); while Peter 'burst into tears; wept . . . the tears running down his cheeks' (39). When alone, Peter feels he could 'now dissolve in tears' (129). Perhaps Clarissa cries the most and for the widest variety of causes. If she makes Miss Kilman want to cry, the feeling is reciprocated: anticipating Doris Kilman's violation of the soul makes

Clarissa 'want to cry' (107). When Peter imagines how Clarissa wrote her note to him, he visualises her 'with the tears running down her cheeks' (132). Finally, when, at the party, Mrs Hilbery tells Clarissa of her resemblance to her mother, we are told: 'And really Clarissa's eyes filled with tears' (149). If Woolf carried on this tradition, she artfully contained it by the tightly controlled form of her novels. *Mrs Dalloway* has as much intense emotion in it as *Wuthering Heights*. It may be significant that the major protagonists in the Dalloway thread were all mature by the end of the Victorian reign. The tears they shed are caused by the emotions they felt during their adolescence. Modern emotional experiences are also given, primarily through the Septimus Warren Smith thread.

There is an enormous shift in attitudes from those of her Victorian parents as expressed through her juvenilia, to those expressed as an adult. The extraordinary aspect of this revolution is that there is little evidence of how her transformation was affected. The process of turning into an intellectual modernist, while still feeling her emotional roots lay in her Victorian past, is almost seamless. Doubtless it occurred when the Stephen siblings moved to Bloomsbury, but she was not instantly converted to Cambridge values. We may glimpse, perhaps, the process of transformation in her early short story, 'Phyllis and Rosamond', where she compares the Victorian and the Modern ways of life and their values through the experiences of two sisters (perhaps loosely based on the two Stephen sisters). Woolf seems to have suggested that our relationship with the past changes as we grow older and change ourselves. She comments that the past is affected by the present and what she would write today about the past would not be the same as it would be in a year's time (*SP*, 75).

For several years following the rediscovery of Woolf in the 1970s, it was her claims to be a Modernist writer and a feminist which most critics emphasised. In my own educational institution during the 1980s, two academics taught *To the Lighthouse*. The divide was even then becoming apparent: one of the academics taught the novel as 'about' Victorian marriage, whilst the other focused on its modernist techniques. I adumbrate the structure of this book, provide an account and justification of the contents of each chapter, and a sketch of the method pursued in this study. I then engage with the critics I find most relevant to my area of exploration. Towards the end of the twentieth-century voices, like that of Janis Paul in 1987, began to reorient responses to Woolf's works by relating them to the Victorian period. During the twenty-first century this critical approach gradually accelerated. All of the critics I consider explicitly or implicitly subscribe to the view that the present can only be fully understood in terms of the past. I will conduct a brief chronological survey of critics from 1987, beginning with Janis Paul right up until 2022, with Anne Reus's book upon Woolf's Victorian inheritance.

PAST CRITICS ON VIRGINIA WOOLF AS A VICTORIAN

Janis M. Paul's book, *The Victorian Heritage of Virginia Woolf: The External World in Her Novels* was groundbreaking. Paul asserted that: 'Virginia Woolf's response to the past was intense and personal, for her early life could not have more accurately mirrored the age'. Paul closely focused on the novels, as the title of her book indicated she would. She rarely quotes, refers to, or discusses any of Woolf's essays, which might have been usefully used to illuminate certain attitudes or decisions Woolf adopts based on her Victorian heritage.

It is interesting that Paul halts her study with *To the Lighthouse* (1927). (Steve Ellis may have been influenced by this decision, for he subsequently argues that Woolf became more critical of Victorianism and the Victorians after this 1927 novel.) Paul divides her book into four parts:

1. 'The background', dealing with Victorianism in various cultural aspects
2. Tackles the early novels, viz., *The Voyage Out, Night and Day,* and *Jacob's Room*
3. Considers 'Two mature novels': *Mrs Dalloway* & *To the Lighthouse*
4. Conclusion

Paul's central thesis is that 'the external world' was 'Woolf's personal Victorian past transformed into the material of fiction' (4). Opposed to this, Paul asserted, was Woolf's 'Modernist exploration of consciousness'. Paul also regards Woolf's novels as an attempt 'to merge inner and outer realities' (4). Paul contends that Woolf's 'innovativeness is everywhere counterbalanced by a strong traditional identification' (5). Like her successors, Paul perceived Woolf's ambivalence to her Victorian past. Paul wished to place Woolf 'into the English novel tradition'. At the 'heart of her uniqueness' is her clear vision of 'the future of literature, yet she never ceased to look over her shoulder at the ghosts of the past' (47). Paul attempts to explain what 'Modern' meant to VW: perhaps not very helpfully, she concludes it meant 'un-Victorian' (51).

Paul states that: 'The Victorian Age defined itself in terms of great men and their deeds and set them in a medium of cultural progress' (13). The major influence in the formation of this concept was Thomas Carlyle, as is made clear in *Jacob's Room*. All this changed with the bloody conflict which broke out in the world in 1914. The shock of the First World War destroyed the Victorian view that civilisation was continuously progressing.

Jacob is seen as a transitional character. Paul argues that he is neither Victorian nor modern. Like most critics, Paul distinguishes between Woolf's pre- and post-war settings in her novels. Nevertheless, Paul also sees *Jacob's*

Room as continuing the eighteenth-century tradition of narrators, particularly Henry Fielding's *Tom Jones* and Laurence Sterne's *Tristram Shandy*. Paul identifies Woolf with these authors because they also forged a 'new narrative form' and like them, 'she is defining her genre and teaching her reader a new way of interpreting it' (117).

This actually places Woolf within a far wider context of the cycle of literary revolution and literary conservatism. It also implies that the novel form, established by the eighteenth-century novelists, continued and evolved naturally and unproblematically into the Victorian novel. This, it seems to suggest, continues harmoniously until the modern age, marked off by the First World War. After this Woolf finds this form inadequate to portray contemporary society.

Paul highlights how Woolf's ambivalence towards Victorianism and modernism are reflected in the structure of her novels and criticism: many of them 'use a dynamic of departure and return as their organizational pattern, beginning with a sense of order, taking off in a flight to freedom, and ending with a return to order. Often, they take flight into imagination and return to empirical reality' (37). Simultaneously, we recognise with Paul that 'Woolf's personal revolution was tame indeed . . . even later in life she approved of freedom and frankness in theory more than she could carry it out in practice' (26).

All Woolf's novels reveal the same ambivalence towards the 'Victorian world of time, place and society'. From this arises the structure of all her novels. Ultimately, Paul concludes that 'the enduring value of Woolf's novels is not predicated upon their Modernism—or their Victorianism, or any other "ism"' (189). Great art survives not because it faithfully portrays its own age, but because it transcends it. This conclusion strangely tends to undermine Paul's argument about the importance of the Victorian period to Woolf's fictional world. Although some of Paul's comments are insightful, her focus is on Woolf's fiction, whereas mine concentrates on her nonfiction.

Like the other critics I consider, Jane de Gay in *Virginia Woolf's Novels and the Literary Past* (2006) acknowledges that as well as being 'an innovative novelist and a radical thinker' who rejects the aesthetics of her literary ancestors, Woolf also 'looked backwards' and was 'immersed in the literary past' (1). Both influence her as reader, critic and novelist. Nevertheless, Woolf's experiments often lead her to draw upon the literary past, rather than unambiguously repudiating it. De Gay's aim is to examine these influences on Woolf's novels by examining her non-fiction material: diaries, essays, notebooks, and letters. This approach enables us to discover what and how she read texts from the literary past. De Gay quotes from Woolf's 1926 essay, 'How Should One Read a Book': 'Do not dictate to your author; try to become him. Be his fellow-worker and accomplice' (5).

Unlike some of the critics I examine, the word 'Victorian' is not included in de Gay's title. This accurately reflects the book's content: de Gay is ambitiously interested in tracing *all* literary influences on Woolf's writing and not just that of the Victorians. Additionally, de Gay argues for the influence on Woolf of a *male* literary tradition.

Like Paul, de Gay stresses Woolf's ambivalent attitude towards her past and her female predecessors: she was 'sceptical and suspicious of the legacy of some of her female precursors' (11). This was intensified by her father's 'qualified sympathy' for such writers as Charlotte Brontë (14). While reading the latter Woolf was ambivalent about claiming her for the female literary tradition.

De Gay devotes a chapter to each of Woolf's novels, in chronological order, in which she investigates her engagement with her literary precursors. De Gay states that how Woolf reacted to these past traditions 'was conditioned by personal, intellectual and political contexts' (17). Several of these chapters are therefore not about Victorianism and its effects on Woolf's novels. Indeed, chapter 3 examines Woolf's engagement with literature from the classical Greek period onwards.

Nonetheless one chapter is highly relevant to my area of research: chapter 4 is titled, '*To the Lighthouse* and the Ghost of Leslie Stephen'. This chapter is full of valuable insights into Woolf's practices as a novelist and critic. How Leslie Stephen influenced his youngest daughter's attitudes towards these forms of writing is built on these perceptions. De Gay's conclusion was that Woolf is less 'original' and 'new' than those who have stressed her modernist credentials. Simultaneously, Woolf appears more 'rooted; less sweepingly radical but more seriously engaged with currents of thought from classical times onward' (215). Thus, de Gay's focus is very wide; far wider than mine. But, inevitably, being inclusive of so extensive a period, de Gay spreads herself rather thinly. There is a breach here into which I intend to step.

Nicola J. Watson's *The Literary Tourist* (2006) devotes one chapter to Woolf's 1904 essay describing her pilgrimage to Haworth. This book is suggestive, but it is primarily a historical account of the origins and development of literary tourism and, in this respect, taps in well to a number of essays Woolf herself devoted to this subject around 1905, and which was returned to intermittently during later periods of her work.

Steve Ellis's self-declared aim in his book, *Virginia Woolf and the Victorians* (2007), is to 'offer an analysis of the comparison and evaluation of the Victorian and the modern that Woolf constantly undertakes in her work', but it is not 'a study of the Victorian literary influence on Woolf'. Ellis proposes to introduce another term to describe the period and world he believes Woolf inhabited: the 'post-Victorian' (7). He says this term was used several times in her lifetime. Nevertheless, he also acknowledges that this phrase was sometimes used with negative connotations. It suggests the continuity which always exists between different artificially constructed epochs, Steve Ellis's title, *Virginia Woolf and the Victorians*, may suggest an uncertainty about the term. He uses the phrase several times throughout his book, but the phrase 'post-Victorian' he excludes from the actual title. However, he wishes it to embrace it as a 'new way to approach the blend of conservatism and radicalism that informed [Virginia Woolf's] outlook' (9).

Additionally, however, Ellis fails to recognise that there is another era between the Victorian and the Moderns: that of the Edwardians. A more recent critic insightfully observes that focusing on the first decade of the twentieth century 'allows us to re-imagine the Victorian /Modern divide as one that is actually bridged by Edwardian literature' (LeeAnne M. Richardson, 83). This is one of the most important insights to emerge from recent studies of Woolf as a historian and historiographer, though these latter two categories are not the primary focus of this book.

Like Janis Paul and Jane de Gay before him, Ellis's main focus in on Woolf's novels, though like de Gay he refers to nonfiction to illuminate her long prose fictions. He shares their perception of the importance of her Victorian past to Woolf: 'It was never her project simply to despatch the Victorian period to the escaped-from regions of the past and congratulate herself on her own modernity'.

It is an important insight that Woolf particularly places herself in relation to her Victorian literary grandparents because of her dissatisfaction with her immediate predecessors whom she labels as 'Edwardians'. Woolf foregrounds the Edwardians (John Galsworthy, H. G. Wells, and Arnold Bennett) by the number of negative observations she makes upon them. I have explored the allusions to them and other writers, which has been revealing. Woolf alludes to Galsworthy thirteen times, H.G. Wells nineteen times, and Bennett twenty-three times. On the whole her allusions to her modernist contemporaries are sparse: three to Katherine Mansfield, thirteen to James Joyce, and five to Dorothy Richardson. There are many more allusions to Jane Austen and Victorian female authors: eighty-nine to Jane Austen, forty-five to the Brontës, and fifty-one to George Eliot. It might be assumed that this simply reflects that books for review were allocated to Woolf, rather than her choosing them, and that she was most often requested to write on canonical authors. In theory this was so, but the actual situation was more complex. Further, when she was an established reviewer, certainly by 1920, she decided what she wished to review. Neither did she always avail herself of the opportunity of writing about canonical authors. For example, in 1940 she declined reviewing a recent biography of George Eliot.

Ellis also perceptively points out that some of the experiences in *Mrs Dalloway* though they are being deployed to highlight the major effect the

First World War has had are actually simply based on Woolf's own experience. One of the most significant characters, Septimus Warren Smith, is supposed to be shell-shocked, but the origins of the description have their roots in Woolf's past, and at least partially from her *Victorian* past.

During the 1920s, Ellis views Woolf as in conflict between the Victorian and the modern. Of *To the Lighthouse,* he argues: 'the ambivalent response of new to old permeates the novel' (80). Ellis is the critic who most clearly detects a change in Woolf's attitudes to the Victorian and Modernist eras; this is important, because Woolf is always evolving. After *To the Lighthouse* he locates a 'more critical examination' of the Victorian past in Woolf's novels (107). It may be significant that I can trace the same movement in Woolf's nonfiction. After the 1920s, Woolf devoted fewer articles to the Victorian woman novelists, particularly the Brontës. During the 1930s she does not write publicly about the Brontës; she is content to leave their vindication to other biographers and critics. She moves on to other things, but she was eager for the Hogarth Press to publish other people's books on the Brontës if she approves of the perspective they adopt. For this reason, I devote a chapter to those works on the Brontës which the Woolfs' Hogarth Press published only: one important book on the Brontë in the 1920s, but they proliferate in the 1930s. The aspect with which Woolf engages most is the recurrent question of the authorship of *Wuthering Heights* (for which there is no extant manuscript). She is peculiarly resistant to the notion that it could have been written by the Brontë sisters' brother, Branwell. She engages with these writers on an emotional level rather than an intellectual one during these years.

Ellis also perceives a movement from Woolf's Victorian mother to her father, which he argues created a 'much less glamorised response' and culminates in the exposure of 'the repressive patriarchal legacy in *Three Guineas*' (107). With regard to the Brontës, Charlotte Brontë appears mainly as an example of the repression of Victorian woman, whose patriarchal father tries to prevent her marriage, because of his 'infantile fixation'. Though the Brontës as writers receive a mention in *Three Guineas* this only exposes their lack of influence in comparison with ladies who have salons attended by politically active figures. Of *The Years*, Ellis truly comments that 'neither modernity nor the Victorian seems a particularly hospitable era' (136). Ellis observes that in *The Years* Woolf ousts romance through the sexuality of the opening chapter. Overall, I think, however, it is possible to make a case for Woolf returning to a world familiar to both herself and the Brontës: that of sibling relationships. The multiple references to Wagner's *The Ring* and Sophocles's *Antigone* might be cited in support of this argument.

Of the vexed matter of Woolf's divided loyalty to the Victorian and the Modern, Ellis has the honesty and insight to accept that finally in *A Sketch of the Past*, there is 'no definite "summing up" of Woolf's Victorian inheritance but a position that is contradictory and indeed inconclusive' (155). This is the only realisation that can follow Woolf's comment about the past and the present. People develop and grow into different people, and so their relationship with the past and the present is never stationary. Woolf indeed sees herself as two distinct beings: 'I now, I then . . . this past is much affected by the present moment. What I write today I should not write in a year's time' (*SP*, 75). Life and memory create a kind of palimpsest of the mental and emotional faculties, which keep being fashioned anew. With the Brontës, who belonged to the Victorian period, Woolf's relationship and estimation kept changing throughout her life, as did her whole past.

Juliette Atkinson's *Victorian Biography Reconsidered: A Study of Nineteenth-Century 'Hidden' Lives* (2010), proposes that it is an oversimplification to view all Victorian biographies as 'wordy hagiographical tomes penned by whitewashing amateurs' (2). As I shall suggest, this prepares the reader of Leslie Stephen's biographical essays to find that they are more complex that has often been thought. Stephen was as ambivalent towards his chosen form, biography, as his daughter was towards hers, fiction. They shared an interest in the recording of the lives of the humble and obscure. Stephen saw such people as those who were not included in his own *DNB*, about whom it was difficult to obtain information. He placed himself in this category and was ambivalent towards the idea of his own life being written.

Marion Dell's task in her book, *Virginia Woolf's Influential Forebears: Julia Margaret Cameron, Anny Thackeray Ritchie and Julia Prinsep Stephen* (2015), was to trace the influence of three Victorian women. Two of them came through the maternal side of her inheritance: her mother, Julia Prinsep Stephen, and her great-aunt, Julia Margaret Cameron. Anny Thackeray Ritchie was an honorary aunt, being the maternal aunt of Woolf's half-sister, Laura Stephen. Ritchie therefore was connected through the paternal side of the Stephen family. I will be considering Julia Stephen as a maternal absence in Woolf's life in chapter 1. Dell rightly insists that our perceptions of Julia Stephen are almost exclusively created through other, mostly family members' constructs of her. Apart from some short stories, letters, and an essay on nursing the sick, which have been retrieved and partly published, Julia left no written record of her life. Prominent among her memorialists were her second husband, Leslie Stephen, and her youngest daughter, Virginia Woolf.

Apart from Dell's assertion that Woolf's rebellions against her Victorian past and to those, literary and familial, within it, were usually only 'tentative and ambivalent', this book does not greatly overlap or assist in my area of the study of Virginia Woolf and the Brontës (177). For my purposes, a study of the paternal inheritance and most particularly Leslie Stephen is more fruitful.

Like Ellis, Corbett in *Behind the Times: Virginia Woolf in Late-Victorian Contexts* (2020) perceives how Woolf constantly rewrites the Victorians.

Although Corbett's book traces the influence of some Victorian writers on Woolf, she focuses on the *late* Victorian women novelists. These were obviously at the other end of the Victorian age from the Brontës. Corbett, however, introduces at the forefront of her discussion the importance of Woolf's gender in her Victorian family and *Zeitgeist*, and how she experienced it differently because of this, as much as because of generational and age differences.

Corbett observes that apart from the four great nineteenth-century novelists (Jane Austen, Charlotte and Emily Brontë, and George Eliot), Woolf's criticism was not very attentive to women writers: 'The first "great" feminist writer of the twentieth century . . . was complicit in the exclusion of others from the women's tradition she did so much to establish'. Early in her writing career, Woolf rejected women writers who combined literature and politics, and those who achieved popular and/or financial success. She did not respond to the early feminism of the last two decades of the nineteenth century. Thus, Woolf's canon of nineteenth-century women writers was highly selective.

In the opening chapters of her book, Corbett focuses on the New Woman novels, which Woolf largely fails to engage with. Amongst these novelists, Corbett believes that Woolf only read Olive Schreiner and Elizabeth Robins. Corbett herself focuses analysis on New Woman novelist Sarah Grand. Corbett sees certain features of Grand's novels, especially her *Heavenly Twins*, as anticipating several of Woolf's concerns. During this period novels' subject matter continues to preoccupy itself with the same questions that lasted for over a century. These preoccupations, Corbett defines as 'questions of marriage, sexuality and conventional morality' (44). Additionally, some of Woolf's and Grand's views of earlier nineteenth-century writers coincide. For example, that Elizabeth Gaskell's novels fail to achieve greatness. Sarah Grand would come to question how far late-Victorian feminists achieve anything, a question which would come to preoccupy Woolf much later in her writing career.

But Woolf objected to the whole concept of novels written with a didactic purpose or to illustrate a theory. As many of these late-Victorian novels were of this kind, Woolf was not interested in them. Corbett points out that in this, Woolf was close to her father's attitude (as will be shown later, in my chapter on Leslie Stephen and Virginia Woolf as critics of the Brontës). Corbett usefully points out that Woolf's main access to books was through her father's library and that Stephen had no great interest in contemporary women novelists and actually possessed few books written by women. Those he did have were the four 'great' nineteenth-century women novelists. By the time Woolf was publishing reviews of contemporary novels the New Woman novels had fallen out of fashion and out of print.

Most of Corbett's discussion throws no light on Woolf's evolving attitude to the Brontë sisters' novels. Corbett dedicates a substantial amount of space to the professional careers of women novelists whom Woolf despises. These include Lucy Clifford and Mrs Humphry Ward. Corbett suggests that Woolf scorns these two women writers because of 'their doggedly professional approach to the business of literature . . . from which Woolf distanced herself and her generation, in casting it as 'a product of the 90ties' (144).

Corbett extends Dell's consideration of Woolf's maternal forebears; she includes her grandmother's family, the Pattles and a descendant from them, Lady Isabel Somerset. Unlike Marion Dell, however, Corbett does not trace a positive influence from the maternal side. Rather, she sees them as being complicit with 'the patriarchal colonial arrangements on which the empire depended at home and abroad. Corbett also examines Woolf's older contemporaries, particularly Margaret Llewelyn Davies and Janet Case.

Like Ellis, Corbett argues that Woolf turns afresh to a consideration of the influence of the Victorians in the 1930s; it 'was an act of invention that depends on reconceiving the past in new terms' (218). As we shall see, Charlotte Brontë features in this new mental landscape not primarily as a writer, but in terms of her biography as a woman oppressed by the prevailing patriarchy. Again, like Ellis, Corbett perceives that as Woolf moved through time her attitudes towards the Victorian past alters. This is an important insight. Another is that Woolf was idiosyncratically selective in which Victorian women writers she chooses to write about. Overall, though Corbett's book is of interest in its suggestion of the importance of Woolf's Victorianism in her life and work, it is not relevant to my approach to the subject.

Anne Reus's *Virginia Woolf and Nineteenth-Century Women Writers: Victorian Legacies and Literary Afterlives* (2022) is the most recent book on the subject of Virginia Woolf and Victorian women writers. It is also the one most relevant to my own project and that over a longer period than the others, as I was fortunate enough to read it when it was still a work in progress. Unlike the other books on Victorian women writers and Woolf considered above, Reus chooses not to focus on how these authoresses' fictional works influenced Woolf's own novels. The book's area of study is 'Woolf's literary biography' of these Victorian women writers (28). Reus's aim is to illuminate Woolf's 'engagement with nineteenth-century women writers, tracing how the tropes and narratives surrounding the domestic amateur writer constitutes a lasting Victorian legacy in Woolf's articles and reviews' (182).

The fact that Reus focuses on Woolf's 'article and reviews', clearly marks a new departure in the study of Victorian women writers' influence on Woolf (though Reus sees her book as complementing Corbett's). Reus reduces this ambitious project to manageable proportions by examining only those Victorian women writers who 'elicited a strong biographical response' from Woolf (28). The writers whose names appear in chapter headings and to whom she devotes considerable space are Jane Austen, Mary Russell Mitford, Elizabeth Barrett Browning, and Charlotte Brontë. Given less space and lacking a whole chapter focusing on them are Mrs Humphry Ward, Margaret Oliphant and—perhaps surprisingly—George Eliot. (I say surprisingly in connection with George Eliot, as she was one of the 'great four' whom Woolf named in *A Room of One's Own.*) The sixth, and final, chapter turns to the 'logical conclusion' of Woolf's (incomplete) autobiography (182). Reus's intention is also to highlight Woolf's ambivalent feminism, which we can trace in her responses to the Victorians.

Reus does well in emphasising Woolf's lifelong interest in biography and autobiography. Woolf was, of course, a reviewer for a decade before she became a published novelist. She displays a lifelong interest in obscure women's lives. She experiments in these genres as early as 1904 in 'The Journal of Mistress Joan Martyn'. Though Reus mentions this early short story, she begins her study with Woolf's 'Haworth, November 1904' and concludes with *Three Guineas* (1938).

As will be readily perceived, Reus's book analyses a large number of nineteenth-century women writers, canonical and noncanonical. Of greatest interest for my purposes, is the chapter '"That indefinable something": Charlotte Brontë and Protest'. This book focuses entirely on Virginia Woolf's changing attitudes to Charlotte and, to a lesser extent, Emily Brontë as novelists. It will aim to build on insights offered by Reus, particularly Woolf's ambivalence towards Charlotte Brontë.

Finally, some of the questions raised by Anne Besnault are challenging, though not all are relevant or conspicuous in my consideration of the Woolf and the Brontës. At times, the evidence contradicts Besnault's theories (though the exception may prove the rule). She chastises Woolf for not paying tribute 'to the "obscure" work of women historians, biographers and critics, three "masculine" domains that she helps to modernise and feminise while conversing almost exclusively with their male practitioners' (Besnault, 182). This is not accurate in describing Woolf's interactions with the Brontë's lives and works. All Woolf wrote about the Brontës, and Charlotte in particular, is shaped by Eliabeth Gaskell's *Life of Charlotte Brontë* (although Woolf was dismissive of Gaskell's novels). Yet Gaskell may have been an influence by virtue of the fact that Gaskell was primarily a novelist, for she did not object to what other critics saw as a novelistic approach by Gaskell to her subject's life. Similarly, though despising Mrs Humphry Ward's novels, Woolf values and respects her Brontë criticism, which she engages with in her review of the centenary volume of essays on Charlotte Brontë, edited by Ward.

Chapter One

Familial Similarities of the Brontës and Virginia Woolf

Both the Brontë and Stephen children suffered multiple bereavements in their family circles, over a period of several years. The Brontës lost their mother, after a protracted illness, at an early age, and their two eldest sisters, Maria and Elizabeth, a few years later. In adulthood, three of the four surviving children (Branwell, Emily, and Anne) all died within a single year. The series of bereavements which afflicted the Stephen children were similarly relentless. Virginia's mother died after a short illness. Only two years later, her half-sister Stella Duckworth died. In Woolf's early adulthood her father died and, less expectedly, her elder brother, Thoby Stephen. There are both similarities and differences in the nature of these deaths and how the survivors reacted to these multiple losses. This chapter will explore these bereavements and their two main consequences in both the case of the Brontës and Woolf: the tight bonding of the surviving children and Charlotte and Virginia's search for mother-figures or surrogates.

The Brontës' mother remains a shadowy figure. The editor of the most complete edition of Charlotte Brontë's letters, Margaret Smith, described Maria Branwell as seeming to have been 'an attractive, loving woman, capable of gentle liveliness, conventionally educated, and somewhat naïvely pious' (*The Letters of Charlotte Brontë*, volume 1, introduction, 2). The naïve piety is evidenced by Maria Brontë's essay entitled 'The Advantages of Poverty in Religious Concerns'. As Juliet Barker comments, in writing this essay, Maria Brontë supported Patrick Brontë's 'twin passions for conversion and education' (Juliet Barker, *The Brontës*, 69). It rather simplistically argued for the benefits of poverty for the religiously inclined. The intention was to publish this essay, but this project never reached fruition, perhaps because of the rapid series of pregnancies she went through, or perhaps she did submit it and it was rejected. Nevertheless, Patrick Brontë retained this essay, writing at the bottom of it: 'The above was written by my dear wife, and sent for insertion in one of the periodical publications.' He went on to admonish himself: 'Keep it, as a memorial of her' (Quoted by Sharon Wright, 173).

In early 1821, Maria Brontë suddenly became so ill that it was obvious to her distracted husband that she had a terminal disease. Although in the event Maria lingered for seven and a half months, her husband daily expected her death. Juliet Barker notes that 'Mrs Gaskell calls it an internal cancer; having given birth to six children in as many years at a comparatively late age, Maria was probably susceptible to uterine cancer' (Barker, note 49, 854). She was not ready to die; though suffering physically, she was more pained mentally by the thought of leaving her six young children motherless.

Finally, on 15 September 1821, Maria Brontë died. Her children were all very young when she died: the eldest of the children, Mrs Brontë's namesake, Maria, was only seven; the second daughter, Elizabeth was six; Charlotte was five; Branwell, the only boy, was four; Emily Jane was three; and Anne, the youngest child, was under two. Sadly, Mrs Brontë's children retained very little memory of her as a mother or as a woman. In contrast to Woolf's frequent allusions to her mother, references to Mrs Brontë by her children are so rare as to be almost nonexistent. Much later on in life, Charlotte Brontë revealingly and touchingly wrote in a letter: 'We can have but one father, but one mother, and when either is gone, we have lost what never can be replaced' (*L&L2*, no. 421: To W. S. Williams, 16 March 1850, 118)). The immediate catalyst for Charlotte Brontë's reflection on the irreparable loss of a parent was the presentation to her of her mother's letters to her father during their engagement. Their only surviving child was invited by her father to read them. Charlotte Brontë movingly described her reaction to these letters:

> I did read them, in a frame of mind I cannot describe. The papers were yellow with time, all having been written before I was born, it was strange now to peruse, for the first time, the records of a mind whence my own sprang; and most strange, and at once sad and sweet, to find that mind of a truly fine, pure, and elevated order. . . . There is a rectitude, a refinement, a constancy, a modesty, a sense, a gentleness about them indescribable. I wish that she had lived, and that I had known her. (*L&L2*, no. 418: To Ellen Nussey, 16 February 1850, 115)

Mrs Brontë was only thirty-eight when she died. Doubtless it was a blessing that she would never know that five of her six children would not even live to the age she had attained, and that there would be no direct descendants.

The earliest of Woolf's losses began at a later age than those of the Brontë children, but also occurred at a formative period of her development. Woolf's mother died in 1895, when her youngest daughter was thirteen. In her book on the loss of a parent in childhood, Maxine Harris emphasised that:

A child is not yet clear as to who he or she is. A child is totally dependent on family first and only peripherally on friends and schoolmates. A child is incapable of surviving alone . . .

The concepts and the very language of adult loss are inadequate to capture the panic, pain, terror, and confusion of a grieving child. (Harris, 4)

We have much more knowledge about how Woolf experienced her mother's death than we do of the same event on the emotions of the Brontë children. Perhaps because Woolf had twenty more years of life than Charlotte Brontë, she wrote more about the effects of the early deaths in her family. Her first written retrospective account of the family deaths began quite early, in her 1908 *Reminiscences*. For Woolf memories of the death of her mother were inextricably linked with her half-sister who also died only two years after Julia Stephen—Stella Duckworth, who was the only one of her half-siblings she loved all her life. As with the other early deaths in the family Stella was never forgotten. Stella's was a name that constantly recurred in Woolf's private writing, predominantly in her autobiographical pieces and her diary, but also, on occasions, in her letters. Like the four youngest Brontë siblings with Maria and Elizabeth Brontë, Woolf looked up to her older half-sister.

Woolf's first account reveals was ostensibly written for her pregnant sister, Vanessa Bell's expected child. In *Reminiscences*, Woolf wrote of her mother's death as having almost cosmic significance: 'her death was the greatest disaster that could happen; it was as though on some brilliant day of spring the racing clouds of a sudden stood still, grew dark, and massed themselves; the wind flagged, and all creatures on the earth moaned or wandered seeking aimlessly' (*R*, 40). After her mother's death, then, Virginia's very perception of the world was changed. Julia, her mother, had been the central person in her life: 'Certainly there she was, in the very centre of that great Cathedral space which was childhood; there she was from the very first' (*SP*, 81).

In 1939, Woolf related how Stella had taken her into her parents' bedroom to say a final goodbye to the corpse of her mother. Woolf instinctively recoiled from kissing her mother's face: it felt 'iron cold, and granulated'. Stella did not comment on this then, but gave Virginia time to recover by saying that their mother always liked to have a certain button on her nightgown undone, and undoing it. Later, in the nursery, Stella asked Virginia to forgive her as she had seen that she was afraid. But what was Stella asking Virginia's forgiveness for? Then it was Virginia's turn to frighten Stella. The young girl told Stella that when she saw Julia Stephen, she also saw a man sitting beside her mother. Stella evidently considered how she could best reassure the thirteen-year-old Virginia. After a pause, she commented that it was nice that their mother was not alone. At this distance in time, Woolf candidly admitted that she was uncertain whether she really saw this or whether she had been seeking attention (*SP*, 92).

The parties of young people, the laughter, and the summer clothes had all disappeared with Julia Stephen's death. Woolf recalled that it was eventually Stella who dispelled the gloom that had prevailed among the family following Julia's death (*SP*, 95). Woolf reflected that only she, her surviving two siblings, and their former cook at 22 Hyde Park Gate now remembered Stella. Woolf had never met anybody who resembled either her mother or Stella.

Stella became engaged to her long-time suitor, Jack Hills. Victorian marital practices continued to mean more to Woolf than the more casual modern alliances she saw around her. It was the Victorian engagement that for Woolf constituted her initial perception of heterosexual love, which was like a precious stone that she carried with her through her life, and with which she compared other engagements between young couples. Thus, Stella and Jack's relationship established a measurement of love for Woolf. The determinedly unconventional Woolf confessed that 'unofficial love' never raised the same emotions as had 'respectable engagements' in her Victorian past (*SP*, 105). This was not the only time Woolf expressed this view. In her diary she recalled how this vision persisted (*DII*, 22 August 1922, 190).

Stella Duckworth and Jack Hills were eventually married in April 1897. They returned after a fortnight's honeymoon, when Stella immediately became ill. After three months of fluctuating ill-health, Stella Hills died at the neighbouring 24 Hyde Park Gate on 27 July 1897. In some ways this struck Virginia as affecting her more greatly than her mother's death. Towards the end of her life, Woolf reflected that at thirteen she had been too young to understand the full implications of her mother's death, but by the age of fifteen, she was fully aware of its aftermath. She described Stella's death in an image of physical violence: she twice referred to it as a 'blow'. Then she combined this with a beautiful and delicate natural image to express the effect of this blow on her: it 'struck' her when she was 'tremulous' and 'filmy eyed' with her 'wings still creased, sitting there on the edge of my broken chrysalis' (*SP*, 124).

The fate of the children who suffer the early death of a parent seems often to depend on how much love and support the surviving parent or substitute can provide to the children in their continuing journey to adulthood. There have been many myths (began by Elizabeth Gaskell in her *Life of Charlotte Brontë*) about Patrick Brontë and his rearing of his motherless children. We know that Woolf was very familiar with Gaskell's *Life*, a source of many apocryphal tales of Patrick Brontë's bizarre behaviour, his cruel treatment of his children, and the deprivations he imposed upon them. It is not known whether Woolf believed these tales. If she did, Woolf may have felt an emotional bond with the Brontë children, believing them to have suffered from a tyrannical father resembling her own. She may even have thought that their putative experiences contributed to their creativity. She did not have the advantages of more recent scholars who have unearthed evidence of the father's deep interest in, and love for, his children, as well as his involvement in their childhood games. Indeed, the Brontë children seemed to have benefitted from a far more involved and supportive parent than the Stephens.

Stella Duckworth protected her two younger half-sisters from their father's grief to some extent. Her death changed all this. For the remaining females in the house—Virginia and her elder sister, Vanessa—one of the main consequences was that they were now exposed to the full blast of their father's character, and it 'was like being shut up in the same cage with a wild beast' (*SP*, 116). The Stephen girls resented Leslie Stephen's histrionics and the unreasonable demands he made on female family members. Made responsible for easing their father's grief, the Stephen children had neither time nor space to undertake their own mourning. While caring for their needy father, their own needs were overlooked.

This meant that part of the problem for Woolf and her siblings was the intense and self-centred nature of their father's grief. In *Reminiscences*, Woolf described how 'there were dreadful meal-times when, unable to hear what we said, or disdaining its comfort, he gave himself up to the passion which seemed to burn within him, and groaned aloud or protested again and again his wish to die' (*R*, 41). After Julia Stephen's death 'there was nothing left' of 'the common life of the family, very merry, very stirring, crowded with people' that had been created by their mother and which centred on her (*SP*, 84). Twice in the Stephens' juvenile newspaper, *The Hyde Park Gate News*, Julia Stephen was referred to as 'the head of the house' and 'the head of the family' (*HPGN*, 86 and 94).

Throughout her diaries (seriously begun in 1915 and maintained until just before her suicide), Woolf often noted the anniversaries of her mother's death. On 5 May 1919, she recalled the anniversary of Julia Stephen's death 'twenty something years ago.' She recollected the stench of wreaths in the hall at the family home, 22 Hyde Park Gate. In this diary entry, she saw her recurrent thoughts of her mother as being positive; they were 'as good a memorial as one could wish' (*D1*, 268).

Five years later, Woolf again recorded the anniversary of her mother's death. This time she had worked out very explicitly that this was the twenty-ninth anniversary. She recalled in detail her recollections of the morning of her mother's death, which she referred to only, euphemistically, as 'it' and 'that day', as though she could not bring herself to use the word 'death', which occurred on a Sunday. From the nursery window she had watched the retreating figure of their family doctor who had been present when Julia Stephen died. This account by Woolf of her mother's death verges on the blasphemous: imagining what their family doctor might have thought on leaving the house of death, she used the final words of Christ on the cross: 'It is finished'. (Incidentally, she reused these words again on the completion of Lily Briscoe's painting in *To the Lighthouse*, when they are ascribed to this amateur painter.) Woolf herself appeared to have harboured a lifelong guilt that she had not felt anything on the death of her mother, and that she could only laugh when confronted with the corpse of Julia Stephen. The death of Roger Fry in 1934 was the catalyst for the recurrence of this memory of what she saw as her inappropriate reaction to her mother's death: 'I remember turning aside at mother's bed, when she had died, & Stella took us in, to laugh, secretly, at the nurse crying. She's pretending, I said: aged 13. & was afraid I was not feeling enough' (*DIV*, 12 September 1934, 242). In 1939 Woolf once again recycled this recollection: 'I remember very clearly how even as I was taken to the bedside I noticed that one nurse was sobbing, and a desire to laugh came over me, and I said to myself as I have often done at moments of crisis since, "I feel nothing whatever"' (*SP*, 92). It is significant that the apparent inability to feel emotion when someone has died is a major symptom Woolf gave to the shell-shocked and psychotic Septimus Warren Smith in *Mrs Dalloway*.

In *A Sketch of the Past,* written right at the end of her life and left incomplete, Woolf returned to her early memories of loss. She did not modify her 1908 conclusion that her mother's death 'was the greatest disaster that could happen'. In fact, the death of her mother now struck her as having had a greater effect on her than the Cambridge Apostles, the Edwardian novelists, the war, or the gaining of the vote. She asserted that her mother had obsessed her between the ages of thirteen and forty-four. According to Woolf, what finally broke this obsession was the writing of the autobiographical novel, *To the Lighthouse*. She described how, when walking round the square where she lived (Tavistock), the novel suddenly rushed into her mind and rapidly developed. She admitted to being mystified as to the origins of her creativity in this instance and offered no explanation of why it flooded into her mind on one day rather than another. She perceptively recognised the cathartic effect on her of writing *To the Lighthouse*: indeed, she compared it to a patient's talking cure with a psychoanalyst. She could neither understand nor explain the process by which the confronting of her mother's death; the profound emotional effects it had on her resulted in a reduced strength and intensity in her subsequent recollections of these painful memories (*SP*, 80–81).

This weakening of the power of the emotions Woolf experienced surrounding her mother's death was perhaps only temporary. Towards the end of her life, she once more recorded the anniversary of her mother's death—the forty second. Significantly, she got the wrong date: she placed the anniversary on the 4th rather than the 5th of May. While this might appear to indicate that her grief had weakened, this conclusion may not be correct. That the writing of *To the Lighthouse* had not perhaps been as cathartic a process as she had optimistically believed is suggested by the fact that she was writing an auto-biography which dwelt on her early family life, and especially her mother, in the months which led up to her suicide.

Nevertheless, Woolf believed that she had had a positive inheritance from her mother: she valued her own sociability and joy in friendship which came from the maternal side (*DII*, 28 June 1923, 250). Unlike the Brontës, Woolf had been old enough when she lost her mother to be able to remember her. A side effect of her bereavement was (and arguably was for the Brontës too), a rapid development of her perceptions and intelligence. It is likely that the effects on both the Stephens and the Brontës of their experiences of bereave-ment led them to develop their verbal skills and intellects to cope with the all the vast and bewildering array of emotions that so often surround such an early loss of a central figure in the family circle. Woolf herself articulated this growth. She recorded that, for the first time, she understood a poem (whose title she could not now recall). She had the 'queer feeling' that 'poetry was coming true' (*SP*, 93).

Retrospectively, Woolf thought that the real tragedy of Julia Stephen's death was not that it caused her family intense unhappiness. Far worse was that it made their mother unreal, which forced her children to be serious and self-conscious, dulling and obscuring their legitimate emotions. It induced hypocrisy by forcing on them the conventional trappings of grief, while inhibiting its verbal expression (*SP*, 95). If Leslie Stephen obscured the real Julia Stephen by idealising her beyond all recognition, it could be argued that Woolf herself did the same. In 1923, the Woolfs hosted a dinner-party of ill-assorted guests. Woolf recorded that they had the family photographs out. Lytton had commented that Julia Stephen's mouth looked full of complaints and that he found her character unappealing. This criticism clearly upset Woolf; she recorded that it changed her memory of a past she had viewed as colourful and rich (*DII*, 17 March 1923, 239). Other, less congenial friends were valued either because they had liked her parents or because they could add their perceptions of Julia Stephen. Woolf defended Walter Headlam (one of her unsuccessful suitors) because he was 'one of the people who really cared for Father and Mother—he has pictures of them both in his rooms' (*L1*, no. 199: To Violet Dickinson, 6 December 1904, 163).

Later, Woolf was pleased to hear both good and bad things about her mother as long as they conveyed her as a real human being. When Woolf was presented with Femina-Vie Heureuse Prize for *To the Lighthouse*, the main pleasure of the day was meeting her parents' friend, Elizabeth Robins. The actress and writer told Woolf that she remembered Julia Stephen as a beauti-ful woman who was both spiritual and worldly. This apparent dichotomy was unified when, according to Robins, something *'vicious'* emerged from Julia's 'Madonna face' (*DIII*, 4 May 1928, 183).

Woolf had a more complicated experience of grieving when her father died because her attitude towards him was extremely complex. She claimed she also ceased to be obsessed with her father after writing *To the Lighthouse*. She would find herself arguing and raging against him long after he was dead. By the time she wrote *A Sketch of the Past*, she had become acquainted with some of Sigmund Freud's work and had learnt the word 'ambivalence', which described her feelings towards Stephen as a 'violently disturbing conflict of love and hate' (*SP*, 108). (In fact, the concept of ambivalence is applicable to many elements in Woolf's life, including her feelings about the Victorian period.)

These ambivalent feelings for her father made Woolf's grief for him difficult to cope with. He had had a long and gradual decline, before his cancer eventually killed him. After his death, she began to express her sense of loss. She experienced guilt feelings for not having done more for him, for not having assured him of her love. The feelings of bereavement were made even harder for her in that they were not shared by the other Stephen siblings. They were all keen to start life afresh in Bloomsbury and leave their past existence as children and young adults behind them at 22 Hyde Park Gate. Virginia suffered another mental breakdown.

However, as she advanced in age, Woolf took a more adult and mature view of her father. Nevertheless, she could still be defensive about her parents. Once again it was Lytton Strachey who criticised Leslie Stephen (as he had Julia Stephen). Woolf wrote back that she thought that the nineteenth-century was 'a great deal hotter in the head' than in the eighteenth century (in which Strachey had a particular interest). She was provoked into making this remark because Strachey had criticised Stephen for being a Victorian (which for Strachey was a matter of utter condemnation). Woolf wrote back that she was not shocked by Strachey's remark, but she went on to defend her father anyway (*L2*, no. 653: To Lytton Strachey, 16 November 1912, 13).

All six of Mrs Brontë's children survived her; but the two eldest sisters, Maria and Elizabeth, swiftly joined their mother under the stone tablet in the church. As we have seen, the Stephens shared the same experience of losing siblings. Once more Virginia and her siblings were older than the Brontë children were at the deaths of their two oldest siblings. In both families, the impact on the surviving children were formative and had a lifelong effect.

Ten-year-old Maria and nine-year-old Elizabeth had been dispatched to the Clergy Daughters' School at Cowan Bridge in Yorkshire on 21 July 1824. They were joined by Charlotte on 10 August 1824. Finally, these three were joined by six-year-old Emily on 25 November 1824. Charlotte Brontë in adult life blamed the unhealthy site of the school for the deaths of her two elder sisters. Patrick Brontë was informed that Maria was seriously ill in mid-February 1825 and he brought her home. By the time she returned to the Parsonage Maria's so consumption was so advanced that nothing could be done for her, except to allow her to die in a familiar and loved environment surrounded by her family. She survived nearly three months, dying on 6 May 1825 at the age of eleven.

A low fever swept through the Clergy Daughters' School at this time. The consequence was that the majority of the pupils were evacuated to a healthier site in Lancashire. However, that same day, 31 May 1825, Elizabeth was sent back to Haworth. Seeing that Elizabeth, too, was about to die of consumption, Patrick Brontë immediately went to the school and removed Charlotte and Emily. They arrived in time to witness the death of Elizabeth, aged ten, on 15 June 1825. That summer Charlotte was nine; Branwell turned eight that month; Emily was just about to become seven; and Anne was nearly five-an-a-half. Barker astutely comments on the effects of these two deaths on the remaining Brontë siblings:

> The deaths of Maria and Elizabeth had a traumatic effect on the remaining children. It was not simply that they had lost two of their sisters, but that they lost their two *eldest* sisters. The younger children had naturally looked to them for the leadership and support which elder children provide. In their case this role had taken on even greater importance because Maria, and to a lesser extent Elizabeth, had helped to fill the void caused by their mother's death so early in their lives. Once again they had been deprived of the maternal figure in the family. (Barker, 138)

Later Charlotte was sent to school again; this time it was to Roe Head, a boarding school run by Margaret Wooler. This was altogether a happier educational experience for Charlotte. She arrived at Wooler's establishment on 19 January 1831; her first sojourn there ended in June 1832. Certainly, in contrast to the Brontës' silence about their mother, Charlotte Brontë shared her memories of her deceased elder sisters; her friends testified that she often talked of Maria and Elizabeth during her time as a pupil at Roe Head. One of the two friends with whom Charlotte had lifelong friendships, Mary Taylor, recalled: 'I used to believe [Maria and Elizabeth] to have been wonders of talent and kindness'. It is sad to continue with the reading of Mary Taylor's letter, for she recorded a recurrent and distressing dream Charlotte had about her elder sisters, who 'were changed; they had forgotten what they used to care for. They were very fashionably dressed, and began criticising the room, &c' (Gaskell, *Life*, 104–105).

The four surviving Brontës lived on into adulthood, as did the four Stephen children. Both the Brontës and the Stephens forged strong sibling bonds in the face of their bereavements. Again, there are contrasts as well as comparisons. Elizabeth Gaskell had recognised the importance of the sibling bonds between the Brontës, even though by the time she became acquainted with Charlotte her brother and sisters were all dead: they 'were all in all to each other. I do not suppose that there ever was a family more tenderly bound to each other' (Gaskell, 56). Later, in the same biography, Gaskell wrote that the love between the three Brontë sisters 'was stronger than either death or life' (Gaskell, 162). Charlotte confirmed this closeness in a letter to one of her mother-substitutes: 'You, my dear Miss Wooler, know full as well as I do the value of sisters' affections to each other, there is nothing like it in this world, I believe, when they are nearly equal in age, and similar in education, tastes, and sentiments' (*L&L1,* no. 174: To Miss Wooler, 30 January 1846, 315). Charlotte Brontë expressed the same sentiment in a letter to Ellen Nussey's brother, Henry Nussey, when she agreed with his view that it is a hard thing for people who have to leave home to work among strangers. It is particularly hard leaving a '*good* home', though it is neither a wealthy nor splendid one and would not appeal to strangers. But her home gives her what she could not find elsewhere 'the profound, the intense affection which brothers and sisters feel for each other when their minds are cast in the same mould, their ideas drawn from the same source—when they have clung to each other from childhood and when disputes have never sprung up to divide them' (*L&L1,* no. 87: To the Rev Henry Nussey, 9 May 1841, 210–11). Charlotte compares the situation of the Misses Ringrose to her own home: they must have 'a very unhappy home. Yours and mine, with all disadvantages, all absences of luxury and wealth and style, are I doubt not, happier' (*L&L1,* no. 249: To Ellen Nussey, 29 November 1847, 370). Significantly, Charlotte Brontë undermined the attitude her first biographer would take to Mr Brontë, by writing that the Ringrose sisters 'have it is plain, no support in either parent'. (The implication of this internal evidence also confirms modern scholarship's conclusion that Patrick Brontë was a much better father than Gaskell had allowed.)

Their reactions to their different siblings' deaths unsurprisingly reflect the attitudes that had evolved throughout childhood and into their adulthood. The years 1848–1849 saw the deaths of Charlotte Brontë's three surviving siblings in rapid and nightmarish succession. Uncannily, Charlotte Brontë had anticipated just such a bereavement situation in 1840 that would become hers less than a decade later. Charlotte Brontë's lifelong friend, Ellen Nussey, had communicated the death of a young woman called Ann Cook. In her reply, Charlotte said that she had 'cared for' Ann Cook and is distressed by the thought that the deceased woman could not now be found anywhere in the world. Then comes the prophecy: 'A bereavement of this kind gives one a glimpse of the feeling those must have who have seen all drop round them, friend after friend, and are left to end their pilgrimage alone' (*L&L1*, no. 61: To Ellen Nussey, 12 January 1840, 173).

During periods of separation, the Brontë siblings highly valued letters from home, which were sure to be understood. While away from Haworth as a governess, Charlotte wrote to Emily: 'Mine bonnie love, I was as glad of your letter as tongue can express: it is a real, genuine pleasure to hear from home; a thing to be saved till bedtime, when one has a moment's quiet and rest to enjoy it thoroughly'. Only at home could she find 'mental liberty' and a freedom from restraint (*L&L1*, no. 53: To Emily J. Brontë, July —, 1839, 161–62).

While alone in Brussels at the Hegers' school, Charlotte wrote to Emily that she would really have liked to be at home. She imagined the inmates of the parsonage and their occupations, as she wrote. She was concerned for the health of those remaining there. During the same period, she wrote to her brother that she regretted that she had not heard from him, as she had been told to expect a letter from him. She was concerned about the depleted family at the parsonage and wanted to know all about the health and spirits of the family. She requested both Branwell and Anne Brontë to write to her. Interestingly, she wrote to her brother that when she was alone in the dormitory, she frequently recurred 'as fanatically as ever to the old ideas, the old faces, and the old scenes in the world below'. By this she meant the imaginary world they created in their Angrian juvenilia (*L&L1*, no. 123: To Branwell Brontë, 1 May 1843, 267). Emily and Anne wrote diary papers to be opened by each in four years' time. They were written on Emily's birthday. Emily hoped that her father and all her siblings will then all be 'stout and hearty' (*L&L1*, Emily J. Brontë, Diary Paper 30 July1841, 216). Anne was also family-orientated in her diary paper: she listed where her siblings were. Both these sisters, like their older siblings, wrote of their own imaginary kingdom of Gondal (*L&L1*, Anne Brontë, Diary Paper 30 July 1841, 216–17). In another letter to Emily, when Charlotte was a governess with the Sidgwick family, she stipulated that it should only be shared with the other sibling still at home, Branwell (*L&L1*, no. 51: To Emily J. Brontë, 8 June 1839, 159).

Charlotte Brontë was the only sister who made friends with women outside the parsonage. However, all her siblings took the same attitude to these female friends as Charlotte herself. Though Anne Brontë was still a governess at Thorp Green, the other siblings at home had 'unanimously requested' Ellen Nussey to come to the parsonage and stay as long as she is able (*L&L1*, no. 89: To Ellen Nussey, 1 July 1841, 213). In another letter to Ellen Nussey, Charlotte revealed the whole household's involvement with her friend, when she passed on a message from her brother: 'Branwell wants to know why you carefully exclude all mention of him when you particularly send your regards to every other member of the family. He desires to know whether and in what he has offended you, or whether it is considered improper for a young lady to mention the gentlemen of a house' (*L&L1*, no. 116: To Ellen Nussey, 10 January 1843, 252). When all the siblings were reunited at the parsonage in June 1844, Charlotte Brontë wrote that all the siblings want Ellen Nussey to visit them in Haworth (*L&L1*, no. 138: To Ellen Nussey, 9 June 1844, 282). Two years later, Charlotte wished that her two sisters, herself, and Ellen Nussey could all go away together in search of recreation, from which she felt they would all benefit (*L&L1*, no. 200: To Ellen Nussey, 24 July 1846, 333–34).

Many of the comments on the Brontës sibling relationships are also relevant to the Stephen children who grew up during the late Victorian period. Despite advances in the education and employment of girls and women by the time the twentieth century was ushered in, many middle-class lives—including the Stephens'—were marked by the same divisions between male and female siblings. In her brilliant book about the brother-sister relationship in nineteenth-century literature, Valerie Sanders wrote that during this Victorian period it was the 'schoolroom' which was the 'place where the differences between [brothers and sisters] first became manifest'. Sanders argued that a middle-class girl was largely educated at home, while her brother was sent away to be educated at a public school, often followed by university (Sanders, 17). Though this may have been the general trend during the Victorian period, it was not followed but reversed in the Brontë family. It was the Brontë sisters who were sent to boarding schools: Cowan Bridge followed by the Roe Head school, and Charlotte and Emily both went to Brussels to attend a continental boarding school. By contrast, Branwell Brontë did not attend a school at all but was solely educated by his father. He was taught the traditional subjects for boys from which sisters were generally excluded: classical Greek and Latin. Emily and Anne Brontë, however, appear to have acquired some knowledge of Latin.

Like the four surviving Brontë children, though for different reasons, the four Stephen children were also an entirely self-contained unit, as Woolf described it: At Talland House in Cornwall, '[w]e never had friends to stay with us. Nor did we want them. "Us four" were completely self-sufficient' (*SP*, 129). Also, like the Brontës, the Stephen siblings continued to live in harmony when they were young adults. They moved as a single unit from Kensington to Bloomsbury after their father's death early in 1904 and travelled abroad together for their holidays. After the death of Leslie Stephen, Virginia, was comforted by the thought that the siblings still had each other, which made her feel her parents were also nearby (*L1*, no. 165: To Janet Case, 23 February 1904, 129). Virginia conveyed an impression of the irreverent, but harmonious, young Stephens when she described Vanessa reading the most ridiculous novels aloud (which provoked shared laughter) and shared their drawings, decent and indecent (which caused more amusement). Apart from Thoby's and Adrian's predilection for hunting, the four siblings were remarkably united in their interests and pursuits (*L1*, no. 206: To Violet Dickinson, early January 1905, 172).

As with the four surviving Brontë siblings, the Stephens, once they had reached young adulthood, all seemed to appreciate each other's friends. For example, all the Stephen siblings seemed to like and welcome Virginia's special friend, Violet Dickinson. When Vanessa, Virginia, and Adrian were going to Cambridge to furnish Adrian's rooms there, Virginia reported that Adrian humbly requested that Violet would also come (*L1*, no. 92: To Violet Dickinson, 22 July 1903, 86). The following day, Virginia asked Dickinson to come and rejoice all their hearts (*L1,* no. 93: To Violet Dickinson, 23 July 1903, 86). The following month, Virginia told Dickinson that the four Stephen siblings had all benefited in every way from Violet's visit (*L1*, no. 97: To Violet Dickinson, August 1903, 90). On another occasion, Thoby Stephen also sent a message via Virginia to Dickinson asking if he could come and consult her about a long walk in her area that he was planning (*L1*, no. 110: To Violet Dickinson, October/November 1903, 103). A final example may be taken from the period after Leslie Stephen's death when Virginia praised and thanked Violet's benevolence in visiting them and raising their spirits. So much so, that Thoby and Adrian wanted to know why another visit had not been planned (*L1*, no. 180: To Violet Dickinson, 17 September 1904, 142). Ultimately, however, for the Stephens, the most important shared friends were Thoby's Cambridge friends. They all remained friends after Thoby's tragic premature death and formed the nucleus of the now-famous Bloomsbury Group.

It is fruitful to examine the very different reactions of Charlotte Brontë and Woolf to the death of a brother: those of Branwell Brontë and Thoby Stephen. Branwell cannot be excluded from any assessment of the influences on his three surviving sisters' lives and novels. He, and to a lesser extent Thoby, were collaborators in the writing of the juvenilia. As is well known the present of a box of twelve soldiers to Branwell from his father was the immediate catalyst for the beginning of their long saga about imaginary kingdoms. While Emily and Anne Brontë soon retreated into their own individually pursued imaginary world of Gondal, Charlotte and Branwell collaborated well into adulthood. Originally Charlotte and Branwell were secure enough in their mutual regard to satirise each other in their little books. As Christine Alexander wrote, the early juvenilia dated 1829 to 1832 'display a healthy rivalry between the aspiring authors' (*The Early Writings of Charlotte Brontë 1826–1832*, xvi-xvii). As Alexander also pointed out, Branwell's favourite subject was the wars fought in the imaginary kingdoms, but Charlotte 'was tired of war' and her favourite topic was 'the domestic life of her characters' (*The Early Writings of Charlotte Brontë*, 149).

Within their juvenilia, both Charlotte and Branwell explored narrators who were of the opposite sex to themselves. Charlotte created several male narrators including Lord Charles Wellesley. In her first novel, *The Professor* (posthumously published), she would retain a male narrator. Her sisters also used male narrators, though in both *Wuthering Heights* and *The Tenant of Wildfell Hall*, Lockwood and Gilbert Markham share their narration with female narrators (Ellen Dean and Helen Huntingdon). Branwell reversed this process and gave his narrator the female identity of Harriet in his two Caroline poems, 'Caroline's Prayer. On the Change from Childhood to Womanhood' (1842) and 'Caroline' (1845). The former may strike one as a strange subject for a young man to explore; but as Sanders wrote: 'all the Brontës valued the uses of androgyny for what they wanted to say about themselves' (Sanders, 141). This was a narrative position that Woolf argued for in *A Room of One's Own* (1929).

However, Branwell gradually alienated all his sisters, possibly because of an over-identification with him of what were then seen as particularly masculine vices—drunkenness, opium addiction, and the inability to hold down a job or pursue a career. Branwell's decline and death were reflected by each of his novelist sisters: John Reed in *Jane Eyre*, Hindley Earnshaw in *Wuthering Heights*, and Arthur Huntingdon in *The Tenant of Wildfell Hall*. All this, however, lay in the future.

Branwell was the first and perhaps the least lamented sibling to die. Strangely, Branwell, like Charlotte, also sketched out his future life when explaining the subject matter of a poem in a letter to William Wordsworth: he described how he had 'striven to develop strong passions and weak principles struggling with a high imagination and acute feelings, till, as youth hardens towards age, evil deeds and short enjoyments end in mental misery and bodily ruin' (*L&L1*, no. 35: To William Wordsworth, 19 January 1837, 136).

For the last eighteen months of his life, he had abused drink and drugs, and this had disguised the fact that he was in the throes of rapidly progressing consumption. Two days before he died, he was still able to walk down the lane to the village, although he needed help to make the return journey. The following day he was unable to rise from his bed. Patrick Brontë wrestled with his dying son to persuade him to repent of his misspent life, which Branwell eventually did. The following morning, the 24 September 1848, Branwell died at the age of thirty-one. Writing to her publisher, Charlotte Brontë lamented her brother's unproductive life; he had once been 'his Father's and his sisters' pride and hope in boyhood'. She continued:

I do not weep from a sense of bereavement—there is no prop withdrawn, no consolation torn away, no dear companion lost—but for the wreck of talent, the ruin of promise, the untimely dreary extinction of what might have been a burning and a shining light. My brother was a year my junior. I had aspirations and ambitions for him once, long ago—they have perished mournfully. Nothing remains of him but a memory of errors and sufferings. There is such a bitterness of pity for his life and death, such a yearning for the emptiness of his whole existence as I cannot describe. (*L&L1*, no. 306: To W. S. Williams, 2 October 1848, 453)

Nevertheless, it was the first death bed as an adult that Charlotte Brontë had attended, and after witnessing Branwell's death, she succumbed to an illness, which seemed to combine the physical and mental. Yet, after only four days, her bitter tone at wasted talents and bad behaviour had been replaced by better feelings: 'All his errors—to speak plainly, all his vices—seemed nothing to me in that moment: every wrong he had done, every pain he had caused, vanished; his sufferings only were remembered; the wrench to the natural affections only was left' (*L&L1*, no. 307: To W. S. Williams, 6 October 1848, 455).

Like the Brontës expectations of Branwell Brontë, the Stephens had great hopes of Thoby Stephen. He was Woolf's elder, (and favourite) brother who died aged twenty-six on 20 November 1906 of typhoid, which he contracted while on holiday in Greece with his siblings and a family friend, Violet Dickinson. Unlike Branwell who appeared to die burnt out physically and mentally, having failed to achieve anything lasting, Thoby was felt by Woolf to have died before he had had a chance to fulfil his potential. At various stages of her life, she would consider what Thoby might have done or been. Nigel Nicolson has drawn a perceptive parallel between Charlotte Brontë's brother Branwell and Thoby Stephen and Virginia: her 'brother was to her what Branwell had been to Charlotte Brontë before he came dissolute. He was her friend and leader and (within certain limits) her confidant' (*LI*, Introduction, xvii).

As with other losses, Woolf remembered Thoby with regret for his death for the rest of her life. She wrote of the effect of his death on her to her confidante Violet Dickinson: she felt rigidly trapped in grief and the pain remained undiminished (*LI*, no. 376: To Violet Dickinson, 8 August 1907, 303). Thoby makes repeated appearances in both Woolf's letters and diaries over the years. He became that 'queer ghost' and Woolf often thought of her own death 'as the end of an excursion which I went on when he died' (*DIII*, 26 December 1929, 275). Yet in the same diary entry, she perceived that the Thoby who is revealed in some of his letters read out by Clive Bell, made him seem unfamiliar, and 'strange and external'. When her nephew, Julian Bell, died in Spain, Woolf compared and contrasted his death with Thoby's (*DV*, 12 October 1937, 113).

Like the Brontë sisters, the Stephen girls received a different education from their brothers. Marianne Thormählen commented that: 'A component in the protracted ancients-versus-moderns battles', with the former generally confined to a boy's education and the latter to a girl's, 'was a disputed subject for generations' (Thormählen, 130). The argument was not resolved by the time of Virginia's girlhood: her brothers and half-brothers were all sent to public schools and Cambridge University where classical education was considered essential. However, Virginia was aware of what she was being deprived of when she wrote that she had no one to argue with and had to painfully extract knowledge from books. She felt Thoby's talk with peers at Cambridge was a much preferable and more successful way of learning. Lacking that, it was unsurprising how comparatively little she knew (*L1*, no. 81: To Thoby Stephen, May 1903, 77). Woolf came to hold this as a grievance, but she would not use her personal experience in her feminist polemic *A Room of One's Own* (1929) because she believed that no one would take her seriously. However, she stated the position baldly to Ethel Smyth: the fact of the matter was she was ignorant because the education of her brothers had consumed all the Stephen family's funds (*L5*, no. 2746: To Ethel Smyth, 8 June 1933, 195).

Nevertheless, things *had* changed by her youth. In practice, Thoby Stephen discussed English and classical literature (particularly Shakespeare) with his younger sister as well as reading Greek with her when he returned for holidays from school or university. He obviously chose books carefully for her, and for her twenty-first birthday presented her with Montaigne's essays, which she would appreciate throughout her life and which influenced her own essay-writing techniques and priorities. Moreover, Christine Kenyon Jones and Anna Snaith investigated the archives at King's College, London, and discovered that Woolf had enrolled in both Latin and Greek classes there. In the autumn term of 1897 and the spring and summer terms of 1898 she attended classes in 'Greek Elementary'. In the same two terms of the following academic year, Woolf was enrolled for 'Greek Advanced Reading'. In the autumn term of 1899, she was registered for 'Greek Intermediate and private tuition'. In the spring, summer and autumn terms of 1900, she attended classes in 'Greek advanced'. Finally in the three terms of 1901, she enrolled for 'Greek' classes in the autumn term as well as 'Greek (private tuition)' in the summer and autumn terms. She also studied Latin, though she began these classes slightly later and finished them a little earlier than the Greek classes. Although she sat no formal examinations, Snaith and Kenyon Jones concluded that she received the equivalent of a degree level education ('Tilting at

Universities' in *Woolf Studies Annual*, volume 10, 2010, 1–44). Despite this, she presented herself as an autodidact and retained a lifelong grievance at the comparison between the classical education her brothers had received, which she felt was denied to her.

There can be no doubt, though, that during the Victorian years Virginia's life was curiously divided. In the earlier part of the letter to Thoby Stephen above, Virginia had taken a pleasure in discussing the career Thoby might pursue. Evidently, she did not envisage a career for herself and seemed to be resigned to living in the wider world vicariously, through Thoby. She quoted Stella Hills's widower's comment on her elder brother; Jack Hills thought Thoby should go to the bar. Virginia asked him whether this appealed to him and encouraged him by praise of the qualities she thought he possessed which would an asset in the courtroom. Towards the end of her own life, Woolf claimed that from his schooldays Thoby was well aware of both the privileges and responsibilities he would have as a man. Woolf quoted Walter Lamb's quotation from *Hamlet*, which Lamb had applied to Thoby: 'Had he been put on, he would have proved most royally' (*SP*, 139).

Thoby Stephen was also clearly concerned about and accepting of his younger sister. He was evidently aware of Virginia's susceptibility to mental illness and appears to have been supportive. When Stella Hills became intermittently ill and eventually died, Virginia became unstable and had to cut down on her lessons. She obviously assumed Thoby would know why she was limited to this, and reported to Thoby that she was restricted to a few lessons with Stella during the mornings and nothing more (*L1*, no. 5: To Thoby Stephen, 24 February 1897, 6). Similarly, three months later she wrote to Thoby saying that their doctor had forbidden all lessons, assuming her brother would understand the reasons behind this decision (*L1*, no. 6: To Thoby Stephen, 14 May 1897, 7).

Sanders commented on the closeness of the sibling relationships in the Stephen family that it 'helped them to survive the trauma of their parents' and step-sister [sic] Stella's early deaths' (Sanders, 14). Woolf, however suggested that it was the other way round. She believed that the four siblings were not so much separated from each other as many families were when the boys were sent to boarding school and that their closeness, which continued into adulthood, was a *consequence* of their bereavements. She felt that without the deaths of their mother and half-sister which had 'united us' (*SP*, 125), Thoby 'would not have been so genuinely, though dumbly, bound to us' (*SP*, 137). These early bereavements had sensitised Thoby.

As indicated, the three Brontë sisters created negative portraits of men who shared what they considered their brother's weak and dissolute character. By contrast, famously, Woolf tried to recapture Thoby Stephen after his early death in the character of Jacob in *Jacob's Room* and Percival in *The Waves*. Thoby Stephen's death blocked Woolf off from an exploration of his life and her desire to understand his character. He remained elusive and may have contributed to her belief in the impossibility of understanding another person, a theme which first emerged in a clearly burgeoning modernist form in *Jacob's Room* and continued throughout her writing career. Here it can be clearly seen how Woolf embodied emotions largely carried over from her Victorian upbringing in a novelistic experiment that her intellect dictated.

Woolf again drew on emotions from her Victorian past and embodied them in perhaps her most experimental work, *The Waves*. The presence of Thoby Stephen in *The Waves* has long been recognised and in this it resembles *Jacob's Room*. Stuart N. Clarke and Susan Sellers stated that Woolf 'seriously contemplated' dedicating *Jacob's Room* to Thoby Stephen. Further, his name and dates (later cancelled) were placed between the elegy Catullus wrote for his brother, which Clarke and Sellers translated as 'And forever, brother, hail and farewell' (The Cambridge Edition of *Jacob's Room*, xli). Similarly, at the completion of *The Waves*, when she sat weeping, she considered dedicating it to Thoby. For some reason, not specified, she concluded she could not do so (*DIV*, 7 February 1931, 10).

Vanessa Bell confirmed that Percival was based on their dead brother when she commented on 'the feelings you describe on what I must take to be Thoby's death'. Woolf had, however, transmuted the personal into art; Bell believed that her sister had 'found the "lullaby capable of singing him to rest"' (*Selected Letters of Vanessa Bell*, VI-39: To Virginia Woolf, 15 October 1931, *367). This was similar to Charlotte Brontë resurrecting her dead elder sister, Maria, in Helen Burns in Jane Eyre* and her recently deceased sisters, Emily and Anne, in Shirley and Caroline in *Shirley*.

Yet although Woolf described him in very different terms from other men in the family, possibly Thoby Stephen's life, had it been prolonged, might have acted as a restrictive influence on the lives of his sisters. Woolf admitted that Thoby was a typical man in not wishing to hear of domestic details of their father's emotional abuse of his daughters; she thought that because of his sex he was 'aloof'. He felt that his sisters 'should accept our lot'. This would have involved them in taking unwanted walks with their father and accompanying George Duckworth to parties they did not want to attend. When Vanessa Bell cut their interfering aunt and her family in public, Thoby 'pronounced one of his rare impressive judgments'. He thought it was wrong for Vanessa to have behaved in that way (*SP*, 143). Nevertheless, Woolf continued to idolise him (or her memory of him) throughout her life. It is very evident that this was so very different from Charlotte's relationship with Branwell. Charlotte became ill after the death of Branwell and this was a pattern in Woolf's family losses too. Nevertheless, it is a fact that Woolf did not become mentally ill at this time. This was a break with the usual effects of family bereavements upon her. This may be explained by the fact that while Charlotte was torn apart by her ambivalent feelings for Branwell, Virginia had no such divided emotions about Thoby.

Although Charlotte Brontë was conflicted over her brother's death, far more important to her were those of her two surviving sisters, Emily and Anne Brontë. They were emotionally bonded but also united in their creativity. In her biography Elizabeth Gaskell described how the three sisters put away their sewing at nine in the evening and 'commencing their study, pacing up and down the sitting-room . . . they talked over the stories they were engaged upon, and described their plots. Once or twice a week each read to the others what she had written, and heard what they had to say about it' (Gaskell, 316–17). When they came to disguise their sex for publishing their poems and novels, the Brontë sisters still chose to present themselves in a familial way—they were the three Bell brothers rather than the three Brontë sisters.

By the end of October 1848, Charlotte Brontë was more concerned about her sisters' health than her own. Emily had an obstinate cold and cough; Charlotte suspected she had a pain in her chest and quick movements winded her. Additionally, Emily had become 'very, very thin and pale' (*L&L1*, no. 311: To Ellen Nussey, 29 October 1848, 460). Emily maintained her customary reserve and refused to discuss her health or accept any proffered medical advice or treatment. Charlotte Brontë had always considered her youngest sister Anne to have a weak constitution. This and Emily's obviously deteriorating health made Charlotte 'more apprehensive than common' and 'much depressed sometimes'. The emotion behind the next sentence of her letter is revealed by the alterations and deletions she made to it, meticulously observed by Margaret Smith, but which were omitted by Shorter. Smith's edition of the letter is: 'We should not knit human ties too <fast> \close/—or clasp human affection too fondly—they must leave us or we must leave them one day (*Letters of Charlotte Brontë*, volume 2: To Ellen Nussey, 29 October 1848, 131). Shorter's tidying up of the letter's punctuation diminishes the reader's apprehension of Charlotte Brontë's mental state of anxiety (*L&L1*, no. 311: To Ellen Nussey, 29 October 1848, 460).

Exactly what her sisters meant to Charlotte Brontë became even clearer after their deaths. Already in her last days Emily seemed 'the nearest thing to my heart in this world' (*L&L2*, no. 315: To Ellen Nussey, 23 November 1848, 8). Charlotte's attitude was rather different towards her youngest sister; at a much earlier date she had adopted a protective attitude towards her. Interestingly, she shared an anxiety which focused on a particular sibling with Woolf. One of the lessons they both took from their multiple bereavements was the fragility of human life. This probably accounts for Charlotte's tendency to panic at her youngest sister's health, and on one occasion it involved her in a dispute with the owner and headmistress of the school, Miss Margaret Wooler. To Ellen Nussey, Charlotte wrote that she was 'in a regular passion' with Miss Wooler, her own '"*warm temper*" quite got the better of me—of which I don't boast, for it was a weakness; nor am I ashamed of it, for I had reason to be angry. Anne is now much better, though she still requires a great deal of care. However, I am relieved from my worst fears respecting her' (*L&L1*, no. 44: To Ellen Nussey, 4 January 1838, 146). Charlotte Brontë persisted in thinking her youngest sister was physically weak and in need of protection. In 1840, Charlotte Brontë again expressed anxiety about her youngest sister: 'Anne's cold is better, but I don't consider her strong yet' (*L&L1*, no. 63: To Ellen Nussey, 17 March 1840, 175–76). She even expressed doubt as to whether her youngest sister was being honest about her health: 'I had a letter from Anne yesterday; she says she is well. I hope she speaks absolute truth' (*L&L1*, no. 85: To Emily J. Brontë, 2 April 1841, 208). When Anne Brontë left the parsonage to become a governess, Charlotte Brontë's description of her was full of pity and compassion, but she also adopted a patronising tone, suggesting that she was writing of someone whom she clearly did not regard as an equal:

> Poor child! she left us last Monday; no one went with her; it was her own wish that she might be allowed to go alone, as she thought she could manage better and summon more courage if thrown entirely upon her own resources. . . . You would be astonished what a sensible, clever letter she writes; it is only the talking part, that I fear. But I do seriously apprehend that Mrs Ingham [Anne Brontë's employer] will sometimes conclude that she has a natural impediment of speech. (*L&L1*, no. 50: To Ellen Nussey, 15 April 1839, 155)

Charlotte Brontë's over-protectiveness of Anne Brontë continued throughout the latter's life. Her elder sister wrote that the thought of Anne's feelings being hurt made her heart ache and she wished that she could be there to comfort her (*L&L1*, no. 91: To Ellen Nussey, 7 August 1841, 219).

It is arguable that Charlotte Brontë's over-protective attitude outlived her youngest sister's death and led to a prolonged underrating of her achievements. In her *Biographical notice of Ellis and Acton Bell*, Charlotte Brontë said she was unsurprised at the unfavourable response to *The Tenant of Wildfell Hall:* 'The choice of subject was an entire mistake. Nothing less congruous with the writer's nature could be conceived'. Charlotte Bronte added that Anne Brontë's selection of this topic was 'slightly morbid', and that her observation of 'talents misused and faculties abused' led her to write a fictionalised version of what she had witnessed. Charlotte Brontë denied that there was any art in *The Tenant of Wildfell Hall*; rather Anne Brontë 'reproduced every detail' of what she had seen and was determined to write it down 'as a warning to others' (*Biographical Notice of Ellis and Acton Bell*, Appendix I to *Wuthering Heights*, 304). It took until the middle of the twentieth century for critics to differ from Charlotte Brontë and to perceive the high quality of Anne Brontë's *The Tenant of Wildfell Hall*. Virginia Woolf was one of the critics who entirely ignored Anne Brontë's two novels; but in this she was merely in step with the majority of her contemporaries.

If Charlotte Brontë was over-anxious about Anne Brontë's health and wanted to protect her, Woolf manifested much the same emotions over Vanessa Bell. As early as the beginning of 1907, Virginia was worrying about Vanessa's health which she admitted worried and agitated her (*L1*, no. 335: To Violet Dickinson, 2 January 1907, 274–75). During the First World War, Woolf wrote to Bell urging her to take a holiday away from her multiple responsibilities (*L2* no. 776: To Vanessa Bell, 30 July 1916, 108). Just before the end of the First World War, Woolf's brief enquiry was eloquent: she simply asked to be told how Vanessa was (*L2*, no. 985: To Vanessa Bell, 7 November 1918, 289). In 1922, Woolf worried about Bell who was suffering from mumps, remembering Stella's description of the illness (*L2*, no. 1269: To Vanessa Bell, 10 August 1922, 543). Simultaneously, while Woolf was writing in these terms, she was worried that she might sound like their maternal aunt, Mary Fisher, whom the Stephen sisters had mocked for her concern over the most trivial details of health or ill-health. Woolf actually made this comparison in a letter to Bell (*L3*, no. 1708: To Vanessa Bell, 25 January 1927, 318). Sometimes, Woolf's anxiety about Bell sounded aggressive: she severely reproached her sister for what she perceived as Vanessa's self-neglect (*L2*, no. 1178: To Vanessa Bell, 13 May 1921, 468). Ultimately, Woolf's fears for her sister proved unfounded, but the same cannot be said of Charlotte Brontë's anxieties, which came to focus not only on Anne but also Emily.

A series of letters from Charlotte Brontë best unfold the tragic drama playing itself out in Haworth Parsonage. A month later, Charlotte was forlornly adhering to the hope that Emily would recover, for 'she is dear to me as life —' (*L&L2*, no. 316: To Ellen Nussey, Shorter says 'undated', 8: but Margaret Smith's edition queries?27 November 1848 in volume 2, 146). In early December 1848, Charlotte expressed her desperation and despair. This was reflected by the underlining of certain words in her letter in Smith's edition: 'I *must* cling to the expectation of [Emily Brontë's] recovery; I *cannot* renounce it' (*Letters of Charlotte Brontë*, volume 2: To W. S. Williams, 7 December 1848, 147). Once again, Shorter interfered with the presentation: he omitted the underlining of words, which again undermined the reader's perception of Charlotte Brontë's emotional intensity at this time.

Like Virginia Woolf, Emily Brontë had no belief in what she called 'poisoning doctors', and only agreed to see one on the last day of her life, when nothing whatever could be done for her. On the morning of the 19 December 1848, as Emily lay dying, Charlotte wrote a brief note to Ellen Nussey, 'Moments so dark as these I have never known' (*L&L2*, no. 320: To Ellen Nussey, 19 December 1848, 12). Charlotte's publishers were the first people to whom she communicated the death of Emily at two o'clock in the afternoon of 19 December 1848, at the age of thirty: 'Yesterday Emily Jane Brontë died in the arms of those who loved her.' She summed up the events of the immediately preceding three months; since Branwell's death, life had seemed to the surviving Brontës 'like a long terrible dream' (Smith, volume 2: To W. S. Williams, 20 December 1848, 155). Shorter failed to include this stark but emotionally restrained letter. Instead, he quoted Charlotte Brontë's account of Emily Brontë's death, written at a greater distance from the event, as an introduction to a reprint of some of the Brontë novels. Additionally, he quoted substantially from A. Mary F. Robinson's biography of Emily Brontë, which was published as part of the 'Eminent Women Series' in 1890. Shorter suggests that Robinson took her account from Ellen Nussey (*L&L2*, 13–15). It is possible that Shorter did not have access to these letters for his edition of the *Life and Letters* in 1908 (though he and Thomas J. Wise must take some of the responsibility for scattering the extant letters over the globe to whoever would pay for them).

In view of Charlotte's anxiety in anticipating Anne Brontë's death, it is ironic that when it occurred it was not as searing for Charlotte as Emily's had been. For one thing, Anne had a much more pliable disposition and willingly accepted the medical advice desired by her remaining family, which Emily had scorned and rejected. Perhaps, also, Charlotte had for years been unconsciously expecting and preparing for it. Understandably Charlotte could not progress with the writing of *Shirley*. Updating an acquaintance on the deaths of Branwell and Emily and the current decline in Anne's health, she wrote, movingly, that 'there have been hours, days, weeks of inexpressible anguish to undergo, and the cloud of impending distress still lowers dark and sullen above us' (*L&L2*, no. 337: To Laetitia Wheelwright, 15 March 1849, 34).

With the passing of time, Emily's death became an increasingly distressing memory ('She was torn conscious, panting, reluctant, though resolute, out of a happy life' [*L&L2*, no. 345: To Ellen Nussey, 12 April 1849, 42]). Charlotte continued to find it easier to bear the demise of Anne on 30 May 1849, at the age of twenty-nine: her 'quiet—Christian death did not rend my heart as Emily's stern, simple, undemonstrative end did—I let Anne go to God and felt He had a right to her' (*The Letters of Charlotte Brontë*, volume 2: To W. S. Williams, 4 June 1849, 216). This letter was not included in Shorter; this was possibly owing to its unavailability in 1908, or could have reflected the contemporary comparative lack of interest in Anne Brontë. These two letters together provide a considerable insight into Charlotte Brontë's estimate of her younger sisters and it is regrettable that both were unavailable to Woolf.

Close as the sisters were, and despite the fact that they all wished to excel in the same literary forms, there was no jealousy or rivalry among the three women. Charlotte Brontë expressed this in a comment in which the main point was not her sisters, but a comparison with the main topic. She demolished the idea that she should feel in a rivalry for the affections of Ellen Nussey: 'I should as soon think of being jealous of Emily and Anne in these days as of you' (*L&L1*, no. 219: To Ellen Nussey, 21 April 1847, 349–50). When Elizabeth Gaskell stayed at the parsonage in 1853, she recorded that her hostess never tired of talking about Emily Brontë. From what Charlotte said, Gaskell gained the impression that Emily 'must have been a remnant of the Titans, great-granddaughter of the giants who used to inhabit the earth' (Gaskell's *Life*, 619).

Unlike the Brontë sisters, the Stephen sisters saw themselves as rivals and in competition with each other, despite the fact that their chosen arts differed. This competition additionally and regrettably extended into their other personal relationships. Virginia even intruded herself into the marital relationship between Vanessa and Clive Bell, by conducting a strong flirtation with him. This, which Vanessa saw as an act of betrayal, affected the future relationship between the two sisters. Virginia admitted in 1925 that what she called her 'affair' with the Bells had caused more pain than anything else had ever done (*L3*, no. 1542: To Gwen Raverat, 22 March 1925, 172). Yet at the same time Virginia was very close to Vanessa, and moreover extremely dependent on her. In 1917, Woolf admitted to having mythologised her sister: Vanessa Bell was, for Virginia, a Shakespearian character whose actions she often imagined so strongly that it was at times difficult to separate the real Vanessa from the imaginary character she had created as a sort of mythological being (*L2*, no. 825: To Duncan Grant, 6 March 1917, 145). It was perhaps not a great step from the general mythologising of her sister to her imaginary portrait of her in Woolf's second novel. In *Night and Day*, Woolf openly told her sister that her heroine was based on her: she wrote to her sister about what she was doing and put the responsibility on Vanessa for having been so stimulating during Virginia's recent visit (*L2*, no. 776: To Vanessa Bell, 30 July 1916, 108). Woolf also told Vanessa that she had been writing about her all morning; her fear was that she would fail to capture and do justice to her sister's complex and sometimes contradictory qualities (*L2*, no. 923: To Vanessa Bell, 22 April 1918, 232). Woolf dedicated *Night and Day* to Vanessa Bell. This sibling relationship was a creative one for Woolf.

The reverse has been claimed for the close relationships between the four Brontë siblings. Miriam Bailin has suggested that the close bonding of the four surviving Brontë siblings affected both their novels and their ability to adjust and succeed in life outside the Haworth Parsonage. Bailin writes: 'The close identification of lovers is a common feature of [Charlotte] Brontë's novels. (Her sister Emily's famous line, "I *am* Heathcliff!" suggests that it was a familial inclination' (Bailin, 71). Bailin sees this bonding and need to recreate it in the closeness of the two people in the marital relationships which conclude most of the novels, as a regressive wish for the harmony 'found in the tightly knit, exclusive society and joint imaginative lives of the Brontë siblings' (Bailin, 72). The four siblings all found the world outside the parsonage hostile and unresponsive to their wishes and expectations: Monsieur Heger rejected Charlotte's love; Mrs Robinson did not reciprocate Branwell's passion; Emily made no outside friends; and William Weightman never reciprocated Anne's love.

According to Woolf herself, she harboured lifelong feelings for Vanessa Bell which bordered on the incestuous; she also directed a blow at what she perceived was Vanessa's indifference to her. Vanessa apparently was never demonstrative enough to satisfy Virginia's needs (*L3*, no. 1942: To Vanessa Bell, 16? October 1928, 546–47). More seriously, she told Bell, after the latter had praised *The Waves* that, apart from Leonard, Vanessa was the most important person in her life and that she would be devastated if she did not like Virginia's writing (*L4*, no. 2451: To Vanessa Bell, 15 October 1931, 390).

It appears that Woolf did not feel the same about her younger brother, Adrian: he, the youngest of the four Stephen siblings, seems not to have held a special place in the affections of his sisters. There are no extant letters from Virginia Woolf to Adrian Stephen, as there are to her older siblings. Adrian was his mother's favourite and the three older Stephen siblings (and, indeed, their father) may have felt jealous of the maternal love and attention he received. This is certainly the impression that can be derived from the older three children's juvenile paper, *The Hyde Park Gate News*.

Woolf frequently referred to him in early adulthood protectively and as if he were much her junior. During Leslie Stephen's long terminal illness, Adrian was summoned home from Cambridge University, and Virginia reported to Violet Dickinson that while he—'poor little boy'—was clearly distressed at his father's condition, he did not express this verbally (*L1*, no. 127: To Violet Dickinson, December? 1903, 112). To the same correspondent, Virginia reported of Adrian, as if he were a young child, and exaggerating the stammer she claimed he had (*L1*, no. 309: To Violet Dickinson, 28? November 1906, 253). I have not come across any other reference to Adrian's speech being a problem. Indeed, if it had been it seems unlikely that he would eventually train and practice as a psychoanalyst. This is comparable to Charlotte Brontë's conviction that Anne Brontë's new employer will think Anne has a speech impediment. In both cases, it may have arisen from a senior sister's protective but patronising attitude to a younger sibling, rather than to any actual speech defect. Virginia also lamented that she could not be a brother to Adrian in lieu of Thoby (*L1*, no. 346: To Madge Vaughan, 15 February 1907, 283). After Thoby's death, while the bond between Virginia and Vanessa remained strong, Adrian gradually drifted away from his sisters and existed only on the periphery of their lives.

It must be remarked that in the case of the four full Stephen siblings, their unity was fostered by the exclusion of their older half-brothers, George and Gerald Duckworth. Virginia, in early adulthood, expressed the young Stephens' scornful view of their intellectual capacities when she mockingly regretted that they had wool where their brains should have been (*L1*, no. 73: To Violet Dickinson, 1903?, 71). It might be said to be a forerunner of the exclusiveness of the Bloomsbury Group. It is perhaps an irony that it was Gerald Duckworth who, with George Duckworth's support, was the first to suggest that their younger half-siblings should relocate to the Bloomsbury area of London (*L1*, nos. 103 and 106: To Violet Dickinson, late September and early October 1903, 96, 99).

All of her life Woolf seemed to have retained an interest in sibling relationships. Arguably in her last novel published during her lifetime, *The Years*, the main relationships are those between the seven Pargiter siblings (and to a lesser extent cousins). As has been long recognised, there are many allusions to Sophocles's *Antigone* in *The Years*. This Greek tragedy presented a sister who died for ensuring her dead brother's burial against a state prohibition enforced by her uncle, Creon. Woolf may also have paused to consider the relationship between the two sisters, Antigone and Ismene. Additionally, the *Antigone* involved the eponymous heroine's cousin, Haemon, who chose death over life without her. Woolf used this theme; neither Haemon's love for Antigone, nor Edward Pargiter's for his cousin Kitty Malone is requited. Yet it is clear that the Victorian period as it segues into the 'present day', is also very different from the classical Greek world. It is not a tragedy and the Pargiter brothers and sisters and their cousins are seen interacting with each other over the decades as they attend various family gatherings. They all, in their different ways, carry their Victorian childhoods into the present, for example, even their childhood animosities are continued into middle age. While the Victorian Pargiter daughters live the sort of lives that the Brontës' female contemporaries might have done, however, in the next generation we see a woman who has trained for a profession and become a doctor.

The types of consolations for the death of loved ones which Charlotte Brontë and Woolf sought greatly differed. It was not merely the fact of living in a different era. Patrick Brontë was a clergyman and Charlotte clung to the idea of a God and a divine plan. Woolf's father had been a clergyman too, but he renounced holy orders long before he started his second family. Stephen became an atheist and married as his second wife another atheist. Virginia Woolf never revealed any understanding of the religious mind. Charlotte Brontë's refusal to question divine providence persisted until her death. However, her searing pain sounded through that very refusal: 'So I will not ask why Emily was torn from us in the fulness of our attachment, rooted up in the prime of her own days, in the promise of her powers; why her existence now lies like a field of green corn trodden down, like a tree in full bearing struck at the root. I will only say, sweet is rest after labour and calm after tempest, and repeat again and again that Emily knows that now' (*L&L2*, no. 322: To W.S. Williams, 25 December 1848, 16–17). The desperate repetition of the belief that Emily is now at rest, perhaps reveals a scintilla of doubt about this. Charlotte urgently needed to adhere to the religion in which she had been reared. This sense of incomprehension surfaced again after Anne's death: 'Why life is so blank, brief and bitter I do not know—Why younger and far better than I are snatched from it with projects unfulfilled I cannot comprehend—but I believe God is wise—perfect—merciful' (This letter to W. S. Williams was not published by Shorter; it is in Smith's edition, volume 2, 216.) When she remained the sole survivor of the family of six children this would become her mantra: so much was invested in it, that it had to be the truth behind human life and suffering on earth.

Indeed, Charlotte Brontë wrote that if she had not previously believed in an afterlife, her sisters' deaths would have convinced her of it. She also wrote, using the same alliterating adjectives as she had before: 'There must be Heaven or we must despair—for life seems bitter, brief—blank.' She described her desolating experience to her publishers: 'Branwell—Emily—Anne are gone like dreams—gone as Maria and Elizabeth went twenty years ago. One by one I have watched them fall asleep on my arm—and closed their glazed eyes—I have seen them buried one by one—and—thus far—God has upheld me. From my heart I thank him'. (This letter to W. S. Williams was not published by Shorter, but is in volume 2 of Smith's edition, 220.) The omission of these letters meant that Woolf could not have read them and so could not have felt as acutely the depth of Charlotte Brontë's suffering at her loss. Woolf would not have understood or approved of Charlotte Brontë's attempt to find religious consolation in her grief.

Unlike Emily's, Charlotte and Anne Brontë's writings would reflect this underlying religious belief about the creation of the world and humanity. There is a marked change in tone and buoyancy in *Jane Eyre* and *Villette*. The latter is a much darker book; some people are born to suffer in life; others are not. The reason for this is not to be questioned. Miss Marchmont best sums this up, when, the night before she dies, she says to Lucy Snowe: 'We should acknowledge God merciful, but not always for us comprehensible' (*Villette*, 50).

By contrast, Woolf's novels largely rejected Christianity (though as several recent books on Woolf have revealed she had a fairly accurate knowledge of Christianity; for example, see Jane de Gay's *Virginia Woolf and Christian Culture*, 2018). *To the Lighthouse* contains characteristic expressions of atheism, especially in Mrs Ramsay's worldview: 'How could any Lord have made this world? she asked. With her mind she had always seized the fact that there is no reason, order, justice: but suffering, death, the poor. There was no treachery too base for the world to commit; she knew that. No happiness lasted; she knew that' (*TTL,* 87). Interestingly, *To the Lighthouse* is also Woolf's most obviously autobiographical novel.

As a consequence of the early loss of their mothers, both Charlotte Brontë and Virginia Woolf sought out people who would extend a maternal warmth to them. In Charlotte Brontë's case, these figures were older women she met over the years. It was perhaps because she attempted to be a mother-substitute for her younger sisters that they did not seek maternal substitutes. Anne, the youngest, may also have bonded the most strongly of the sisters with their Aunt Branwell. She was their aunt's favourite among the girls and could have had no memory whatsoever of her own mother. Emily did not spend much time away from Haworth Parsonage; and when she was elsewhere, she was apparently unconcerned with making relationships of any sort with people outside her immediate family circle. Branwell was the other favourite of Aunt Branwell. He revealed his deep feelings for her while attending her deathbed, describing her as one 'who has been for twenty years as my mother' (*L&L1*, no. 107: P.B. Brontë to Francis H. Grundy, 25 October 1842, 242). He also described her as 'the guide and director of all the happy days connected with my childhood' (*L&L1*, no. 108: P.B. Brontë: To Francis Grundy, 29 October 1842, 243).

Charlotte Brontë as a searcher for maternal affection is the most interesting of the Brontë siblings. Twice she had been deprived of a mother-figure during her childhood. This same double deprivation occurred in Woolf's life too. Confirmation of this in the Brontës lives is to be found in Gaskell's *Life of Charlotte Brontë,* in which she quoted an 'informant's' remark on little Maria Brontë: 'She was as good as a mother to her sisters and brother' (*Life*, 50).

Woolf seemed to be much more aware of this need to have mother-substitutes in her life than Charlotte Brontë was, and she expressed it in her diary, writing of Vita Sackville-West that though she was not as intelligent and perceptive as Woolf herself, she provided her with the 'maternal protection' which was the thing she most desired from other people, of both sexes (*DIII*, 21 December 1925, 52). Though she wrote she did not know why she felt this, the 'reason' is of course obvious, when we recollect her early history. These multiple women varied from her half-sister, Stella Duckworth; to an older woman, Violet Dickinson to whom she confided in her youth; to

such a near-contemporary as her sister, Vanessa; to a younger woman, Vita
Sackville-West with whom she became intimate in middle age; and finally, in
the 1930s, to the much older feminist composer Ethel Smyth.

Aunt Branwell seemed to function as an unsatisfactory mother-surrogate
for Charlotte Brontë who went outside the parsonage to seek a substitute for
the two maternal figures she had lost within its walls. Woolf, too, after the
death of her second mother surrogate initially looked outside her domestic
circle, particularly during her father's long final illness. In Charlotte's case,
when she became a pupil at Roe Head School, she established a lifelong
friendship with its proprietor and head, Margaret Wooler (1792–1885).
Charlotte Brontë later returned to the school as a teacher. Miss Wooler's
name runs throughout her letters. She seems to have been the most important older woman she selected as a mother-substitute; it is therefore worth
pausing here to consider Miss Wooler. A prominent Brontë scholar in the
late nineteenth and early twentieth century, Clement K. Shorter, was able to
record details of Miss Wooler's life and character supplied by her nephew, in
addition to the testimony of Ellen Nussey, a fellow pupil of Charlotte Brontë
at Roe Head School (Clement K. Shorter, *Charlotte Brontë and Her Circle*,
260–62. Henceforth *CBC*).

Neither Miss Wooler's nephew nor Ellen Nussey mentioned Margaret
Wooler's late (apparently unsolicited) advice to Charlotte Brontë in January
1853. Since gaining literary recognition, Charlotte had been befriended
by Harriet Martineau. Around this time, the latter had co-authored and
published a book with H. G. Atkinson called *Letters on the Laws of Man's
Social Nature and Development*. Despite the fact that Martineau rejected
accusations of atheism, some former friends broke off relations with her.
Miss Wooler probably warned her former pupil and erstwhile colleague not
to accept Martineau's friendship and invitation to stay with her in the Lake
District. Charlotte Brontë, though not in entire agreement with Miss Wooler
about Martineau's character, nevertheless seemed to receive this advice with
gratitude, as she might have done had she had a mother to offer it: 'I read
attentively all you say about Miss Martineau; the sincerity and constancy of
your solicitude touches me very much'. Having acknowledged Miss Wooler's
advice with gratitude, Charlotte Brontë then takes pains to explain why she is
doubtful about accepting it: 'I should grieve to neglect or oppose your advice,
and yet I do not feel that it would be right to give Miss Martineau up entirely.
There is in her nature much that is very noble. Hundreds have forsaken her.
. . . With these fair-weather friends I cannot bear to rank. And for her sin, is
it not one of those which God and not Man must judge?' (*L&L2*, no. 608: To
Miss Wooler, 27 January 1853, 303). Ultimately, however, Charlotte Brontë
never again accepted Martineau's hospitality. The reasons for this were probably a combination of her older friend's disapproval with her own anger at

Martineau's criticism of the type of love Charlotte Brontë displayed in her novels, culminating in *Villette* (1853).

Charlotte Brontë remained loyal to Wooler all her life. Margaret Wooler's nephew confirmed the long-lasting relationship she had with Charlotte Brontë: 'Miss Wooler kept up a warm friendship with her former pupil, up to the time of her death' (*CBC*, 261). After the deaths of all Charlotte Brontë's siblings, Miss Wooler invited her former pupil to stay with her and made return visits to the Parsonage. They even went on holiday together. Margaret Wooler also functioned as a *father*-substitute at Charlotte Brontë's wedding. When on the morning of her marriage Mr Brontë refused to accompany the small wedding party to church, Miss Wooler stepped into the breach when it was discovered that it did not have to be the father who gave away the bride: Margaret Wooler gave away her quondam scholar and colleague.

Similarly, the first woman Woolf attached herself to for a sort of maternal protection was an older, spinster friend called Violet Dickinson (1865–1948). Virginia even wrote a mock-biography of her older friend in 'Friendship's Gallery' (*E6*, 518–44). Virginia felt passionately, though not sexually, towards Violet and created many animal aliases for herself in her letters. Certainly, Dickinson was Virginia's main correspondent between 1902 and 1907. The correspondence waned after this, but continued intermittently after Woolf had discovered her lifelong friends who constituted what came to be known as the 'Bloomsbury Group'. Who was Violet Dickinson? The editors of Woolf's letters give us a potted biography of her. She was the daughter of a Somerset squire, Edward Dickinson, and his wife, the daughter of Lord Auckland. Dickinson was a lifelong spinster and for most of her adult life lived at Welwyn with her brother Oswald, who became Secretary to the Commissioners in Lunacy. (His knowledge might have been helpful to Violet Dickinson who initially took on responsibility for Virginia during the psychotic breakdown which followed Leslie Stephen's death.) On her death, Dickinson bequeathed her whole fortune of £25,000 to Oswald. She published one book, the letters of her great-aunt Emily Eden, in 1919 (but not with the fledgling Hogarth Press). Dickinson was over six feet tall and Virginia frequently teased her about her exceptional height. Though she was clumsy and graceless she was very popular and well-loved both in the literary and fashionable world (*L1*, introduction, xviii).

Violet Dickinson continued to provide emotional support to Virginia after Leslie Stephen's death. When she found it so difficult to talk to her siblings about her conflicted emotions about their father's death, she found she could write about them to Dickinson (*L1*, no. 171: To Violet Dickinson, March 1904, 133). Virginia was tormented by self-reproach about her behaviour to her father, which she expressed to Dickinson in letters which make painful reading. She became obsessed with the conviction that she should have done more for him and assuaged his loneliness in the years following Julia Stephen's death (*L1*, no.167: To Violet Dickinson, 28 February 1904, 130). Over a month later, Virginia wrote in similar terms expressing her guilt and remorse (*L1*, no. 175: To Violet Dickinson, 31 March 1904, 136).

When Virginia's mind gave way under the strain of all this emotion and she became psychotic, Violet Dickinson provided the support that one might expect only a mother to give: she took Virginia into her home, so that she could be looked after. When one considers that at one stage Virginia required the care of three nurses and was suicidal, it will be obvious that Violet was no fair-weather friend. Virginia remained at Welwyn from April to September 1904, at which point she was sufficiently well to join her siblings who were on holiday in Nottinghamshire. Her first extant letter after her breakdown was written to Violet Dickinson.

Violet Dickinson also helped Virginia to launch her literary career. It seems to me unfair of Nigel Nicolson to claim that Virginia's letters to a male (Clive Bell) after pages of letters to Violet Dickinson and her cousin Emma Vaughan 'come as a relief' (*L1*, Introduction, xx). Before Clive Bell at least two women recognised Virginia's talent as a writer and offered encouragement. One of these was Violet Dickinson who introduced Virginia to Kathleen (Margaret) Lyttleton, editor of the *Women's Supplement* of the Anglo-Catholic *Guardian*. It is surely significant that Virginia did not approach any of the contacts of Leslie Stephen who had had an extensive literary connection but preferred to go through a woman. Perhaps this was connected with her comment to Violet that although she found anybody's criticism hard to bear, she was best able to accept it from her (*L1*, no. 207: To Violet Dickinson, early January 1905, 173). (It will be observed that it was much easier for Virginia to launch her literary career than it was for the Brontës.) As Woolf's career progressed and she began to write short stories for the Hogarth Press (which the Woolfs set up in 1917), Dickinson loyally supported the press by subscribing to all its publications. She also kept up with Woolf's later novels, though they had long since ceased to be intimate friends. There was no obvious breach in the friendship; they simply grew apart. It seems that Woolf had outgrown Dickinson.

After the deaths of her two younger sisters, Charlotte Brontë's growing fame brought her into contact with other contemporary women writers who to some extent occupied the position of mother figures to her. Woolf's trajectory sometimes also led her to find mother-substitutes in other writers, or aspiring authors. In the case of Charlotte Brontë, the above-mentioned Harriet Martineau (1802–1876) seemed to wish to nurture the younger writer, after receiving a copy of *Shirley* from its author. Martineau particularly wanted to penetrate the mystery of the identity of Currer Bell since she herself had been suspected of writing *Jane Eyre*, or at least of supplying some of the material from her own childhood, for the first part of the novel (Harriet Martineau's *Autobiography*, volume 2, 21). As with Gaskell, Martineau's first impression of Charlotte Brontë was her diminutive size: 'I thought her the smallest creature I had ever seen (except at a fair)' (Harriet Martineau's *Autobiography*, volume 2, 23). This quotation gives the unfortunate impression that Martineau initially viewed Charlotte Brontë as a physical freak, of the sort on display at travelling fairs, to see whom people were willing to pay a fee.

Both Gaskell and Martineau were disposed to be sympathetic to Charlotte Brontë because of her overwhelmingly tragic family history. But Martineau had not anticipated how moved she would be by this small sole survivor of the original six siblings: 'When she was seated by me on the sofa, she cast up at me such a look,—so loving, so appealing,—that, in connexion with her deep mourning dress, and the knowledge that she was the sole survivor of her family, I could with the utmost difficulty return her smile, or keep my composure. I should have been heartily glad to cry' (Harriet Martineau's *Autobiography*, volume 2, 23).

In letters to friends, Martineau adopted a protective tone when writing of Charlotte Brontë. Martineau expressed concern about her visitor: 'I hear, from one of her acquaintance in London, that she is in a very unsatisfactory state of health. She herself wrote lately that she was much better than a year ago. I shall do my best to take care of her' (*The Collected Letters of Harriet Martineau*, volume 3, To Lady Shuttleworth, December 1850, 179. Henceforth *CLHM*). In 1851, Martineau was even more maternal in her desire to protect Charlotte Brontë; she feared for she would die should she be 'detained long in her most dreary and unhealthy house. . . . She throve here so here she must come again & again' (*CLHM*, volume 3, To Leigh Hunt, 24 January 1851, 187). In the same letter Martineau also heaped excessive praise on Charlotte, like some doting mother on a favourite child:

A fairer specimen of the true heroic mind I never saw: large & strong,—gentle & composed,—meek & self-possessed,—so sympathising that her consciousness seems to pass into others, leaving none for herself,—she is as opposite to the creature of passion & prejudice as to the marble-hearted self seeker. Very fine as her ideas & the expression of them are, I forget them in her most moving goodness.—By the way, Mr Atkinson & I have often said that we wished we had known any one who cd be liberal beyond his or her point of belief. In Miss Brontë we have found the last. You wd say so if you saw her last two letters,— the noblest, I think, I ever saw. (*CLHM*, volume 3, To Leigh Hunt, 24 January 1851, 187)

It might cross the mind of the impartial reader that no mere mortal could ever have been what Martineau thought her new friend to be. When Charlotte

Brontë died, Martineau continued to lay on praise with a trowel: 'Vast as was her genius, and infinitely as I admired it, I honoured yet more her integrity and unspoiled uprightness, simplicity, and sense. She was a noble woman, such as society can ill spare' (*CLHM, The Collected Letters of Harriet Martineau*, volume 3: To John Greenwood, early April 1855, 354).

Two years later, however, Martineau reversed her high praise of Charlotte Brontë. The cause of this peripetia was the publication of Gaskell's *Life of Charlotte Brontë*. The biographer's account of Martineau's relationship with Charlotte Brontë, embittered Martineau, who completely turned against her former friend, and ended with an attempt to blacken Charlotte Brontë's character. This is most apparent in two of Martineau's letters written after the publication of Gaskell's *Life* (1857). Martineau felt that she had been misrepresented in the biography. In the first letter, which was to Patrick Brontë, she conceded that Charlotte Brontë had been well-disposed to her and was even affectionate. The sting came in the qualification: 'but it is not the less true that, as I have publicly & privately said, there is scarcely a statement concerning myself in her letters which is altogether true: & I may add that some of them are more like hallucination than other statement' (*The Collected Letters of Harriet Martineau*, volume 4, To Patrick Brontë, 5 November 1857, 46). Martineau is virtually telling the bereaved father that his recently dead daughter was out of touch with reality, was effectively insane!

To another correspondent, Martineau wrote that she sorrowfully affirmed 'that I have long ceased to consider C. Brontë truthful'. Although it is impossible to know how far people consciously lie (but Martineau uses the euphemistic 'untruths'), she is now certain that 'C. B. made no point of saying what was true'. Martineau added: 'On all hands, her want of sincerity & good faith is coming out'. Martineau cited as proof her own dealings with Charlotte Brontë, who had encouraged the publication of Martineau and Atkinson's book, but was simultaneously condemning it to another correspondent. This she labelled as 'double-dealing', which had long since 'compelled' Martineau to conclude that Charlotte Brontë lacked 'integrity' (Volume 4: To R. P. Graves, 27 November 1857, 56). Taken together, these two letters give the impression that Martineau had been pushed beyond her limits by a formerly much-loved daughter. They express disappointment as well as chagrin.

An early literary confidante and mother-substitute for Virginia Woolf was Madge Vaughan (1869–1925), the wife of her cousin, Will. The Stephens had known Madge before her marriage. During her childhood and adolescence, Virginia had cherished an infatuation for Madge. During her convalescence from her 1904 breakdown, Virginia went to stay with the Vaughans in Giggleswick School in Settle in Yorkshire. Her first impression was that Will Vaughan thought Virginia a bad influence on his wife. In turn, Virginia thought Will's constant reminders to Madge that she had the duties of a headmaster's wife were bad for her creative instincts. However, while Madge often said she longed for the company of unconventional artists and writers, Woolf already suspected her sincerity. She does wonder, though, if Madge would have been happier married to someone else or had remained a spinster. Five days later, Virginia reversed her opinion of the Vaughans' marriage: everyday she had witnessed their happiness. Madge admitted that the life she led suited her better than any other life would have done, though she liked to complain.

Madge was an intermittent writer herself, and after Virginia had returned to London, they sent each other their manuscripts for comment. By this time Virginia was viewing Madge as a mother-surrogate. Her first letter after her return to London addressed Madge as 'Mama Vaughan', whose 'infant' Virginia claimed herself to be (*L1*, no. 197: To Madge Vaughan, 30 November 1904, 161). Presumably Madge did not object to this mode of address, for less than two weeks later, Virginia opened her letter with 'Dearest Foster Parent' (*L1*, no. 201: To Madge Vaughan, 11 December 1904, 165). Madge was the first reader of Virginia's writing (not Clive Bell) who called her a 'genius'. This gave Virginia 'enormous pleasure' and she promised that she would recall Madge's words of encouragement when feeling depressed about her writing (*L1*, no. 198: To Madge Vaughan, 1 December 1904, 162).

Two years later it was also to Madge that Virginia confided what she was trying to achieve in her writing and how she saw reality. While claiming to agree with Madge's criticisms, she defended what Madge thought revealed narrowness and a lack of sexual passion. Whilst she admitted that her world might seem dream-like to Madge it was what she cared about and was her own personal vision of reality. Virginia cited George Eliot as a late developer whose first novel was published when she was nearly forty years old. She thought George Eliot an encouraging example: Virginia herself still had plenty of time to develop. She did not want Madge to think she was complacent and stressed that she was dissatisfied with her writing. At the same time, she believed it was better to write about what seemed real to her than to attempt to write about things of which she had no understanding. Virginia ends with a personal appeal to this mother-figure: 'I only want to be treated like a nice child' (*L1*, no. 272: To Madge Vaughan, June? 1906, 227).

These letters indicated a fundamental disparity between the two women's perceptions of the nature of reality and the world. Thus, it is not surprising that Virginia soon dispensed with Madge Vaughan as a surrogate-mother. Virginia's passion for Madge cooled as it had done for Violet Dickinson. The final breach with Madge Vaughan, however, was definite and bitter, like Martineau and Charlotte's, and contrasted with the way in which Woolf had gradually withdrawn from Violet. Madge chose to query the morality of

Vanessa Bell's domestic arrangements. As ever, when Vanessa was attacked, Virginia took her side.

Here we might state that Vanessa Stephen Bell remained a permanent mother-figure for Virginia, despite the fact that there was only three years' difference in their ages. Of course, their relationship had been forged in their Victorian past, and though both aspired to embrace modernism in painting and writing, Virginia was faithful to the emotions she had felt for Vanessa during their shared childhood. Since then, both women had married. Virginia was frankly jealous of the Bell children as they threatened to absorb all their mother's maternal instincts. In her mid-thirties, Woolf wrote to Vanessa that she had a right to receive her physical demonstrations of love before Julian and Quentin Bell (*L2*, no. 784: To Vanessa Bell, 10 September 1916, 114). When Vanessa's third and last child was born, Virginia referred to herself as her sister's 'firstborn' (*L2*, no. 1000: To Vanessa Bell, 31 December 1918, 312). Aged nearly forty, Woolf demanded of Vanessa Bell why she had given birth to her in a world whose crises were so hard to negotiate (*L2*, no. 1169: To Vanessa Bell, 17 March 1921, 458). Woolf would continue to regard Vanessa Bell as a surrogate-mother until her own death—and one of her two suicide notes was to her sister. After Leonard Woolf, Virginia most loved Vanessa Bell, with whom she shared all the baggage they had brought with them from the Victorian world into the modern world.

Another woman writer, Elizabeth Gaskell (1810–1865), also clearly felt maternal towards Charlotte Brontë, pitying her solitary state. The two writers first met at the Kay-Shuttleworth's holiday home, Briery Close, in the summer of 1850. On a subsequent visit to the Haworth Parsonage, Gaskell bribed one of the two servants to show her the slab in the church under which the remains of the Brontë family, except Anne, were interred. Gaskell also related the old servant, Tabby's, account of how the three writing sisters had, from childhood, put away their sewing in the evening and paced round the dining room table. Anne and Charlotte had continued this practice, and then Charlotte alone paced round the table. Tabby confided that 'now my heart aches to hear Miss Brontë walking, walking, on alone' (*LMG*, no. 166: Mrs Gaskell to ?John Forster, September, 1853, 247). Gaskell's choice of anecdote before embarking on her *Life of Charlotte Brontë,* suggests that her subject had already become a tragic heroine in her mind. In her *Life,* Gaskell wished to extend a sort of maternal protection over Charlotte Brontë. The pity she felt for Charlotte Brontë had soon been transmuted into love and she was determined to make others see her subject as she did.

As with Harriet Martineau, Gaskell was struck by Charlotte's smallness and shyness which appealed to Gaskell's protective maternal solicitude for her. She described Charlotte as being '(as she calls herself) *undeveloped*; thin and more than half a head shorter than I' (*LMG*, no. 75: Mrs Gaskell to

Catherine Winkworth, 25 August 1850, 123). While both writers were the guests of Sir James and Lady Kay-Shuttleworth, they were included in an invitation to the Arnolds at Fox How in Ambleside. Gaskell observed with pity how Charlotte's nerves were severely taxed by the demands of a gathering of unknown people. Although the party was to be limited to twelve, 'she suffered the whole day from an acute headache brought on by apprehension of the evening' (*LMG*, no. 76: Mrs Gaskell to Unknown, August 1850, 127).

Gaskell retained a high enough opinion of her fellow-writer to devote herself to the arduous task of writing Charlotte Brontë's biography. In her *Life of Charlotte Brontë*, Gaskell divided her subject's life into two: the domesticated Victorian daughter and the writer. It was this dichotomy that Woolf inherited, as she was very familiar with Gaskell's biography. Apart from its subject, doubtless Woolf would also have been interested to see how a female fellow-novelist had approached the task of writing a biography of another woman—a form Woolf wanted to revolutionise as well as the novel genre.

Woolf's final mother-figure, who came to be central to her life in the 1930s, was the considerably older feminist composer Ethel Smyth (1858–1944). Smyth grew to maturity during the Victorian era, but she challenged many of its assumptions about women. She believed that women should be able to practise a profession; she fought to have her compositions performed and published: between 1878 and 1930, Smyth published:

> two sets of lieder, several songs for voice and chamber, and a choral symphony. Today we also know of her unpublished works for solo, piano, organ, and various chamber ensembles. In addition to composing, Smyth was also a devoted letter-writer, and she turned to writing memoirs and essays later in life, publishing ten volumes of prose between 1919 and 1940. (https://www.ethelsmyth.org /about/ Accessed 23 October 2021)

Woolf was more self-aware—or franker—about her emotional needs than Charlotte Brontë. She was conscious of the role she wanted Smyth to play in her life, and it was a maternal one, as she candidly acknowledged in a letter to Ethel herself (*L4*, no. 2204: To Ethel Smyth, 16 July 1930, 188). The following year, Woolf elaborated further on the maternal qualities of Smyth and her protective attitude towards her (*L4*, no. 2342: To Ethel Smyth, 1 April 1931, 302). She was a marked contrast to some of Woolf's earlier mother surrogates. Unlike Violet Dickinson and Madge Vaughan, Smyth was a public figure and a well-known practitioner in one of the arts. Additionally, Smyth was, and continued to be, an unconventional rebel against her Victorian upbringing. Here again she was different from most of Woolf's other surrogate mothers, who tended to be more conservative and traditional in their lives and work.

During Woolf's last decade, Smyth was her main correspondent. Woolf had been attracted to Smyth before they met because she so enjoyed the multiple volumes of Smyth's autobiography, and read them as they were published. In her turn, Smyth's initial attraction was to Woolf's *A Room of One's Own*. After reading this feminist polemic, Smyth wrote a fan letter to Woolf and the two women first met in February 1930. They also knew each other's families; in one of her autobiographical memoirs, *Impressions That Remain* (1919), Smyth had immortalised an apocryphal tale about Woolf's maternal great-grandfather.

To some extent, Smyth further radicalised Woolf. In 1909, Woolf had rather half-heartedly addressed envelopes to support the struggle for female suffrage. By contrast, Smyth had been completely caught up in the movement for a time and even went to prison for it. Smyth possibly influenced *The Years*, in which Woolf wrote of the militant suffragette Rose Pargiter; and *Three Guineas*, where Woolf exposed the restrictions that men had put on women's lives. It was perhaps under Smyth's influence Woolf learnt to write out her anger about the disabilities of women in a patriarchy.

In Woolf's letters to Smyth, she confided much more about her character, beliefs, and formative experiences than she did to most of her other correspondents. Woolf was able to write of her mother: having written to Smyth, 'Yes, I think your mother adorable', she added, 'So was mine' (*L4*, no. 2138: To Ethel Smyth, 13 February 1930, 137). A month later, Woolf was pleased and impressed when Smyth quoted the very quotation about her mother that was in Woolf's mind (*L4*, no. 2154: To Ethel Smyth, 10 March 1930, 149).

The topics Woolf discussed with Smyth in her letters were sometimes more like her diary entries than the letters she wrote to her other correspondents; they were more self-revealingly personal and intimate. She confided important feelings, for example, about her own sexuality. Woolf revealed what she herself believed was her own sexual cowardice and lack of experiment and exploration in this area of her life (*L4*, no. 2194: To Ethel Smyth, 22 June 1930, 180). Woolf elaborated on this in another letter, when she described her feelings for men. Perhaps surprisingly, she admitted that the men whom she had found sexually attractive were the most conventional and conformist of their sex. These men terrified her and she felt safer with the type of man with whom her main interactions were mental. (Regrettably, Woolf did not name the former, nor where she had met them.) She added that she got 'exquisite pleasure' from holding hands and making contact with either men or women's bodies. She added a warning (that Woolf scholars would be wise to heed) about sexuality generally when she wrote that she viewed it as a mistake to try to pigeon-hole and label complex sexual relationships (*L4*, no. 2218: To Ethel Smyth, 15 August 1930, 200).

In another letter to Smyth, Woolf directly asked her to rehearse the arguments against suicide. Woolf here confessed the extreme variability and volatility of her emotional thermometer during a single day. Woolf hastily added that she was not about to take her own life, but merely wants to know (*L4*, no. 2265: To Ethel Smyth, 30 October 1930, 242). However, she later told her how having been dragged to a party by Smyth had inflicted such suffering that she had felt suicidal. Only Leonard Woolf's presence had prevented her from killing herself (*L4*, no. 2341: To Ethel Smyth, 29 March 1931, 302). Only at this stage of her life was Woolf able to go through the phase of fairly aggressive adolescent rebellion against a mother-substitute, of which she had been deprived by her mother's early death. (This may be compared to Charlotte Brontë turning on one of her surrogate-mothers, Margaret Wooler, when she thought the latter did not understand why Charlotte was so worried about her youngest sister.) Woolf's outspokenness in this instance marked a great change from her relationships with earlier mother-substitutes. Woolf may have been vaguely aware of this, because she told Smyth this incident had triggered memories of her adolescence when she had been forced to attend society parties with her half-brother George Duckworth.

Smyth's behaviour also reminded her of how her father had behaved after he had been widowed for a second time. As a mature adult, she was no longer prepared to tolerate excessive emotional demands; she made the protest to Smyth that she had been unable to voice to her father. Stephen's insecurity about the value of his work and his despair at being widowed skewed his children's relationships with him. She associated Smyth with the worst aspect of her Victorian past, with its emotional intensity and hypocrisy (*L5*, no. 2859: To Ethel Smyth, 26 February 1934, 279). In fact, Woolf's complex response seems to have reflected her ambivalent feelings about both her parents in the Victorian past. Further, Smyth's Christianity brought back memories of her Stephen cousins and their perpetual attempts to convert Virginia and her siblings to their faith. Again, Woolf had fought back against this as an adult and the theme of forced conversion is important in *Mrs Dalloway*.

Woolf also particularly distrusted egotism of which Smyth had remarkably large quantities. Several times Woolf told Smyth how much she loathed the egotism in her writing, when Smyth persisted in putting forward her own experiences of sexual discrimination. Woolf described the effect Smyth's egotism had on her: it caused her one of her severest types of headaches, so that she had to shut down Smyth's monologue, which was entirely composed of personal grievances, for her own mental survival (*L4*, no. 2375: To Vanessa Bell, 23 May 1931, 334). Ultimately, though for different reasons, Smyth failed as had Woolf's earlier surrogate-mothers. Their relationship confirmed Woolf's view about the general impossibility of understanding between people. On one occasion, Woolf listed the adjectives suggested by Smyth's description of her: she was 'chill, cold, immaculate, inapproachable'; a with-drawn 'statue' (*L4*, no. 2420: To Ethel Smyth, 16 August 1931, 368). Yet against this negativity were set two positives which remained and prevented a complete rupture between the two women. Smyth acknowledged Woolf's importance to her, which Woolf appreciated. Then Smyth gave her what was withheld by Bloomsbury friends, who were silent about their personal emotions. By contrast, Smyth showed and openly revealed what she felt (*L4*, no. 2498: To Ethel Smyth, 29 December 1931, 422).

The Brontës' experience of being motherless was one that filtered through into the majority of their mature novels, as well as being present in their juvenilia. Perhaps most significantly in the juvenilia the motherless children recreated themselves as powerful presences in the imaginary kingdom of Angria, who were able to resurrect their characters after they had succumbed to violent deaths. They could only achieve in fantasy what they must have longed to be able to do in their real lives—to raise their dead mother and sisters.

In *The Professor*, neither the hero nor the heroine has any parents. *Jane Eyre*'s eponymous heroine has the same lack of both parents. In *Shirley*, whose second half was written after the death of both Emily and Anne Brontë, Caroline Helstone's mother miraculously materialises just in time to save her daughter from dying from lack of love. This wish-fulfilment must have been a reflection of Charlotte mental state at this time. The eponymous heroine of *Shirley* has also lost both her parents. In her final novel, *Villette*, Lucy not only lacks both parents but has no living relatives at all. Charlotte Brontë imaged Lucy Snowe's multiple bereavements (as Woolf would do later) in terms of changes in the physical world: we get no details other than the presentation of the first-person narrator's (metaphorical?) view of herself as the sole survivor of her family from a ship wrecked at sea. At the end of *Villette*, the storm imagery recurs, and surely confirms the reader's instinctive belief that Paul Emanuel had perished at sea, despite the ambiguous ending (which was apparently written this way at Mr Brontë's request). Charlotte learnt to use storms as effectively as Shakespeare to highlight when a character's life is completely convulsed. Sadly, by this time Charlotte was so chronically depressed that she could not even envisage a happy outcome for her heroine, who also was depressed.

In Emily Brontë's *Wuthering Heights*, the first generation of characters die before the main story of their descendants really begins. It is easy to forget that the main protagonists are still adolescents when major decisions about marriage are taken. In the second generation, Hareton's and the younger Catherine's mother both die either giving birth or shortly afterwards. The other major second-generation character, Linton Heathcliff, only enters the world of *Wuthering Heights* when his mother, Isabella Heathcliff (née Linton) dies offstage in the south of England. This is one of the rare instances in the Brontës' novels that a death is used as a plot device.

Anne Brontë's eponymous heroine, Agnes Grey, is the sole heroine who is blessed with a mother from beginning to end of the novel. As suggested earlier, this may be because Anne found it easier to accept Aunt Branwell as a mother-substitute, being so young at the time of Mrs Brontë's death that she can have had no memory of her. The heroine of *The Tenant of Wildfell Hall* mirrors Anne's situation: Helen Graham is also reared by her aunt; her mother having died at some indeterminate time before the novel opens. The hero, Gilbert Markham has a mother but no father.

Similarly, in Woolf's first novel, *The Voyage Out*, the heroine, Rachel Vinrace, is a very young twenty-four-year-old. It is implied that this is because her mother died when she was only eleven and she was reared by her two spinster aunts who completely failed to equip her to function in the adult world of relationships—and especially the marital one. The novel sees her try, and fail, to overcome the limitations imposed on her. Other novels reveal quite a large number of characters who lack at least one parent, be it father or mother. Most interesting are the female protagonists whose mothers are dead or absent: Clarissa Dalloway's mother is notably missing from *Mrs Dalloway* in the memories of youth that occupy a number of characters in that book. (though she too has an aunt, Miss Parry). Delia Pargiter is another variation on the theme; we see her ambivalent attitude towards her dying mother in *The Years*.

Chapter Two

Shared Life Experiences of the Brontës and Virginia Woolf

It is an undeniable fact that the Brontës and Virginia Woolf all suffered from poor health. Woolf actually published an essay in 1930 on the subject of illness: 'On Being Ill'. In this essay, she expressed her surprise that though illness was so common it occupied a very small place in fiction. She thought that it should have received equal treatment with such universal themes as love, battles, and jealousy (*EV*, 195). Certainly, it was a marked feature in the lives of both the Brontë family and that of Woolf. In a letter Charlotte Brontë passed the striking observation that they had been so accustomed to ill health that they virtually ignored it and were unaware of their deterioration: 'Unused, any of us, to the possession of robust health, we have not noticed the gradual approaches of decay; we did not know its symptoms: the little cough, the small appetite, the tendency to take cold at every variation of atmosphere have been regarded as things of course' (*L&L2*, no. 326: To W. S. Williams, 15 January 1849, 21). For Charlotte Brontë and Virginia Woolf physical and mental ailments seem to have been inextricably linked. As Carol A. Senf has commented, although the three Brontë sisters' novels written between 1846 and 1853 are in some respects very different, they all 'depict physical and mental illness . . . and often represent social factors that contribute to physical and mental illness, especially for women and other marginalised characters' (Senf, in *A Companion to the Brontës*, 372). In Woolf's case, her ill health began with the death of her mother when she was thirteen and had her first breakdown. As with Charlotte Brontë, it is difficult at times to distinguish between physical and mental illness: some of Woolf's illnesses were psychosomatic in origin. Hermione Lee comments of Woolf: 'All her life, severe physical symptoms signalled and accompanied phases of agitation or depression' (Lee, *Virginia Woolf* [London: Chatto & Windus], 185). Together these illnesses had a very marked impact on Woolf's life: at the beginning of 1922, she calculated that she had lost five years to illness (and there was much more to come) (*L2*, no. 1210: To E. M. Forster, 21 January 1922, 499).

Ann Dinsdale and Kathryn White have written of the unhealthiness of Haworth in the Brontës' time and explained the reasons for this. At Patrick Brontë's request, Benjamin Babbage as a representative of the General Board of Health, compiled a report on living conditions in Haworth, which was published in 1850. Babbage reported that living conditions were overcrowded and sanitation utterly inadequate, there being only one privy to every four and a half households. The sewerage system was nonexistent and sewage ran down Main Street in open channels. Further, the water supply at the bottom of the hill was contaminated both by sewage and by the decomposing bodies buried in the graveyard at the top of the village. Babbage found that the average age of death in Haworth was twenty-five which was as low as that in some of the worst London slums. Just over 40 percent of Haworth's children died before they had attained their sixth birthdays. While the Brontës had a private two-seater privy and a well the water of which came from the moor, they were still affected by the badly drained and crowded graveyard, which they could see from the parsonage (*Brontë Parsonage Museum, Haworth, A Souvenir Guide*, 9).

Illness was a recurrent event in the lives of the Brontës, both during their childhood and their adulthood. Not only they themselves were often ill, but they were surrounded by family members who were sick, often resulting in their deaths. Janis McLarren Caldwell has justly commented: 'The imaginary worlds of the Brontës were profoundly shaped by the chronic ill-health and early deaths that plagued the family' (Caldwell in *The Brontës in Context*, 335). The ill-health which the Brontë children experienced was not only physical: Caldwell advanced the theory that all the Brontës suffered from some kind of neurosis:

> Each experienced a different kind, attributing his or her distress to one of the multiple types of mental illness described in the Victorian period. Patrick acknowledged a tendency to melancholy, often associated with stress in his job as a clergyman combined with the task of supporting his motherless children. Branwell, disappointed in love, consumed alcohol and opium at a suicidal rate. Under the stress of leaving home for school at Roe Head, Emily suffered a homesickness expressed as wasting and weakness, which frightened Charlotte enough to have her sent home. When Anne was sent to Roe Head instead, she also experienced a form of depression, in her case identified as religious melancholy.

Anne, too, had to be sent home, because Charlotte became 'extremely alarmed' by Anne's 'severe symptoms'. Charlotte Brontë 'herself often classified her various depressions as hypochondria' (Caldwell, 344).

The connections between the mind and the body had been disputed during the Victorian period. Andrew Skull baldly stated that the problem of distinguishing 'between neurological and psychiatric' illness was not satisfactorily resolved by the Victorians (Andrew Scull, *Hysteria*, 87). Many specialists viewed women's biological functions as causing much female ill-health. Lisa Appignanesi comments that in 1921: 'As if trapped in the swing of a vast pendulum, the mind doctors focused their attention on physical or biological explanations only to be corrected by their followers, who emphasised the psychological and mental, and then back again' (Appignanesi, 153).

This debate, therefore, was still very much alive in Woolf's adulthood. In her youth, Virginia became mentally unwell as Stella Duckworth's health fluctuated. She was examined by the Stephens' family doctor, Seton, who stopped Virginia's lessons and prescribed milk and some medicine (Virginia was unsure what this was) (*PA*, 9 May 1897, 83). Dr Seton also recommended physical, outdoor activity. Gardening was suggested—not something that Woolf pursued as an adult. Leslie Stephen took up this suggestion '& the back garden is to be reclaimed—that will be a truly gigantic work of genius'. This sounds as though none of the combined family looked after the garden, that it was neglected. However, Virginia added, 'nevertheless we will try'. To this end 'a fork, a spade, a hoe & a rake' had been ordered in preparation for the next day's commencement of gardening (*APA*, 11 May 1897, 84). Throughout May and June, Virginia recorded progress in the gardening, in which Vanessa also participated.

No doubt their early experiences dictated the sort of illnesses they explored in their novels. The medical doctor became increasingly important as the Victorian period progressed. Charlotte Brontë would put a doctor centre stage in her final novel, *Villette*, whose central character and first-person narrator certainly suffered from severe depression. Physical as well as mental illness were explored. As both the Brontës' elder sisters had died of consumption, for example, this fatal illness recurs in a number of their novels. Patrick Brontë had a great respect for the medical profession and was an amateur student of medicine himself. Sally Shuttleworth has suggested that the name of Charlotte Brontë's doctor in *Villette* was taken 'from the text which held the place of a secular Bible in the Brontë household' (Shuttleworth, 10). This book was, to give it its full title: Thomas John Graham's *Modern Domestic Medicine: A Popular Treatise, Illustrating the Symptoms, Causes, Distinctions, and Current Treatment of the Diseases Incident to the Human Frame; Embracing the Modern Improvements in Medicine*, which was written to be used by 'clergymen, families, and students in medicine' (Graham, title page). No doubt Patrick Brontë consulted it both for his own family and those of his parishioners. Like his daughters, Patrick Brontë was intrigued by the relationship between physical and mental illnesses. Every symptom of either was carefully researched in the parsonage copy of *Domestic Medicine*. Mr Brontë added to the margins of the pages of this book his own comments on and experiences of illnesses as he met them, both physical and mental, among his own family and in the lives of his parishioners. As Shuttleworth commented: 'Fear of mental instability was not a peculiar quirk of the Brontë household, occasioned by Branwell's illness and too much isolation in a moorland landscape, but was rather a widespread cultural phenomenon' (Shuttleworth, 33).

Shuttleworth's study of the awareness of the Brontës' knowledge of current theories of mental and physical illness makes the point that 'By the nineteenth century nervous disorders had become nervous disease, a threatening state of organic pathology which seemed to menace bodily, mental and social health' (Shuttleworth, 47). It is fascinating that Virginia Woolf made a similar connection between the individual's ill health and the general condition in the third decade of the twentieth century. She, however, applied it not just to society, but the whole human race, and seemed much more accepting of it. She believed that every ten years there was 'one of those private orientations which match the vast one which is, to my mind, general now in the race' (*L3*, no. 1337: To Gerald Brenan, 25 September 1922, 598–99).

Charlotte Brontë's early experiences affected her from her childhood until her death. At Roe Head School, a fellow pupil and close friend of Charlotte Brontë, Mary Taylor, noticed that Charlotte already suffered from depression: 'When in health she used to talk better, and indeed when in low spirits never talked at all' (Quoted in Gaskell's *Life*, 121). Mary Taylor also stated that Charlotte's 'feeble health gave her her yielding manner, for she could never oppose any one without gathering up all her strength for the struggle' (quoted in Gaskell's *Life*, 154). Gaskell herself was struck by the 'absence of hope' in Charlotte Brontë's letters to Ellen Nussey, even in the early ones (*Life*, 119). Gaskell suggests that Charlotte Brontë's early hopelessness was either 'so to speak, constitutional' or that perhaps 'the deep pang of losing two elder sisters combined with a permanent state of bodily weakness' caused it (Gaskell's *Life*, 120). It is worth noting both that Charlotte's depression was not related to her early loss of her mother by Gaskell and Taylor and that they both speak of a combination of poor physical and mental health in Charlotte Brontë. Later on in her *Life*, Gaskell wrote that it was inevitable that 'the intensity of her feeling should wear out her physical health (*Life*, 202). Later, Charlotte Brontë suffered from a physical illness, described as a 'fever', in which a 'depression of health produced depression of spirits' (*Life*, 452).

Even before the loss of her three siblings who had survived to adulthood, Charlotte Brontë was no stranger to depression. She described the nature of the illness, based on her own experience of what she called 'hypochondria', both in a letter and in her novel *The Professor.* The editor of Charlotte Brontë's letters, Margaret Smith, explained that her subject 'uses this word to mean intense depression, not necessarily accompanied by preoccupation with imaginary ailments' (*Letters of Charlotte Brontë*, vol. 1: footnote 7, 506). Caldwell also contributed to our understanding of the term hypochondria, though she ascribed physical symptoms, commenting that in Victorian times it was defined as 'a specific physical and mental illness characterised by pain under the ribs and low spirits' (Caldwell in *The Brontës in Context*, 344). Caldwell did not offer an opinion as to whether or not these bodily symptoms were psychosomatic or not. However, Charlotte Brontë appeared to have viewed it primarily as a mental condition. It is worth quoting both passages about hypochondria to emphasise this. In her letter to Miss Wooler, Charlotte expressed her pity for Margaret Wooler's younger brother, Thomas Wooler, who has suffered from 'the tyranny of Hypochondria' for more than a decade:

> a most dreadful doom, far worse than that of a man with healthy nerves buried for the same length of time in a subterranean dungeon. I endured it but a year, and assuredly I can never forget the concentrated anguish of certain insufferable moments, and the heavy gloom of many long hours, besides the preternatural horrors which seemed to clothe existence and nature, and which made life a continual waking nightmare. Under such circumstances the morbid nerves can know neither peace nor enjoyment; whatever touches pierces them, sensation for them is suffering. A weary burden nervous patients become to those about them; they know this and it infuses a new gall, corrosive in its extreme acritude, into their bitter cup. When I was at Dewsbury Moor I could have been no better company for you than a stalking ghost, and I remember I felt my incapacity to *impart* pleasure fully as much as my powerlessness to *receive* it. (*L&L1*, no. 210: To Miss Wooler, no date, (but Smith gives November/December 1846), volume 2, 505–506)

William Crimsworth, the hero of *The Professor*, enlarges on a 'reaction' to the 'sweet delirium' he had been experiencing on becoming engaged to Frances Henri, the novel's heroine:

> A horror of great darkness fell upon me; I felt my chamber invaded by one I had known formerly, but had thought for ever departed: I was temporarily a prey to Hypochondria. She had been my acquaintance, nay my guest, once before in boyhood; I had entertained her at bed and board for a year; for that space of time I had her to myself in secret; she lay with me, she eat with me, she walked out with me, shewing me nooks in woods, hollows in hills, where we could sit

together, and where she could drop her drear veil over me, and so hide sky and sun, grass and green tree; taking me entirely to her death-cold bosom, and holding me with arms of bone. (*The Professor*, 191)

Hypochondria (to whom both Crimsworth and Brontë give the female sex) talked of death and even attempted to persuade him to take his own life. Retrospectively, Crimsworth understands why he suffered from hypochondria when a boy. Then he had been a lonely orphan and without sympathetic siblings. Now, however, when his prospects appear to be prospering, he cannot comprehend why hypochondria should assault him again. He tells the reader of his struggle with this personified 'demon': 'I repulsed her, as one would a dreaded and ghastly concubine coming to embitter a husband's heart towards his young bride; in vain; she kept her sway over me for that night and the next day, and eight succeeding days. Afterwards my spirits began slowly to recover their tone; my appetite returned, and in a fortnight I was well' (*The Professor*, 191–92).

Like the Victorian doctors and her contemporaries, Woolf pondered on the connections between the mind and the body. Like Charlotte Brontë, she created a female doctor in *The Years*, the last novel published during her lifetime. Dr Peggy Pargiter's view of the medical profession very probably resembles her creator's: Peggy tells Eleanor that doctors 'know very little about the body; absolutely nothing about the mind' (*TY*, 365). Certainly, Woolf was frustrated that the medical experts practising in Harley Street (and therefore at the top of their profession) could offer no solution to her health problems (*DIV*, 15 January 1933, 143). Like Charlotte Brontë, at times of particular stress Woolf experienced physical and mental symptoms. Maurice Craig, a modern psychiatrist, was consulted by the Woolfs about Virginia's mental illnesses. He demystified the vocabulary of mental specialists. He avoided the word 'mad'. He also tried to change old attitudes to the insane: 'the student will be constantly reminded to look upon mental disorders in the same way that he views disease in general. This warning is very necessary, as so many men regard the insane as if they were the victims of some strange visitation, and not sufferers from ordinary illness' (Craig, iii). He also offered a definition of insanity which he borrowed from Henry Maudsley's (1835–1913) *Pathology of the Sane*.

By insanity of mind is meant such derangement of the leading functions of thought, feeling, and will, together or separately, as disables the person from thinking the thoughts, feeling the feelings, and duties of the social body, in, for, and by which he lives. . . . Insanity means essentially then such a want of harmony between the individual and his social medium, by reason of some defect or fault of mind in him, as prevents him from living and working among his kind in social organisation. Completely out of tune there, he is a social discord of which nothing can be made. (quoted by Craig, 24)

What is disturbing about this definition is that insanity is not only an individual state of mind but is socially defined as well. This seems to suggest that disregarding society's values or behaviour could on their own be considered to arise from insanity. This is particularly relevant as, as Appignanesi points out, the late nineteenth century was a time of social upheaval, in which women were rejecting the Victorian status quo which defined women in terms of their biological and reproductive functions. Women were demanding not only 'the vote and for equality within marriage', but also an education which equalled that of their male counterparts, and generally a greater freedom (Appignanesi, 106). This led to 'a moral panic which envisaged that middle-class women's attempts to change their lives' resulting 'in madness and the decline of the species' (Appignanesi, 110).

Craig did, however, mention several of the symptoms which Woolf experienced. Examples of these include fatigue, insomnia, loss of control, refusal of food, and headaches (Craig, 75, 85, 93, 121, 244). He was in harmony with the more old-fashioned Savage in applying a modified treatment of confinement to bed and rest to the mentally unwell. As we shall see (below), this treatment originated in America from Dr Silas Weir Mitchell. Leonard Woolf's autobiography confirmed that his wife did manifest the symptoms identified by Craig, and that the rest cure was apparently the only treatment that they had recourse to, and that it was generally effective.

A new diagnosis was introduced at the turn of the nineteenth century into the twentieth: 'neurasthenia' or 'nerve exhaustion'. As Appignanesi explained it viewed a number of different catalysts, primarily heredity, gender, and modern life (Appignanesi, 101–102). Leonard Woolf confirmed that his wife acquired this label: 'The doctors called it neurasthenia' but he commented that none of the mental specialists understood what caused this disease, or its nature. He said it was an umbrella term, 'which covered a multitude of sins, symptoms, and miseries' (Leonard Woolf, *Beginning Again*, 76).

Unlike Charlotte Brontë, Woolf several times in her adult life appears to have crossed the boundary between sanity and insanity. Some doctors who treated mental diseases were actually hostile to the women they treated. An eminent American specialist, Silas Weir Mitchell (1828–1914), was one such, and he invented the 'rest cure' which (in a modified form) was several times inflicted on Woolf. Michell's attitude towards the female patient is summed up by his biographer:

Mitchell's world is a microcosm illustrating how gender politics deformed the benevolent authority of medicine and sustained myth, idealisation, and fantasy.

While medicine made remarkable advances as a science and a profession, it also became the most powerful weapon in the fierce nineteenth-century fight against women's rights outside the home. Mitchell's assumptions represent the attitudes of an age that attempted to bridle a force that was ultimately impossible to restrain. (Nancy Cervetti, 2–3)

Woolf was treated with some elements of Mitchell's regime, including bed rest, no intellectual activities, and overfeeding.

One of Virginia Woolf's long-term psychiatric advisors was the eminent Dr George Henry Savage (1842–1921). His dates show that he overlapped with the Brontës, as well as with Virginia Woolf. His major book, *Insanity and Allied Neuroses: Practical and Clinical* was first published in 1881. This publication intersected the time between the Brontës and Virginia Woolf's writing careers. Savage's views of mental illness are particularly interesting in suggesting the consequences which could result from 'fright and nervous shock', which may be applicable to Crimsworth. Crimsworth's attack of hypochondria seems to be an anticipation of what Savage referred to as 'post-connubial insanity' which are 'due to the shock of marriage' (Savage, 55). Brontë seemed to hint at this by the choice of metaphor she ascribed to her first-person narrator: he referred to a 'dreaded and ghastly concubine' who embittered 'a husband's heart towards his young bride'. It appears that Crimsworth was destabilised by the thought of lived domesticity with Frances Henri and particularly sexual intimacy. Savage's comment on love in 1881, was also highly applicable to the time when Brontë was writing *The Professor* in the 1840s: 'Education and the restrictions of society have done much to suppress the appearances of emotion, and have controlled most markedly the exhibitions of sexual longing. But the root of the evil lies deeper, and as soon as self-control is lost, one sees the passion manifested in all their naked truth (Savage, 53). It may be this which persuaded Crimsworth not to confide in anyone about his tussle with hypochondria.

It is of great interest that many things had not changed between Savage's book and the experiences of the Brontë sisters. Of particular interest are Savage's comments of the high incidence of insanity among governesses, and his explanation for this:

In Bethlem we have a very large number of governesses. . . . To my mind, the governess's life is a very good example of the predisposing causes of insanity, as seen in action. Thus we see a girl of nervous temperament, with high powers of receptivity, anxious, self-sacrificing, and with emotional and artistic feeling, thoroughly good and hardworking.

He gives the example of a girl who has a marked gift for music. She is forced to exhaust herself in taking advantage of the music masters her parents provide. She comes to suffer from 'dyspepsia, constipation, and sleepless-ness', her head bothers her, 'menstrual irregularity' occurs. 'In this unstable condition she obtains some engagement, or, more disastrously, I would say, a situation. Here she is better fed, and has regular hours; but, on the other hand, there are no means of drawing herself out of her herself.

> The child, or children, are more or less trying to her temper, and she, the enthu-siast, is hourly annoyed by the utter lack of interest exhibited by her pupils. She often has no companions of her own age and station, the heads of the household look down upon her as belonging to an inferior grade, and her own education and position prevent her from associating with the domestic servants. In this manner she becomes only one degree better than the prisoner in solitary confine-ment. She is thrown into a purely subjective life, building castles in the air . . . till at last the castles in the air become to her no longer fairy ideas, but actual realities. She thinks herself wedded to some wealthy nobleman. (Savage, 34–35)

This description of the governess's life in a situation in a family can aptly be applied to Charlotte and Anne Brontës' experiences in such a position. Charlotte Brontë wrote in terms recognisable from Savage's description of such a situation: 'I see now more clearly than I have ever done before that a private governess has no existence, is not considered as a living and rational being except as connected with the wearisome duties she has to fulfil. While she is teaching the children, working for them, amusing them, it is all right. If she steals a moment for herself she is a nuisance (*L&L1*, no. 51: To Emily J. Brontë, 8 June 1839, 159). The same month, she again described her expe-riences as a governess with the Sidgwick family: 'imagine the miseries of a reserved wretch like me . . . all strangers, people whose faces I had never seen before—in this state of things having the charge given me of a set of pampered, spoilt, & turbulent children'. Although Mrs Sidgwick is generally thought to be an agreeable person, 'does this compensate for the absence of every fine feeling, of every gentle and delicate sentiment? . . . she does not know my character, and she does not wish to know it (*L&L1*, no. 52: To Ellen Nussey, 1 July 1839, 160–61). The year before Charlotte Brontë had expressed the dreariness of life 'passed amidst sights, sounds, and compan-ions all alien to the nature within us' (*L&L1*, no. 37: To Ellen Nussey, 2 April 1837, 138–39. Smith dated this letter 2 October 1838). Although Charlotte soon left her post at the Sidgwicks, she did sometimes display a determina-tion to endure and succeed. In the letter quoted above (1 July 1839), she had added: 'I said to myself I have never yet quitted a place without gaining a friend. Adversity is a good school. . . . I resolved to be patient'.

Both Charlotte and Anne Brontë wrote novels in which the heroine was a governess: *Jane Eyre* and *Agnes Grey*. Arguably, Jane acquired the husband of her choice and the independent income that Charlotte Brontë wished for. It is at least worth considering whether Charlotte avoided madness by projecting her possibly subjective fantasies of a governesses' 'rags to riches' stories into a fictional representation of the governess's rise in the social and financial scale. It is conceivable that she aimed to transform imaginatively her own life, as she transformed her bereavement and grief after her two sisters' deaths by imagining happy marriages for them.

In Anne Brontë's *Agnes Grey*, the eponymous heroine actually voiced many of the situations and inconveniences that Savage described as involved in the life of a governess. Savage could almost have read *Agnes Grey* and based his description of the governess's experience on Anne Brontë's heroine! Savage described how a young woman's family's financial situation might take a turn for the worse, forcing the daughters to seek a financially remunerative employment outside the home and away from her family:

> many who lead the life of governesses have been compelled to do so by some domestic misfortune which has suddenly compelled them to turn their education to account, as being the only sure source of livelihood enabling them to preserve the vestiges of their former social position. (Savage, 35)

This aptly describes the Grey family's circumstances. Richard Grey, a clergyman, had married a woman who was his social superior. Mrs Grey's family then disinherited her. Richard Grey wanted to provide for his wife and family an improved financial standard of living. When a merchant friend persuaded Mr Grey that he can greatly increase his wealth, Richard Grey sold his patrimony and invested the proceeds in 'mercantile pursuits'. Agnes's father was cheerfully convinced that his wealth would be substantially increased, but Agnes tells us that his expectations were bitterly disappointed. The ship had been wrecked at sea with the loss of all the Greys' fortune and the merchant himself. Agnes herself remained buoyant under this affliction, but her father's mental and physical health were undermined. He did not go mad, but he did not survive his loss beyond about a year and dies in the course of Agnes's narrative.

Agnes's experiences as a governess amply bears out Savage's description: 'The name of governess, I soon found, was a mere mockery as applied to me; my pupils had no more notion of obedience than a wild, unbroken colt (*AG*, 24). Though she persevered she found that 'my best intentions and most strenuous efforts seemed productive of no better result, than sport to the children, dissatisfaction to their parents, and torment to myself' (*AG*, 26). Agnes became isolated when the only person she could talk to, Betty the nurse, is sacked for physically chastising the children. However, even Betty belonged to a lower social class than Agnes, which is reflected in the fact that Anne uses Betty's forename, while Betty calls Agnes 'Miss Grey'.

Agnes, too, was eventually sacked. She found another post with the Murray family. There was an inauspicious beginning when Mrs Murray did not deign to introduce herself to Agnes until the day after her arrival. She reflected that her mother would have behaved better than this even to a new kitchen servant. Agnes observed, with some surprise, 'that while Mrs Murray was so extremely solicitous for the comfort and happiness of her children, and continually talking about it, she never once mentioned mine, though they were at home surrounded by friends, and I am an alien among strangers' (*AG*, 61). Rosalie never loses sight of the fact that Agnes is 'a hireling' and the daughter of 'a poor clergyman' (*AG*, 61).

The children's friends never noticed her when they are all out walking. Agnes commented on this:

it was disagreeable to walk beside them, as if listening to what they said, or wishing to be thought one of them, while they talked over me or across, and it their eyes, in speaking, chanced to fall on me, it seemed as if they looked on vacancy—as if they either did not see me, or were very desirous to make it appear so. (*AG*, 106)

Savage's insight that the governess cannot mix with the servants either, is well born out in Agnes's experiences:

The servants, seeing in what little estimation the governess was held by both parents and children, regulated their behaviour by the same standard.

I frequently stood up for *them*, at the risk of injury to myself, against the tyranny and injustice of their young masters and mistresses; and I always endeavoured to give them as little trouble as possible; but they entirely neglected my comfort, despised my requests and slighted my directions. (*AG*, 69)

Agnes retained her sanity by asserting her sense of moral superiority to the whole household and cherishing her growing love and preoccupation with the good clergyman, Edward Weston, whom she will eventually marry. Her sanity is never under threat.

Charlotte Brontë did not show a major insane character in *Jane Eyre*, but driving the plot is the mad character Bertha Mason Rochester, first wife of Edward Rochester. In a letter, Charlotte wrote that she agreed with her contemporaries, Julia Kavanagh and Leigh Hunt, in the view that Bertha ('the "'Maniac'"') is:

shocking, but I know that it is but too natural. There is a phase of insanity which may be called moral madness, in which all that is good or even human seems to disappear from the mind and a fiend-nature replaces it. The sole aim and desire of the being thus possessed is to exasperate, to molest, to destroy; and preternatural ingenuity and energy are often exercised to that dreadful end. The aspect, in such cases, assimilates with the disposition—all seems demonised. It is true that profound pity ought to be the only sentiment elicited by the view of such degradation, and equally true is it that I have not sufficiently dwelt on that feeling: I have erred in making *horror* too predominant. Mrs Rochester, indeed, lived a sinful life before she was insane, but sin is itself a species of insan-ity—the truly good behold and compassionate it as such. (*L&L1*, no. 260: To W. S. Williams, 4 January 1848, 383–84)

Elaine Showalter and Sally Shuttleworth have both traced ideas about mental ill-health current in the nineteenth century and have argued that Charlotte Brontë knew and accepted the theories and terminology of the psychiatric experts of her age. She evidently knew of James Cowles Prichard's (1786–1848) theory of 'moral insanity' which he had propounded in a *Treatise on Insanity and Other Disorders Affecting the Mind* (1835). Shuttleworth quoted Prichard's definition of this particular form of mental illness: 'moral insanity', according to Prichard, was 'a morbid perversion of the natural feelings, affections, inclinations, temper, habits, moral dispositions, and natural impulses, without any remarkable disorder or defect of the intellect or knowing or reasoning faculties, and particularly without any insane illu-sion or hallucination' (quoted by Shuttleworth, 49). If the reason and intellect still functioned in 'moral madness', then it suggested that madness was only partial and could be cured. It also put pressure on the lunatic to co-operate with the psychiatrists who were treating them to regain their sanity. The individual had to take responsibility for their condition. Unfortunately for the lunatic, this could lead to others passing moral judgement on their state. It is to this category Bertha Rochester supposedly belonged and Rochester certainly delivered judgement on her and utterly condemned her for bringing on her own insanity. What the modern reader might find disturbing is that by Rochester's own admission Bertha has periods of sanity which may continue for weeks. He did not adjust her treatment according to whether she is well or ill. At these times she was not released from her imprisonment in the attic or provided with anything to do. No wonder during these lucid intervals she abused Rochester (*JE*, 309)!

The exposure of Bertha's hitherto secret confinement in the upper storey of Thornfield creates a moment of intense drama in *Jane Eyre*. The conduct-ing of the wedding service between Rochester and Jane is interrupted by Richard Mason and his lawyer, who register the objection to the marriage on the grounds of an already existing wife. Wood, the clergyman, initially disbelieves Mason. Rochester, however, admits he married fifteen years ago in the West Indies; he expects Wood has 'many a time inclined your ear to gossip about the mysterious lunatic kept there under watch and ward' (*JE*, 291). The degree of wealth and space possessed by the mad person's family determined how a lunatic at this time was treated. As Rochester suggests, many wealthy families of higher social status preferred to conceal their lunatic relative within the confines of their own homes. This perfectly describes the case of Bertha. By the time Dr Savage was writing, this method of confining lunatics in private houses was frowned upon. He commented: 'Home cure is only suitable for cases in which there is hope of speedy recovery, and where there are judicious friends and sufficient space. . . . Care should be taken that the patient is, if possible, on the ground floor, so as to avoid accidents from precipitation . . . the success of home treatment depends upon the quiet of home, with the absence of relations' (Savage, 480). The chronic lunatic's welfare is not best served by keeping him alone with keepers in a private house, for this puts him in 'the position of a man controlled by his servants, and having no companionship or occupation' (Savage, 481). (It is of interest to note, however, that he complied with Leonard Woolf's desire to keep Virginia Woolf at a private house with the stipulation that four nurses should be employed at the worst stage of her long intermittent period of insanity during the First World War. In *Mrs Dalloway*, Septimus is not so fortunate; it is his projected forced removal from Rezia that precipitates his plunge to death.)

Rochester's view of Bertha's insanity as subject to moral judgement combines with the early Victorian view that madness was hereditary. (However, Dr Savage still retained this view in the 1880s, writing that inherited insanity 'stands first in importance' (Savage, 37). He makes this point several times.) Rochester states: 'Bertha Mason is mad; and she came of a mad family: —idiots and maniacs through three generations! Her mother, the Creole, was both a mad woman and a drunkard! . . . Bertha, like a dutiful daughter, copied her parent in both points' (*JE*, 292).

Psychiatrists of this period, according to Showalter, viewed women as being 'more vulnerable to insanity than men because the instability of their reproductive systems interfered with their sexual, emotional, and rational control' (Showalter, 55). Rochester ascribes voracious sexual desires to Bertha, which shame and disgust him. Bertha Mason was 'the true daughter of an infamous mother', who 'dragged me through all the hideous and degrading agonies which must attend a man bound to a wife at once intemperate and unchaste' (*JE*, 306). Rochester further describes her as possessing 'a nature the most gross, impure, depraved I ever saw' (*JE*, 306). When he tells Jane that Bertha's 'excesses had prematurely developed the germs of insanity', he presumably meant sexual excesses (*JE*, 306). While he himself admitted that he had 'tried dissipation,' he insists he avoided 'debauchery', which he hated and hates as he associates it with Bertha: 'rooted disgust at it and her restrained me much, even in pleasure. Any enjoyment that bordered on riot seemed to approach me to her and her vices, and I eschewed it' (*JE*, 311).

Rochester then takes Jane, Wood, and Mason to the top storey where Bertha is confined with her sole attendant, Grace Poole. Bertha is described in Gothic rather than in realistic terms. She is dehumanised and is presented in terms of a wild animal, which grovels and growls and seems to have no language. Jane repeatedly refers to Bertha not as 'she' or 'her' but as 'it.' This is a caricature of 'a mad woman'. Charlotte Brontë herself seemed horrified and repelled at the behaviour, appearance, and reported speech of Bertha. Unlike Woolf's Septimus, the view of Bertha is from the outside; we are not presented with a view of psychosis as it is experienced subjectively. It is an objective view of Bertha. Charlotte did not seem to feel any pity for nor empathy with Bertha. Jane, however, does at one point rebuke Rochester for his extreme language about his insane wife: 'you are inexorable for that unfortunate lady: you speak of her with hate—with vindictive antipathy. It is cruel—she cannot help being mad' (*JE*, 301).

Although Showalter wrote that these ideas of female sexuality and insanity were dominant between 1830 and 1870, this idea lingered on. Once again, we find Dr Savage ascribing to these views. He regarded the different reproductive stages that women went through—puberty, pregnancy, childbirth, and the menopause —as particularly dangerous phases for the sanity of women. Simultaneously, as noted earlier, he recognised that society compelled people to suppress their sexuality, through an exertion of self-control. Savage seems to hold the same view as Rochester about a woman's uninhibited sexuality leading to madness. According to Savage, what he calls 'hysteria' may develop into insanity if the patient loses 'self-control'; the symptoms developing out of an 'unrestrained or ill-regulated passion, which disturbs first the emotional side of the character', and which later affects 'the associated social relations, thereby destroying first the ideas of propriety as regards the sexes, and next the requirements of organised society regarding truth and honesty' (Savage, 82–83). Insanity here seems to have been defined by a person's deviation from the rules of society.

In *Wuthering Heights*, Emily Brontë not only introduced numerous physical ailments but created the psychotic state of 'monomania' to account for Heathcliff's obsession with Cathy and her death. Graeme Tytler usefully supplied us with information about the origins of the word and condition. My discussion of 'monomania' is deeply indebted to Tytler's article. It was coined by the French psychiatrist, Jeanne-Etienne-Dominique Esquirol (1772–1840), who, as Tytler informed us, was viewed as one of the 'founders of modern psychiatry'. The word was first used by Esquirol in 1819 and then percolated into the vocabulary of those interested in mental illness. Esquirol cited the causes of monomania:

> Monomania is essentially a disease of the sensibility. It reposes altogether upon the affections, and its study is inseparable from a knowledge of the passions. Its seat is in the heart of man, and it is there that we must search for it, in order to possess ourselves of all its peculiarities. How many are the cases of monomania caused by thwarted love, by fear, vanity, wounded self-love, or disappointed ambition. (Quoted by Graeme Tytler, 'Heathcliff's monomania: An anachronism in *Wuthering Heights*', *BST*, 20:6, 331–43, 335)

Emily Brontë may have read Esquirol's book *On Insanity*—in which he discussed monomania—as there was a copy in the Keighley Mechanic's Institute. The causes of Heathcliff's monomania may be attributed to 'thwarted love', 'wounded self-love', and 'disappointed ambition.' He himself talks of his 'immortal love', of his 'wild endeavours to hold my right', his 'degradation', and his 'pride' (*WH*, 354). Heathcliff is obsessed with Cathy both when she is alive and when she is dead and is desperate to remain in some sort of communication with her.

However, as Tytler suggested, Heathcliff only began to show definite signs of mental illness eighteen years after Cathy's death. Again, Dr Savage's comment on the insidious nature of madness is helpful here. Savage wrote that people do not generally become suddenly insane, 'the whole thing, as a rule, is a morbid development. . . . Sleeplessness may lead to the use of stimulants, and these in their turn upset the digestive functions, and the patient, thus weakened and exhausted, loses all self-control and becomes mad' (Savage, 18). Although we have no knowledge of Heathcliff using stimulants, we do know that he experienced insomnia and hallucinations and he must have been weakened by his rejection of food for several days. As Nelly Dean observed: 'he might have had a monomania on the subject of his departed idol; but on every other point his wits were as sound as mine' (*WH*, 354). Because, as the word suggests (*mono*mania), Heathcliff was only partially affected by his madness, Nelly Dean was deceived as to the severity of his mental illness. Nevertheless, when he died, she was cautious as to what she told Dr Kenneth of Heathcliff's final illness, 'fearing it might lead to trouble' (*WH*, 365). The implication is that Heathcliff's death, like Catherine's, might be seen as suicide by the doctor.

Katherine Frank suggested that Emily Brontë refused to eat until she became so ill that she had to return to the parsonage from both Roe Head school, where she was a pupil and from Law Hill where she was a governess (Frank, 99, 126–27). In the light of this it is of interest to look at the deaths of Cathy and Heathcliff. Though both Cathy and Heathcliff starved themselves,

each was differently motivated in their abstinence from food. After an irre-
vocable falling out between Edgar Linton and Heathcliff, Cathy told Nelly
Dean: 'I'll try to break their hearts by breaking my own' (*WH*, 104). After
Edgar told Cathy she must choose between him and Heathcliff, Cathy started
fasting. On the third day of self-starvation, Nelly Dean told Cathy that Edgar
'does not fear that you will let yourself die of hunger' (*WH*, 107). Cathy asked
Nelly to inform Edgar otherwise, but Nelly refused. Cathy also now began to
show signs of mental illness: her moods shifted alarmingly and she appeared
not to know where she was—confusing Wuthering Heights and Thrushcross
Grange. She failed to recognise the image of herself reflected in the mirror,
which actually is at Wuthering Heights, not at Thrushcross Grange. Cathy
thought she would once again 'be myself were I once among the heather on
those hills' (*WH*, 111). Like Emily, (though she is the least autobiographical of the three sisters), Cathy could not live away from the moors. Cathy
became violent and physically struggled with Nelly when she tried to prevent
her from opening the window. Nelly referred to her mistress's 'ravings', and
Cathy was, indeed hallucinating (*WH*, 111). Nelly told Edgar that Cathy's
mind wandered (*WH*, 113).

When Emily sickened, Charlotte admitted that she was (understandably) depressed: 'Moments so dark as these I have never known' (*L&L2*,
no. 320: To Ellen Nussey, 19 December 1848, 12). The darkness image
was repeated when Charlotte described the days as passing 'in a slow dark
march'. The same letter described sleeping problems: she suddenly wakes
'from restless sleep' to 'the revived knowledge that one lies in her grave, and
another not at my side, but in a separate and sick bed' (*L&L2*, no. 325: To
Ellen Nussey, 15 January 1849, 19–20). After Emily had died and Anne was
ailing, Charlotte admitted, 'You are right in conjecturing that I am somewhat depressed. At times I certainly am' (*L&L2*, no. 338: To Ellen Nussey,
16 March 1849, 34).

Susan Anne Carlson states that 'There is agreement among biographers
that Charlotte Brontë probably suffered from a major depressive disorder,
a form of depression that can cause suicidal episodes and become progres-
sively worse over a lifetime' (Carlson, 'The Impact of Clinical Depression on
Charlotte Brontë's *Villette*', *BS*, 45:1, 13–26, 13). Understandably, Charlotte
Brontë's depression increased after the deaths of Branwell and her two surviving sisters, Emily and Anne Brontë. Winifred Gerin believed that only the
writing of *Shirley* after the death of Anne Brontë kept her alive and prevented
her suicide (Gerin, *Charlotte Brontë: The Evolution of Genius*, 390).

As Charlotte Brontë became the only survivor of the six siblings her
depression which had been episodic became chronic. She found the solitude
difficult to bear and wrote to her publisher's reader, 'Late in the evenings,
and all through the nights, I fall into a condition of mind which turns entirely

to the past—to memory; and Memory is both sad and relentless' (*L&L2*, no. 472: To W. S. Williams, 2 October 1850, 174. The date suggested by Smith is 19 November 1849). She also found the task of editing new editions of *Wuthering Heights* and *Agnes Grey* lowered her spirits still further: 'I found the task at first exquisitely painful and depressing' and reading over her sisters' papers 'brought back the pang of bereavement and occasioned a depression of spirits well-nigh intolerable' (*L&L2*, no. 475: To Ellen Nussey, 3 October 1850, 178). She added that she classified it as 'quite a mental ailment'. The anniversaries of her three siblings' deaths provoke 'dejection' and a mixture of physical and mental symptoms (*L&L2*, no. 540: To Mrs Gaskell, 6 November 1851, 237).

Carlson argues that Charlotte Brontë's depression can be detected in *Villette*; it 'influenced the author's writing process, her subject matter and the construction of her narrator, Lucy Snowe' (Carlson, *BS,* 46.2, 13). *Villette's* heroine is a first-person narrator who shares her creator's depressed attitude towards life. Lucy never descends into actual psychosis, but she is obviously extremely unwell mentally. Her mental sufferings are presented realistically. Unlike Bertha Rochester, who was a caricature and used as a plot device, mental illness is the subject of *Villette* and is presented directly. Carlson suggested that 'The miracle is that *Villette* is not a creative disaster, but a masterpiece, beautifully written, but darker and more brutal than *Jane Eyre.* . . . [Charlotte Brontë] took a hard look at the mental illness that was destroying her art and described it truthfully through the character of Lucy Snowe. The reader is trapped in Lucy's mind from the first page and must suffer as the heroine suffers fighting off mental illness only to face a life of isolation and hardship' (Carlson, *BS,* 17).

Bearing in mind Charlotte Brontë's depressed mental state while writing *Villette*, it seems likely that that was reflected in the inconclusive closure of the novel. She had been unable to envisage a happy outcome of Paul Emanuel's mission abroad. She had intended to detail his drowning at sea, but in deference to her father's wish against such a resolution, she agreed to leave Paul's fate to the decision of the reader. Charlotte definitely did not possess a 'sunny imagination' herself at this point in her life. Carlson's reading is more convincing than that of such critics as Jian Choe, who writes of Lucy Snowe's time with Miss Marchmont: 'The caring relationship eventually enables Lucy to affirm her inner strength and to regain the will to live' (Choe, 179). Charlotte Brontë had become far more pessimistic since writing *Jane Eyre*. She could no longer believe in the possibility of a happy and fulfilling marriage for her heroine. Like Charlotte Brontë herself, Lucy seems utterly crushed by the experience of the deaths of all of her family.

Like Virginia Woolf, Charlotte Brontë, after her two younger sisters'
deaths, recorded suffering with 'nervous headaches', which were particularly bad when she was staying in London, when the company she so much
desired was available, but which she could no longer face with equanimity.
She complained of this trip that London had not agreed with her; she suffered
from 'the oppression of frequent headache, sickness, and a low tone of spirits'
(*L&L2*, no. 518: To Ellen Nussey, 19 June 1851, 220). This psychosomatic
affliction evidently became a permanent burden in her continuing depression
over the loss of her siblings. In 1854, she still suffered from 'the frequent
head-aches which often haunt sedentary people' and they were 'my chief
cross as regards health' [This is not included by C. K. Shorter's *L&L2;* but
is in Smith's *Letters of Charlotte Brontë*, volume 3, To Mrs Gaskell, early
January 1854, 221).

Charlotte Brontë, in the years between her siblings' deaths and her marriage, also frequently referred to her difficulties in sleeping and her sufferings during sleepless nights. These she had in common with Virginia Woolf.
Charlotte Brontë experienced these at the parsonage, but also when away. She
spent three weeks alone at the seaside. For the first ten days she had a continuous headache and 'some dreary evening-hours and night-vigils (*L&L2*,
no. 578: To Miss Wooler, 23 June 1852, 270). Of course, the real problem was
that she took this holiday alone. Charlotte herself recognised that solitude and
her consequent loneliness resulted in ill-health: 'I am well aware myself that
extreme and continuous depression of spirits has had much to do with the origin of the illness; and I know a little cheerful society would do me more good
than gallons of medicine' (*L&L2*, no 544: To Ellen Nussey, 17 December
1851, 241). It is significant that as marriage with Arthur Bell Nicholls
approached, with the prospect of the end of her solitary life, Charlotte Brontë
was less afflicted with headaches and her general health improved.

In her novels, Woolf, too, used her experience of madness, but disguised
it in both instances as something else. *The Voyage Out* employs what were
presumably her own experiences in the descriptions of the fatal illness of her
heroine, Rachel Vinrace. The latter's illness is purely physical, but its symptoms reveal the interaction of bodily and mental health. Woolf's periods of
mental illness were often heralded by a headache. Leonard Woolf confirmed
this: he described how difficult it was to maintain the balance between the
demands of her writing and of society. When the balance was lost, the first
'threat was almost always a headache', which indicated 'mental strain'
(*Downhill All the Way*, 49).

Similarly (though from a different cause) Rachel's first symptom is also a
headache (*VO*, 381). Her mind is affected by her fever so that she is delirious,
hallucinating, and sunk in a world inaccessible to anyone else. Woolf attributes to Rachel a complete loss in the ability to accurately assess the passing

of time: when Terence Hewet replaces Helen Ambrose by her bedside, she is unaware of when one departed and the other one arrived. More startlingly, Rachel's nights 'do not end at twelve, but go on into the double figures—thirteen, fourteen, and so go on until they reach the twenties, and then the thirties, and then the forties. She realised that there is nothing to prevent nights from doing this if they chose' (*VO*, 385).

Rachel is fearful and suspicious of Nurse McInnis, who has been engaged to help look after her. The nurse's very ordinary pastime when not actually tending her patient is playing cards: Rachel finds this action 'inexplicably sinister' and she cries out (*VO*, 385). Similarly, Leonard Woolf wrote of his wife when 'mad' that she 'believed that the doctors and nurses were in conspiracy against her' (Leonard Woolf, *Beginning Again*, 164). Rachel has for some days intervals of lucidity, but she is increasingly drawn into her own, unshared, world. Almost from the beginning of her illness, Rachel's language starts to become incomprehensible. She strives to recall some lines from Milton's *Comus,* but she experiences anxiety 'because the adjectives persisted in getting into the wrong places' (*VO*, 384). This a minor symptom in *The Voyage Out*, but it was no doubt based on a similar and more intense symptom of Woolf's own illness. Indeed, Leonard Woolf described how in mid-1915 her talk gradually 'became completely incoherent, a mere jumble of dissociated words' (Leonard Woolf, *Beginning Again*, 173).

The other Woolf character whom she endowed with some of her own experiences of madness, again in a disguised form, was Septimus Warren Smith. In *Mrs Dalloway* he displayed clear signs of shellshock though the war had officially been over for five years (but not for him). Andrew Scull informs us that the term 'shell-shock' was coined by a Cambridge medical practitioner called Charles Samuel Myers (1873–1946) (Scull, *Hysteria*, 153). Those in authority supporting the government in pursuing the war were initially puzzled by this new condition. Some of the establishment thought victims of this disease were simply trying to shirk their duty of supporting the war effort by serving at the front. Something of this attitude spills over into the treatment of Septimus, especially by the ignorant general practitioner Dr Holmes, who delivered the opinion that 'there was nothing the matter with [Septimus]' (*MD*, 20).

Scull gives a thorough and moving account of the causes of shellshock: 'it was not just the pointless sacrifice, the mass slaughter, and the sight of the maimed and frightfully wounded that wore on men's nerves. Almost worse was the daily sense of fear and loss of control, and the tension caused by the inability to escape from an intolerable situation' (Scull, *Hysteria* 156). Jane Marcus's research into Sir George Savage discovered that he lectured shortly after the end of the First World War at the Royal Society of Medicine, which included the effects of shellshock on a soldier he had spoken to. This soldier resembled Septimus Warren Smith in that both men, when medics were sent to remove them, had thrown themselves out of a window. Savage's soldier lingered on for a few hours, unlike Septimus (Jane Marcus, 103).

Again, Woolf attributed to Septimus several of her symptoms of mental illness. Like her, he heard birds chirping Greek words (*MD*, 21). In fact, Woolf's ascribing to Septimus her own knowledge of Greek appears to be inconsistent with other information we are given about him; he is described as 'one of those half-educated, self-educated men' who educated himself after a day's work through books borrowed from public libraries, which he had been advised to read by 'well-known authors consulted by letter' (*MD*, 71). Of course, Thomas Hardy's Jude was an autodidact who taught himself some of the ancient classical languages, but there is no evidence that Woolf's character did the same. In fact, the reader is told that Septimus read 'Aeschylus (translated)' (*MD*, 75). His most apparent acquisition of highbrow culture is manifested in his former love of Shakespeare and Keats, among others.

Another attitude of mental specialists towards their patients which had particularly offended Woolf's sensibility was what she saw as their need to impose their own views on the mentally ill. This was clearly applied to her when she was recommended to 'practise equanimity'. In the early 1930s she wrote in a letter how much she disliked the whole matter 'of preaching, of causes; of converting' (*L4*, no. 2372: To Ethel Smyth, 12 May 1931, 329). A few days later, she again expressed her detestation of those who wanted to convert other people; 'tampering with belief' seemed to her to be 'impertinent, insolent, corrupt beyond measure' (*L4*, no. 2374: To Ethel Smyth, 18 May 1931, 333).

The closest we can get to periods of complete breakdown are to be found in *Mrs Dalloway*. In this novel, Woolf criticised the developing psychiatric profession. Dr Bradshaw is shown to possess this desire, which is revealed as sinister and threatening. Sister to the desire to teach the mentally ill a sense of proportion is 'Conversion'. This undesirable quality is applied to Bradshaw's insensitive treatment of Septimus but also more widely to British imperialism and the British Empire which 'is even now engaged in dashing down shrines, smashing idols, and setting up in their place her own stern countenance' (*MD,* 85). This quality in Bradshaw is expressed in an image of cannibalism: 'Conversion . . . feasts on the wills of the weakly' and endeavours to impose its own features on the nation's face (*MD*, 85). Bradshaw's own wife had 'gone under' fifteen years ago. Rezia instinctively disliked Bradshaw (*MD*, 87). Mrs Dalloway, too, disliked him, and reflected she would not like him to see her when she was vulnerable (*MD*, 155). Having heard of Septimus's suicide (this is the only point where their stories actually join), Clarissa's opinion of Bradshaw becomes even more negative: he is 'obscurely evil'; one who 'capable of the indescribable outrage' of 'forcing your soul' (*MD*, 157).

THE IMPORTANCE OF WORK (WRITING)

For Charlotte Brontë and Woolf writing was of paramount importance in their lives, although it could also be a cause of mental anguish. Because there is so little surviving about the private thoughts of Emily and Anne Brontë we will never know exactly what their writing and publications of poems and novels meant to them. There is much more evidence about Charlotte Brontë's attitude towards her writing, particularly after the deaths of her younger sisters. During her sisters' declining health and then immediately after their deaths Charlotte Brontë could not continue with writing *Shirley*: 'both head and hand seem to have lost their cunning; imagination is pale, stagnant, mute' (*L&L1*, no. 310: To W. S. Williams, 18 October 1848, 458). After Emily Brontë's death, Charlotte Brontë still hoped her youngest sister might survive. During this period, she wrote that if Anne Brontë were spared she thought she might yet achieve something in writing (*L&L2*, no. 341: To W. S. Williams, 2 April 1849, 38).

Woolf was rather more self-analytical a writer than Charlotte Brontë. Her life span was also more than twenty years longer than Charlotte Brontë's and she was consequently far more productive of books. Almost from the outset of her career as a novelist Woolf expressed her pleasure in being a writer. As usual though, she was perfectly capable of contradicting or even reversing her opinions concerning her work within a very short period. In 1915 she recorded that writing all morning had given her 'infinite pleasure' (*DI*, 6 January 1915, 9). She heartily agreed with Lady Ottoline Morrell's view that 'the pleasure of creation' transcended 'all others' (*DI*, 29 July 1918, 175). She used the same phrase to describe the effect that writing had on her: it gave her 'infinite pleasure' (though she qualified this by the phrase 'on the whole'). But she continued and said that any other work she would regard as 'a waste of life' (*DI*, 3 November 1918, 214). Eighteen months later she confided to her diary that she believed that successful writing was connected with good health and that the soul's primary function was to produce that work (*DII*, 21 January 1920, 10). She reiterated the connection between work and being well and happy: it is 'the root & source & origin' of both 'health and happiness' (*DII*, 28 July 1923, 259).

When she was ill, Woolf was forbidden to work. During the writing of *Night and Day* she was restricted to a single hour's writing daily because she had suffered a long period of mental illness (*L2*, no. 1016: To Katherine Arnold-Forster, 5 February 1919, 325). She resented this and experienced it as a deprivation. During another period of enforced idleness, she wrote that she detested being unable to write for it took away the purpose of her life (*L4*, no. 2196: To Ethel Smyth, 26 June 1930, 181). Again, she wrote to the same correspondent when illness returned and she was forbidden to work, asking what purpose had life without writing (*L4*, no. 2426: To Ethel Smyth, 2 September 1931, 372).

When she remained as the only survivor of the six siblings, Charlotte Brontë (like Virginia Woolf) would see her work as a writer as the main task and motive in her life. She expressed this repeatedly as she resumed work on *Shirley*. She wrote to W. S. Williams (her main contact at her publishers): 'Labour must be the cure, not sympathy. Labour is the only radical cure for rooted sorrow' (*L&L2*, no. 356: To W. S. Williams, 25 June 1849, 54). To the same correspondent, Charlotte gives a hint that without her writing she would have taken her own life:

> Lonely as I am, how should I be if Providence had never given me courage to adopt a career—perseverance to plead through two long, weary years with publishers till they admitted me? How should I be with youth past, sisters lost, a resident in a moorland parish where there is not a single educated family? In that case I should have no world at all: the raven, weary of surveying the deluge and without an ark to return to, would be my type. As it is, something like a hope and motive sustains me still. I wish all your daughters—I wish every woman in England had also a hope and motive: Alas! there are many old maids who have neither. (*L&L2*, no. 358: To W. S. Williams, 3 July 1849, 59)

Later in the same month, in a letter which makes sad reading considering her relative youth; Charlotte owned she expected no future human companionship; now her writing was her 'best companion' (*L&L2*, no. 362: To W. S. Williams, 26 July 1849, 62). At the end of August 1849, she wrote in the same vein, specifically about *Shirley*: 'Whatever now becomes of the work, the occupation of writing it has been a boon to me. It took me out of dark and desolate reality into an unreal but happier region' (*L&L2*, no. 368: To W. S. Williams, 29 August 1849, 67). Finally, she acknowledged that in the aftermath of Anne's death '[t]he faculty of imagination lifted me' and it has continued to keep her buoyant (*L&L2*, no. 378: To W. S. Williams, 21 September 1849, 74). In this letter she also searingly referred to the deaths of her two sisters which had deprived her of those whom she understood and who understood her. In another letter, Charlotte wrote that once Emily Brontë was dead her absence seemed to make writing pointless as she would be unable to read anything Charlotte might write in future (*L&L2*, no. 346: To W. S. Williams, 16 April 1849, 44). Unlike Woolf, Charlotte believed that God had given her the ability of writing and 'it is for me a part of my religion to defend this gift and to profit by its possession' (*L&L2*, no. 378: To W. S. Williams, 21 September 1849, 74).

In a nightmare scenario, however, Charlotte Brontë's writing gradually ceased to be a positive in her life and became another source of depression and suffering: she often experienced writer's block. This was especially true of the writing of *Villette*. It was particularly galling because in the absence of her sisters, writing would have distracted her from sadness, but she finds herself unable to write (*L&L2*, no. 418: To Ellen Nussey, 16 February 1850, 114). Although Charlotte often suffered from minor physical illnesses at this time, she recognised that much of the writer's block was caused by a 'mental ailment'. She despairingly wrote that she had expected to occupy and interest herself with writing, but she completely lacked any stimulation and failed to produce anything (*L&L2*, no. 475: To Ellen Nussey, 3 October 1850, 178–79. Smith dates this letter 23 October 1850).

By the autumn of 1852, writing is not only an unpleasant occupation but *itself* deprived Charlotte Brontë of any and all pleasure. She uses imagery of imprisonment and physical restraint. She is tormented by *Villette* which will not get written: 'But oh! I don't get on; I feel fettered, incapable, sometimes very low'. She tries to dismiss her writing because 'it presses me too hardly, wearily, painfully. Less than ever can I taste or know pleasure till this work is wound up' (*L&L2*, no. 585: To Ellen Nussey, 1852, 275. Shorter could not pin this letter to any month in 1852; Smith suggests 24 September 1852). Patrick Brontë was aware of his daughter's mental depression and urged her to invite Ellen Nussey to the parsonage, which she did. Prior to this visit, she had refused to go and stay with Margaret Wooler who would have provided her with some congenial and restorative companionship because the writing of *Villette* was not progressing. She was aware that her writing was 'a matter not wholly contingent on wish or will, but lying in a great measure beyond the reach of effort and out of the pale of calculation'. She also stressed in this letter the pressure she felt her publishers were exerting on her to complete *Villette* (*L&L2*, no. 565: To Miss Wooler, 12 March 1852, 258).

In 1851, Charlotte Brontë had conveyed her attitude to her writing to Elizabeth Gaskell, who wrote to Maria James, and said she wished Charlotte had some means of support other than writing. Gaskell thought this had a detrimental effect on her fellow novelist's writing, which had to be 'pumped up instead of bubbling out; and very bad for her health'. Gaskell agreed with Charlotte Brontë's assessment of her own situation: had she had to earn her own living she would have preferred to become a governess again, though she strongly disliked that occupation. She had added Charlotte Brontë's view was that 'one should only write out of the fulness of one's heart, spontaneously' (*The Letters of Mrs Gaskell*, no. 105: To Maria James, 29 October 1851, 167–68).

Even early in her writing career Woolf sometimes felt negatively towards her writing. She acknowledged to her diary that writing imposed a great strain on her (*D2*, 11 August 1921, 129). She also admitted that writing could be an 'agony' (*D2*, 10 September 1921, 135). She asked herself why she persevered with novel-writing when she had so many faults and it was such a struggle (*D3*, 27 November 1925, 47; 22 July 1926, 96). Earlier, she had been deeply depressed by the suggestion of her Greek teacher, Janet Case, that she should abandon novel-writing in favour of the more useful genre of biography (*L2*, no. 987: To Vanessa Bell, 13 November 1918, 293).

As the 1930s advanced, Woolf became increasingly desperate to continue with her writing; she clung to it as the best method of her mental salvation. She feared that she could no longer write (*DV*, 30 October 1936, 26). Writing became more difficult; she became bogged down in *The Years*, which caused her intense misery and suffering, and brought her to the verge of breakdown (*DV*, 10 November 1936, 31). She employed the image of medicine and admonished herself: 'Work, work, work—that's my final prescription' (*DV*, 10 January 1936, 50). The following month: 'Work is my only help' (*DV*, 12 February 1936, 54). Three years later Woolf still felt 'the dominant theme is work' (*DV*, 5 January 1939, 197). She also felt that her writing was her small contribution to the war effort (*DV*, 6 September 1939, 235).

Thus, like Charlotte Brontë, but for different reasons, when life became difficult, writing also became difficult. Charlotte Brontë found bereavement disabling for her writing; for Woolf it was the unstable condition of Europe throughout the 1930s which culminated in the Second World War. Indeed, she identified with Charlotte Brontë's experience as a writer: 'My books only gave me pain, Ch. Brontë said. Today I agree' (*DV*, 16 August 1940, 311). By the following month, Woolf had concluded that no writers were happy. She has also lost faith in the medium of her profession, language: she concluded, that only those who avoided words attained happiness (*DV*, 5 September 1940, 315).

In common with Virginia Woolf, Charlotte Brontë displayed an inability to judge her own writing. She admitted that although she thought she would know whether *Shirley* attained equality with *Jane Eyre*, in the event she could not tell: 'it may be better; it may be worse'. She sought the opinion of W. S. Williams, since she felt her own was valueless (*L&L2*, no. 368: To W. S. Williams, 29 August 1849, 67). Over a year later, she reported to another employee of her publisher that the reception of *Shirley* had not been as positive as that of *Jane Eyre*. She was puzzled by this; for she had taken greater pains with *Shirley*, about which she now ventured to express her opinion: she did not think it was an inferior achievement to *Jane Eyre*. She had given *Shirley* 'more time, thought and anxiety' (*L&L2*, no. 466: To James Taylor, 5 September 1850, 167).

Charlotte Brontë was equally uncertain about the value of *Villette*. She wrote to Ellen Nussey that she had finally 'finished my long task', that is, she had completed *Villette*. It had been posted to her publisher in London. She confessed to Ellen that she was unable to determine whether she had done it 'well or ill', and awaits the critical responses to it (*L&L2*, no. 598: To Ellen Nussey, 29 November 1852, 288. Smith dates this letter a week earlier).

Woolf also resembled Charlotte Brontë in her inability to assess and pass judgement on her own books. While she often included accounts of the positive and negative attitudes of both herself and others towards her publications, she confessed that she more often dwelt on their faults. Woolf thought about withdrawing her experimental short story from publication because she was uncertain of its worth (*L2*, no. 950: To Vanessa Bell, 8 July 1918, 258). Equally, she expected that her first novel would be condemned and she felt it deserved that condemnation (*D1*, 27 January 1915, 29). (This was very similar to Charlotte Brontë's anticipated hostile criticism towards *Shirley*. They both used variations of the same two words: deserved and condemned). She was apprehensive about the reception of *Night and Day* (*D1*, 5 December 1919, 315–16). She confided to her diary her anxiety about the publication of her short story collection, *Monday or Tuesday* (*D2*, 6 March 1921, 98). The response to these short stories was such as led her to consider abandoning fiction writing for literary criticism (*D2*, 8 April 1921, 106–107). Neither, however, could Woolf pass any judgement about the worth of her essays. She wrote that her essay, 'Character and Fiction' that on reading it over it had appeared 'superficial and flippant' (*L3*, no. 1472: To T. S. Eliot, 23 May 1924, 110).

Repeatedly, Woolf viewed *Orlando* in terms of a failure: she vividly described it to Vita Sackville-West in several different images and adjectives: on 6 March 1928 as 'addled egg: too hasty, too splash-dashery, and all over the place' (*L3*, no. 1868: To Vita Sackville-West, 6 March 1928, 468) and as 'all over the place, incoherent, intolerable, impossible' (*L3*, no. 1873: To Vita Sackville-West,?20 March 1928, 474). Writing to her nephew, she condemned *Orlando* as 'an extremely foolish book' (*L3*, no. 1888: To Julian Bell, 2 May 1928, 491). To Vanessa Bell's other son, Woolf described *Orlando* as a 'bad joke' (*L3*, no. 1901: To Quentin Bell, 5 June 1928, 506). Finally, she dismissed it as a revelation of 'the entire worthlessness' of her own words (*L3*, no. 1906: To Edward Sackville-West, 24 June 1928, 510).

On the Cambridge lecture which formed the basis of *A Room of One's Own*, Woolf advised Pernel Strachey not to attend as it was so dull (*L3*, no.

1914: To Pernel Strachey, mid-August 1928, 516). Having finished making
the final corrections to *A Room of One's Own* she asks herself whether it is
good or bad; she sums up what she regards as its strengths and weaknesses
(*D3*, 19 August 1929, 241–42). Similarly, Woolf criticised *The Waves*: she
thought it failed because it was 'too difficult: too jerky; too inchoate altogether' (*L4*, no. 2230: To Clive Bell, 21 February 1931, 292). Less than two
months later, *The Waves* had become 'the worst novel in the language' (*L4*,
no. 2347: To Quentin Bell, 11 April 1931, 309). Having finished writing
The Waves, Woolf stated she was thinking of abandoning writing altogether
because of this 'bloody book' which was 'fundamentally unreadable' (*L4*, no.
2404: To Ethel Smyth, 12 July 1931, 357). She returned to her description of
it as a 'failure', which was now intensified into 'a complete failure' (*L4*, no.
2434: To John Lehmann, 11 September 1931, 377).

In 1935 Woolf was insecure about her future writing: supposing it merely
became increasingly feeble and silly? (*DIII*, 15 September 1935, 342).
Similarly, she questioned herself as to whether she could still write (*DV*,
30 October 1936, 26). Having published *Three Guineas*, and received the
usual contradictory reviews, she admitted she was completely 'in the dark' as
to its 'true merits' (*DV*, 19 December 1938, 193). Although *Roger Fry* met
with public approval, Woolf stressed her awareness that her friends thought it
'a dud' (*DV*, 1 August 1940, 308).

Towards the end of her life, Woolf recorded her assessment of her 'position
as a writer'. Her starkest estimate was that she was 'secondrate' and 'likely . . .
to be disregarded altogether'. The best judgement she was able to arrive at
was that 'my position is ambiguous' (*DV*, 22 November 1938, 188–89). It
was partly her inability to judge her final novel, *Between the Acts* which
contributed to her suicide. She wrote to John Lehmann (who had bought out
her share of the Hogarth Press) that although Leonard Woolf disagreed with
her opinion that the novel was 'much too slight and sketchy', she wanted his
independent judgement (*L6*, no. 3703: To John Lehmann, 20 March 1941,
482). Lehmann responded with enthusiasm and praise, but Woolf had concluded that *Between the Acts* was 'too silly and trivial' to publish in its present
form (*L6*, no. 3709: To John Lehmann, 27? March 1941, 486).

Generally speaking, Woolf summed up her inability to judge her writing by
a comment made in 1922, in which she wrote she was unable to judge whether
what she wrote was 'good or bad' (*L2*, no. 1238: To T. S. Eliot, 14 April 1922,
521). She used the same phrase about being unable to determine whether
To the Lighthouse was 'good or bad' (*L3*, no. 1717: To Vita Sackville-West,
18 February 1927, 333). She again commented in a general way to another
writer, asking him whether he could estimate the quality of his writing, for
she 'never knew' about hers (*L5*, no. 2910: To Stephen Spender, 10 July 1934,
314–15). Rather touchingly, she admitted to a writer with whom she had no

direct involvement that she was always 'surprised' when people responded positively to her writing, and so must thank him for telling her that he had (*L3*, no. 1403: To Richard Aldington, 24 June 1923, 48).

Generally, Charlotte Brontë was less anxious about critical responses to her novels than was Woolf. From Charlotte's letters we can trace her reactions to her critics. They provoked a surprising variety of emotions in her. Sometimes she was philosophical and even grateful to the critics: 'censure, though not pleasant, is often wholesome' (*L&L1*, no. 242: To W. S. Williams, 10 November 1847, 366). Simultaneously she felt that if *Jane Eyre* had 'any solid worth in it, it ought to weather a gust of unfavourable wind' (*L&L1*, no. 243: To Messrs. Smith, Elder and Co., 13 November 1847, 367). She calmly accepted that posterity would decide on the value of the Brontë sisters' novels: 'As to the critics, if the Bells possess real merit, I do not fear impartial justice being rendered them one day' (*L&L2*, no. 349: To W.S. Williams, 8 May 1849, 47). On other occasions she derived pleasure from reviews which she felt understood what she was aiming for (*L&L*, vol. 1 no. 247: To Messrs. Smith, Elder and Co., 1 December 1847, 369). Endearingly, at times she found it hard to believe that a novel she had written was 'worthy' of the admiration of such distinguished men as Thackeray and others (*L&L1*, no. 252: To W. S. Williams 11 December 1847, 372). Some critiques, though they were negative, she accepted as a 'just punishment' for the faulty planning and structure of *Jane Eyre* (*L&L1*, no. 253: To W. S. Williams, 13 December 1847, 373). Other reviews of this type saddened her by their failure to recognise *Jane Eyre*'s real values: 'I feel a sort of heart-ache when I hear the book called "godless" and "pernicious" by good and earnest-minded men'. But she also hoped to profit from their criticism: 'but I know that heart-ache will be salutary—at least I trust so' (*L&L1*, no. 259: To W.S. Williams, 31 December 1847, 379). Another way Charlotte Brontë reacted to criticism was with defiance and an anger she would not quite admit to feeling: she would not let negative reviews change her writing and 'if the spirit moves me in future to say anything about priests etc., I shall say it with the same freedom as heretofore' (*L&L1*, no. 274: To W. S. Williams, March 3 1848, 400. Smith dates it, with a query, as 3 April 1848). Understandably between the deaths of Emily and Anne Brontë, critics' responses were not of paramount importance to Charlotte Brontë: she expressed a 'sorrowful independence of reviews and reviewers' (*L&L2*, no. 323: To W. S. Williams, 2 January 1849, 17). During that period, though she claimed her indifference to the reviews, veiled anger is again present though not directly expressed as such; that a critic is not a 'gentleman' seems irrelevant to literary assessment. (*L&L2,* no. 329: 4 February 1849, 25).

After her sisters' deaths the responses of critics to *Shirley* and *Villette* became harder to bear; she no longer had her sisters with whom she could share critics' opinions. She apologised to W. S. Williams for her 'hasty' response to a review of *Shirley*, and explained that if her sisters had been alive, they would laugh with her over the review (*L&L2*, no. 384: To W. S. Williams, 1 November 1849, 78–79). Both Charlotte and Virginia at times referred to criticism of their works in terms of physical violence. Even before she was the sole survivor of the original six Brontë siblings, however, she once used the image of physical assault to anticipate the effect of the critical response of G. H. Lewes to *Jane Eyre*: 'if any part of your censure galls me too keenly to the quick—gives me deadly pain—I shall for the present disbelieve it, and put it quite aside, till such time as I feel able to receive it without torture' (*L&L1*, no. 244: To G. H. Lewes, 22 November 1847, 368). Later, she became even more anxious about what the critics would 'do' to her and that she feared 'castigation' by a brutal Austrian Field Marshall' (*CLCB3*: To Mrs Elizabeth Smith, 25 November 1852. This letter is not quoted by Shorter. But it is important as it is the first reaction to her critics' responses being a physically violent one). As she awaited the critics' reviews of *Shirley* to appear, she bent her head in anticipation of the response she would receive: she anticipated, and believed she deserved, 'the lash of criticism. I shall wince when it falls, but not scream' (*L&L2*, no. 371: To W. S. Williams, 10 September 1849, 69). This is even more pronounced in her request to Harriet Martineau for her truthful response to *Villette*, she elevated it to a moral and beneficial act which Martineau would bestow on her. She stipulated for as much frankness as if 'you spoke to some near relative whose good you preferred to her gratification'. Charlotte Brontë followed this up with disturbing images of physical brutality: 'I wince under the pain of condemnation, like any other weak structure of flesh and blood; but I love, I honour, I kneel to truth. Let her smite me on the one cheek—good! the tears may spring to the eyes; but courage! there is the other side, hit again, right sharply' (*L&L2*, no. 609: To Harriet Martineau, 21 January 1853, 304). Predictably, when Martineau did respond with what seemed to her to be the truth about *Villette*, Charlotte permanently ended the relationship!

Woolf remained particularly sensitive to criticism and usually agonised over the possible critical reception of her work. She stated her dependence on critical judgements of her work and the necessity of critics' praise (*D1*, 12 May 1919, 271). She struggled throughout her writing career to find 'the right attitude' towards the criticism of her writing; it appears that she did not find this any easier as she became an established writer (*DIV*, 17 May 1932, 100). Fearing a published attack on her in Wyndham Lewis' *Men without Art*, she asked Leonard Woolf what comprised the 'sensible attitude to criticism'. He replied succinctly, but supportively, that she should not read it (*DIV*, 15 October 1934, 140).

Quentin Bell suggested that Woolf was particularly sensitive to criticism of her work because for her it was a verdict on her sanity:

> Her novels were very close to her own private imaginings; she was always conscious that, to the outside world, they might simply appear to be mad, or, worse still, that they really were mad. Her dread of the ruthless mockery of the world contained within it the deeper fear that her art, and therefore her self, was a kind of sham, an idiot's dream of no value to anyone. For her, therefore, a favourable notice was more valuable than mere praise; it was a kind of certificate of sanity. (*Virginia Woolf: A Biography*, volume 2: 1912–1941, 28–29)

Later critics have failed to pick up this insight, but it seems to me to be of crucial importance. Because she did not write letters or diaries when she was at her most mentally unwell, it is easy to overlook just how seriously and frequently she became ill. One of the most striking features of the recollections of her contemporaries who knew her, is how often they allude to her mental instability and even insanity. John Lehmann described such episodes: 'They began very slowly with headaches, and increasing depression. She seemed withdrawn behind a veil, and all her gaiety and lively interest in the outside world disappeared. Everyone in the house sensed the accumulating tension of anxiety and distress. We knew that she was in great danger, and that Leonard was all too keenly aware of it' (Noble, 31). Rosamund Lehmann stated succinctly that Woolf 'lived under the shadow of the fear of madness' (Noble, 63).

Barbara Bagenal relates a distressing incident when Woolf was 'near to a mental breakdown'. On this occasion, Woolf, while eating a meal, started flicking meat on to the table cloth, 'obviously not knowing what she was doing'. Leonard at once took control of the situation. He warned Barbara to stop talking to Virginia and not to mention her behaviour. Then he took Virginia upstairs to rest and stayed with her until she fell asleep. By the teatime 'the danger was passed' and Virginia had no memory of the incident (Noble, 152). Equalling distressing is Louie Mayer's description of Virginia's behaviour when she was mentally ill. Mayer described Woolf coming into the kitchen to tell her something, but forgetting what she had wanted to say. Then Virginia would wander off and walking in the garden was so unaware of her surroundings that she would bump into trees (Noble, 159).

Frances Partridge claimed that Woolf's insanity was reflected in her face and body: her face 'bore the stigmata that are to be seen in many who have been gravely mad—a subtly agonised tautness, something twisted; the way she held herself, turned her head or smoked a cigarette struck one as awkward even while it charmed and interested one (Stape, 92).

More than one of these observers linked her insanity with her creativity. Woolf herself had evidently considered her illnesses very closely; often
stimulated her creativity and vision. She emphasised this both in the privacy
of her diary and to Ethel Smyth, a confidante in the 1930s. Woolf recorded
that after being confined to bed for six weeks, she had spent her accumulated
energy to complete the final draft of her essay 'Women and Fiction' (*DIII*,
28 March 1929, 218–19). That same year, Woolf expressed the idea that her
illness was partly caused by 'suppressed imagination' (*L4*, no.1998: To Vita
Sackville-West, 12 February 1929, 21). Later that year, Woolf expressed
the benefits of her illness: she believed her headaches were partly mystical.
During these headaches she plumbed the depths of personal failure and a
more generalised human misery. When this knowledge had descended into
her unconscious mind, she resumed the novel she was then writing. (*L4*, no.
2056: To Vita Sackville-West, 15 August 1929, 78).

The following year, Woolf confided to her diary that had she been able to
remain in bed for another fortnight she thought she would have perceived
the whole of *The Waves*. She would have been ashamed if she followed her
inclination to stay in bed and sleep, though she is aware that her mind often
worked best 'in idleness. To do nothing is often my most profitable way'
(*DIII*, 16 February 1930, 286–87). Woolf repeatedly stressed how her illnesses fuelled her creativity and provided her material. Referring to the long
period of mental ill-health which followed her marriage, Woolf commented
'As an experience, madness is terrific . . . and in its lava I still find most of
the things I write about. It shoots out of one everything shaped, final, not in
mere driblets, as sanity does' (*L4*, no. 2194: To Ethel Smyth, 22 June 1930,
180). Woolf also told Smyth that if her headache reached its third and ultimate stage, it led her to become 'visionary' (*L4*, no. 2199: To Ethel Smyth,
1 July 1930, 183). In a letter to Clive Bell, too, she traced the pattern of her
headaches: it had three stages which were 'pain; numb; visionary' (*L4*, no.
2198: To Clive Bell, 30 June 1930, 183).

Woolf recorded her experiences in completing the composition of *The
Waves*, where creativity and madness seemed almost indistinguishable: 'having reeled across the last ten pages with some moments of such intensity &
intoxication that I seemed only to stumble after my own voice, or almost,
after some sort of speaker (as when I was mad). I was almost afraid, remembering the voices which used to fly ahead' (*D4*, 7 February 1931, 10).

It was also Leonard Woolf's conviction that there was a connection between
his wife's illness and her creativity: 'I am quite sure that Virginia's genius was
closely connected with what manifested itself as mental instability and insanity' (Leonard Woolf, *Beginning Again*, 80). This is perhaps a continuation
of a romantic view of madness. Be that it as it may, Leonard Woolf took the
lead in promoting this view. He stressed that it was essential to remember that

Virginia had been insane three times. He pointed out that since the classical Greek period it has been thought that 'sanity and genius are closely allied'. He commented on this with an odd use of a double negative: 'one could see clearly that the two things were not disconnected' in his wife (Stape, 148). David Garnett supported this view: 'her genius owed much to her nervous instability' and 'her wildly poetical imagination was often only just this side of borderline' (Stape, 154). Ethel Smyth was convinced that Woolf's 'terrific gift' depended on 'the slightly insane streak in her' (Stape, 42).

In moments of despondency and depression, it would be understandable if Woolf suspected that material tapped through psychosis was just that: mad fantasies which no readers could access. It seems that Woolf suffered considerably from the threat of psychosis returning. Vita Sackville-West wrote to Harold Nicolson that Woolf 'was *so* sane, when not mad. And *so* how [pathetic], about going mad again'. Sackville-West truly added: 'What a nightmare it must be' (Nigel Nicolson, *Vita and Harold* 155). Nicolson expressed concern about Woolf's relationship with his wife 'from her point of view as I can't help feeling that her stability and poise is based on a rather precarious foundation. I mean it would be rather awful if your coming out [to Teheran] made her ill' (Nicolson, *Vita and Harold*, 176). Vita Sackville-West's relationship with Woolf was clearly limited by the former's knowledge of Woolf's mental illnesses. They first met in 1925, when Woolf was suffering from headaches and exhaustion. Matthew Dennison, a recent biographer of Sackville-West, quotes from one of her letters to Harold Nicholson about her relationship with Woolf. In it she said she had bedded Woolf twice only because 'I am scared to death of arousing physical feelings, because of the madness' (Dennison, 181). Nicolson replied feelingly, praising Sackville-West's caution: 'it's not merely playing with fire; it's playing with gelignite' (Dennison, 181). Victoria Glendinning also sheds light on Woolf's relationship with Sackville-West: in 1936, when Sackville-West visited Woolf, the latter 'was on the brink of another severe bout of nervous illness' and she was so upset by the visit that 'she had to take chloral afterwards' (Glendinning, 284).

A professional view was offered from the psychoanalyst, Alix Strachey: 'Virginia's imagination, apart from her artistic creativeness, was so woven with her fantasies—and indeed with her madness—that if you had stopped the madness you might have stopped the creativeness too'. She added that when Woolf 'intensified her fantasies . . . to such an extent that they had probably become uncontrollable' (Noble, 117). Alix Strachey also wrote that friends and acquaintances made special allowances for Woolf because of her psychological fragility: 'Sometimes [Woolf] said things that made people very angry, but nobody contradicted her vehemently. We felt somehow she was too vulnerable, too easily injured mentally to lose one's temper with' (Noble, 113).

Several of the Woolfs' contemporaries also described or commented on the strain this mental fragility of Virginia imposed on Leonard Woolf. Beatrice Webb's diary explicitly expresses a scenario which Virginia must have feared above all: that Leonard would not be able to keep her out of some sort of asylum, as they approached a second world war (Stape, 30). Ironically, in this sense, she might be seen as partly a victim of the Second World War, as her character Septimus Warren Smith was of the First World War. Nigel Nicolson observed the care Leonard Woolf took of his wife, for he knew that 'she was always on the point of going mad again' (Stape, 75). She would be aware that two of her friends—Roger Fry and T. S. Eliot—had committed their wives to institutional care. Her suicide was precipitated by her awareness that she was on the verge of complete mental breakdown. Sackville-West said Leonard had told her that Virginia 'had not been well for the last few weeks and was terrified of going mad again' (Stape, 80).

In both *Mrs Dalloway* and in her volume of essays, *The Common Reader: First Series*, Woolf wrote on Montaigne's essays. What she particularly took from him was the utmost importance of communication to him. She believed that in his essays he attempted to communicate his own soul. She expressed his underlying belief as: 'Communication is health; communication is truth; communication is happiness' (*E4*, 76). These ideas—and some of their language—are attributed to Septimus. He mutters to himself: 'Communication is health; communication is happiness. Communication.' Ironically, he is unable to communicate with his wife and his mutterings only serve to make Rezia 'mad with terror' (*MD*, 79). Woolf shared with Montaigne and Septimus a preoccupation with the seeming impossibility of communication between people (*L6*, no. 1380a: To Mary Hutchinson, 'perhaps Wednesday 18th April 1923', 503).

It seems she was always haunted by the idea that her attempt to revolutionise the form of the novel and convey her own unique vision might simply be her own mad attempt to convey something that nobody else shared. She confided to Molly MacCarthy that she had been enormously relieved to find that in her sequence of sentences one followed another in *The Voyage Out* and that it was not the 'pure gibberish' she had convinced herself it was (*L2*, no. 716, To Molly MacCarthy, 15 December 1914, 56). She had a similar reaction to *Jacob's Room*: she had doubted whether it would 'convey anything to anybody' (*L2*, no. 1306: To Philip Morrell, 29 October 1922, 575). Two days later, Woolf conveyed the same idea, in almost exactly the same words to another correspondent (*L2*, no. 1311: To Lady Ottoline Morrell, 1 November 1922, 579).

Woolf expressed her apprehension about the anticipated responses to her critical essay collection, the *Common Reader*. Partly this self-mistrust arose because she felt her education had been insufficient, but she also feared that it might not make sense to other people, that it might be classified as 'nonsense' (*L3*, no. 1552: To G. Lowes Dickinson, 9 May 1925, 182). She was equally nervous about *To the Lighthouse*; but about this novel she expressed doubt during its composition. She twice used the word 'mirage' to communicate her apprehension that it might be totally unreal (*L3*, no. 1621: To Vita Sackville-West, 1 March 1926, 241). Woolf returned to her word 'gibberish', which she used twice in a single letter to describe *The Waves* (*L4*, no. 2145: To Quentin Bell, 17 February 1930, 142). She expressed her conviction that it created an impression that she was insane: she feared that it was a 'failure' which would not 'convey anything to anybody' (*L4*, no. 2437: To John Lehmann, 17 September 1931, 380–81).

Resembling Charlotte Brontë, Woolf described criticism of her works in terms of physical assault. These references tended to occur in the 1930s, when the political situation was deteriorating and she appeared to have felt generally more vulnerable. When Wyndham Lewis negatively reviewed *Mr Bennett and Mrs Brown*, Woolf experienced it as more than purely verbal abuse; she had 'my back against the wall'. This is an image which creates a picture of someone being physically cornered, perhaps to be then violently attacked. She felt she had been 'publicly demolished' by what our own contemporaries call the cancel culture; she will have no future existence at Oxbridge (*DIV*, 11 October 1934, 251). Three days later she referred to being flagellated by Wyndham Lewis's review (*DIV*, 14 October 1934, 251). She fearfully anticipated the critical reception of *The Years*: although she will experience the reviewers' 'violence'; she will find her personal circles' lack of approval harder to bear (*DV*, 20 February 1937, 58). Later she recorded that she will be 'beaten', she will be laughed at, ridiculed and scorned by the reviewers (*DV*, 2 March 1937, 64). Even more disturbingly, Woolf appeared to think that the reviewers would hang her when she metaphorically referred to 'the drop' not being 'fatal' (*DV*, 7 March 1937, 65). Edwin Muir's review in *The Listener* and Scott James's in *Life and Letters*, she received as a smack on her face (*DV*, 2 April 1937, 75). Queenie Leavis's hostile review of *Three Guineas* affected her as a 'violent attack' (*DV*, 1 September 1938, 165).

Another aspect of writing which Woolf would increasingly share with the Brontës as she aged was that of anonymity. Although it is easy to assume that the Brontës published anonymously because of their sex—and as we shall see, this was the explanation Charlotte Brontë gave—in fact, male authors also often published incognito, for a variety of reasons. In the Brontës' own time, John Mullan tells us that: 'Literary history exhibits few more obstinate practitioners of anonymity than the author of the so-called "Waverley novels"'

(Mullan, 20). The Brontës much admired Sir Walter Scott, who continued to conceal his identity until 1827, so doubtless they would have been aware of this precedent (and its advantages in provoking the reading public's curiosity). Like Scott, too, Charlotte Brontë would go to extraordinary lengths to preserve her anonymity: neither writer scrupled to actually lie in denying their authorship when directly challenged. In fact, it appeared to have been an acceptable falsehood: readers were expected to understand 'that an author's denial of an anonymous book might be as conventional, as respectable, as a gentleman's refusal to speak ill of a lady' (Mullan, 37).

Charlotte Brontë herself had written in her own name and sex to Robert Southey after having written a letter in which she concealed her female identity. Then she received the now-famous rebuff: 'Literature cannot be the business of a woman's life, and it ought not to be' (*L&L1*, no. 28: Southey to Charlotte Brontë, March 1837, 128). After this it was unsurprising that she and her sisters published anonymously under names which were ambiguous if not downright masculine. She herself explained their motives: 'we did not like to declare ourselves women, because—without at the time suspecting that our mode of writing and thinking was not what is called "feminine"—we had a vague impression that authoresses are liable to be looked on with prejudice' (Appendix 1 to *Wuthering Heights*, 302). When Charlotte submitted the sisters' poems to publishers, she deftly avoided using any pronouns which would establish their sex: 'You will perceive that the poems are the work of three persons, relatives; their separate pieces are distinguished by their respective signatures' (*L&L1*, no. 179: To Aylott & Jones, 6 February 1846, 319). By the time their poems were being reviewed, Charlotte Brontë boldly described the three poets as 'brothers', in a letter to the editor of the *Dublin University Magazine* of 6 October 1846. (Shorter did not include this letter in his *Life and Letters*.) She also referred to the three sisters as 'the brothers Bell' (*L&L1*, no. 242: To W. S. Williams, 10 November 1847, 366). She added that were the mystery of the real identity of the Bells solved, it would probably be thought not worth resolving. Nevertheless, she will not interfere with it as 'it suits ourselves to remain quiet, and certainly injures no one else'.

Sometimes Charlotte Brontë seemed to derive a mischievous delight in her anonymity (rather like Sir Walter Scott). She wrote that an elderly clergyman had recognised Lowood School in *Jane Eyre*. He also identified the originals of Brocklehurst (who, he said 'deserved the chastisement he had got') and Miss Temple. But he was unable to discover the real name of Currer Bell. She gleefully commented: 'What author would be without the advantage of being able to walk invisible?' (*L&L1*, no. 260: To W. S. Williams, 4 January 1848, 384). More seriously, Charlotte experienced her anonymity as liberating and would regard its loss as a very great 'misfortune': 'mental tranquillity would then be gone; it would be a task to write—a task which I doubt I could continue. If I were known—I should ever be conscious in writing that my book must be read by ordinary acquaintances—and that idea would fetter me intolerably' (*LCB*, volume 2: To W. S. Williams, 20 April 1848, 51. Shorter does not include his letter, which is of crucial importance for an understanding of Charlotte Brontë's pseudonym).

As Charlotte Brontë made clear part of her reason for not publishing under her real name was because she did not want to be considered as a gendered author. She stressed this when she wrote of what she would wish to say to critics of her novels: "To you I am neither man nor woman—I come before you as an author only. It is the sole standard by which you have a right to judge me—the sole ground on which I accept your judgment' (*L&L2*, no. 364: To W. S. Williams, 16 August 1849, 64). To another correspondent at Smith, Elder and Co. she put this question about her critics: 'Why can they not be content to take Currer Bell for a man?' (*L&L2*, no. 389: To James Taylor, 6 November 1849, 82). She protested to a critic about his review of *Shirley* in the *Edinburgh Review*: 'after I had said earnestly that I wished critics would judge me as an *author*, not as a woman, you so roughly—I even thought so cruelly—handled the question of sex' (*L&L2*, no. 409: To G.H. Lewes, 19 January 1850, 106). Charlotte Brontë was appalled when she was revealed locally as Currer Bell (*L&L2*, no. 416: To Ellen Nussey, 5 February 1850, 112–13).

It is of interest to compare the importance of anonymity to the Brontës and its changed application in the case of Virginia Woolf. It is likely that it was Emily Brontë was the one among the sisters who insisted on their poems and novels appearing anonymously before the public. It has to be admitted that Charlotte Brontë also increasingly appreciated it, as it enabled her to speak out more freely. Woolf was one of the earlier generations of women writers who published under their own names. Since she never commented on it in her own case, the reader can only assume she did not perceive it as a problem. Neither did she publish any of her novels before her marriage to Leonard Woolf in 1912, so no change of her name as an author was involved. Nevertheless, she was familiar with the great female Victorian writers who had used pseudonyms whose sex was at the least ambiguous, as in the case of the Brontës or downright deceptive as in the case of George Eliot.

Woolf's literary criticism was rather different from her novels, though. Much of her early journalism was published anonymously when she had yet to make a name for herself as a writer of any kind. By the time she collected her essays for the first *Common Reader* she published under her own name, but she clearly indicated she did not wish to be known as an individual. She wrote in her diary that in this book she aimed to investigate literature with specific questions about 'ourselves', but that 'personality must be avoided at all costs' (*D2*, 5 September 1923, 265). She confirmed the importance of this

perception to her the following year: she must avoid the personal and egotistical and write formally, respecting her art (*D2*, 18 November 1924, 321).
She added to this that the critic should not lay any emphasis on the sex of the
author of the book under review: it is 'dangerous' and, if the sex is revealed, it
immediately arouses likes and dislikes which are not connected with aesthetic
judgement. The greatest writers do not stress the question of sex, one way or
the other (*E4*, 453–54). In this, she was in complete accord with the motives
of the Brontë sisters' use of pseudonyms, which she would develop further in
her first feminist polemic, *A Room of One's Own* (1929).

That Woolf had formerly, however, considered the uses of anonymity was
richly suggested in *A Room of One's Own*. In this polemic, Woolf slipped
in the perhaps subversive idea that 'Anon' who produced poems without
the naming of the author was frequently 'a woman' (*AROOO*, 48 [Panther
Triad]). Then, rather cryptically, she wrote that 'at last' she had grasped her
'philosophy of anonymity'. It appeared, as before, to involve the rejection
of the personal and the personality in writing (*DIV*, 29 October 1933, 186).

This theme grew in importance to Woolf throughout the 1930s. She and
Ethel Smyth clashed over the issue. Woolf appreciated what she identified as
the 'personal objective part' of a volume of Smyth's autobiography, *Female
Pipings on Eden*. Woolf (which would be surprising had she not evolved into
a different sort of writer as a world war again approached)) placed a growing
importance on statistics and facts. Indeed, they were to be central to *Three
Guineas*. She loathed Smyth's recital of personal grievances against the musi-
cal establishment; she thought they not only did not valuably contribute to the
book, but they also made it less forceful and convincing. Further, she found
such personal comments embarrassing. She stated that she adored anonymity
(*L5*, no. 2743: To Ethel Smyth, 6 June 1933, 191). She reflected further on
this topic in another letter to the same correspondent two days later. Again,
she stressed that she did not want to be focused on Smyth the individual;
she once more emphasised the need for facts, statistics, and objectivity. She
would have welcomed details about the difficulties experienced by female
musicians—how many women were in orchestras, the number of their musi-
cal instructors, and so forth. She warned that such writing would lead to her
being disregarded and dismissed as a woman with a personal grievance. She
told Smyth that although she had felt strongly about her own lack of education as a girl and a young woman, in *A Room of One's Own* she had eschewed
her own private history. She apparently viewed the readership of such works
as hostile men who would say that her personal complaints simply proved the
vanity of women who were incapable of omitting their own personality (*L5*,
no. 2746: To Ethel Smyth, 8 June 1933, 194–45). Later that year, Woolf raised
the subject again. She said she could only write unconsciously and with total
anonymity. She had to lose the sense of herself and since her friends militated

against this, she avoided them (*L5*, no. 2811: To Ethel Smyth, 29 October 1933, 239). Nearly five years elapsed before Woolf wrote of anonymity again. She wrote that she did not want her life to be written about during her lifetime, nor did she want to write about herself. She needed to embrace her 'private, secret' self, and desires to remain 'anonymous and submerged' (*L6*, no. 3443: To Ethel Smyth, 17 September 1938, 272). In 1939 she advised her correspondent to act as she does: to attempt to produce something 'impersonal' without caring about its fate (*L6*, no. 3506: To Ling Su-Hua, 17 April 1939, 328).

Woolf's growing need for anonymity during the 1930s culminated in an unfinished writing project, the first chapter of which she called 'Anon'. The idea of this work was vaguely stated as early as 1930 when she envisaged writing a 'history of English literature' as something she would write in her old age (*D3*, 11 March 1930, 297). Ten years later, she had, while picking blackberries, envisaged a book on the history of literature, from its earliest manifestation to its modern form, in a more definite and detailed way (*DV*, 12 September 1940, 318). Brenda R. Silver wrote that the following day Woolf started a new notebook with the heading *Reading at Random/Notes,* dating it 18 September 1940. Silver traced the origins of this critical work back to 1938 when Woolf had looked over her published essays on literature; but believed that Woolf did not actually start it until 1940 (Silver, 1979). Six months later, Woolf referred to writing another 'C[ommon] R[eader] twice in March 1940, on the 24 and 29', which suggests that she intended her new critical book to be the third in the series of this title (*DV*, 274, 276). Simultaneously with her critical reading of literature, she, however, began writing her final novel, *Between the Acts*. In this she dramatically represented each age of England's history in a village pageant. In this novel she parodied the literary styles and preoccupations of different periods. She was doing in fiction what she was also pursuing in a critical context. The reader feels that she wanted to control her private world in a way that was impossible in the outside world which was heading inexorably for the Second World War. From her father, she had learnt the importance of the social and historical context of literature and this last fragment reveals how well she had learnt his lesson. Readers who are interested in the evolution of this fragment are directed towards Brenda R. Silver's ground-breaking article. My purpose branches off here on another route—it is to trace Woolf's ideas about 'Anon', to seek its process of evolution since the Brontës' practice of it.

According to Woolf, anonymity was 'a great possession'. It produced writing in an impersonal and general way. In its earlier manifestations it led to the creation of ballads and songs. The recipient knew nothing about the writer's life and so was not distracted from their work. One of Anon's privileges was a lack of responsibility and self-consciousness. They can repeat and express general emotions and shared experiences. No one wishes to discover the details of Anon's biography, of their individual experiences. Anon gains vitality by a quality provided by the audience and, Woolf argues this quality still remains in writers (*E6*, 598).

Besnault views Woolf's incomplete 'Anon' as a response to and a product of the time in which it was written. Besnault suggests that in 'Anon' Woolf attempted to construct a 'cultural bridge' between 'vernacular culture and the utopian project of healing the scars of a community that needed to hold together in the face of a terrifying future. . . . The estrangement of a community from its collective memory and instincts, the separation of the reader from the writer, the erasure of the once heard voices from the recordings of official history all illustrate the personal and collective fear of loss and disconnection' (Besnault, 173). It is possible to read *Between the Acts* as a fictional embodiment of these fears, with its sense of isolation and fragmentation.

All these arguments (except the last) can fruitfully be applied to Charlotte Brontë who, like Woolf, appreciated anonymity. Unfortunately, by the nineteenth century the writer had long found it difficult to claim it. Woolf traces the demise of anonymity for the writer to the introduction of the printing press in the late fifteenth century by Caxton. Once there were printed books, the contents of them were beyond change (*E6*, 583). Woolf argued that the 'first blow' in the killing of anonymity was that it attached the name of the writer to the book. Paradoxically, though, it also preserved literary works. Additionally, it created a past and led to the establishment of a tradition, dating itself from the Spencer's *Faery Queen* (*E6*, 591) and Shakespeare (*E6*, 598–99). Woolf mainly applied herself to these dramatists. In modern times, the literal theatre becomes a theatre created in the reader's mind; the playwright is replaced by the novelist and the audience by the individual reader. Woolf concludes the essay with the succinct statement that 'Anon is dead' (*E6*, 599).

There were a number of differences between Woolf's and the Brontës' views on anonymity. For Charlotte Brontë it was an urgent and pressing need to preserve anonymity for as long as possible. Above all, she needed to prolong it so that she could (as Woolf pointed out) speak out boldly behind the shield of a pseudonym, which would hide her sex. For Woolf such anonymity was not felt to be necessary; but, while she put her own name on her books, she also disliked her writings being considered as the production of a woman. Overall, though, anonymity did not occupy her as consistently as it did the Brontës. At the end of her life, she was more concerned with tracing the history of the decline and fall of Anon as a literary phenomenon.

JUVENILIA

Adults frequently write about children, but in juvenilia it is the children themselves who write about themselves and adults in their world, or indeed in a world of their own creation. The writing of juvenilia was quite a marked occupation of middle-class children throughout the nineteenth and into the twentieth century. Both the Brontë and the Stephen children wrote juvenilia. There is no fixed age at which juvenilia is deemed to belong outside this classification. Charlotte continued writing juvenilia until the age of twenty-three, while Branwell was still writing it when he died at the age of thirty-one. Emily Brontë's sole novel shows her continuing preoccupation with the juvenile imaginary world of Gondal which she had created with her younger sister, Anne.

While the Brontë juvenilia seems to have developed after their childhood bereavements, the death of Mrs Stephen resulted in the abandonment of the family newspaper, the *Hyde Park Gate News* in 1895, when Virginia was thirteen. The death of their mother virtually marked the end of their childhoods as life after it became serious and difficult. As Hermione Lee eloquently wrote: the *Hyde Park Gate News* 'is the story of what happened to the Stephen children before the tragedies' (Lee, xiv).

The four surviving Brontë children wrote a huge amount of juvenilia. Much of Charlotte and Branwell Brontë's accounts of the imaginary worlds of Glass Town and Angria are extant. While Charlotte and Branwell formed a writing partnership, so, too, did the youngest two sisters. We know the latter pair created a fictitious world they called 'Gondal'. Unfortunately, beyond a few diary papers and some of Emily Brontë's poetry, nothing survives. Scholars believe there was also a prose account of Gondal, which was posthumously either destroyed by Charlotte Brontë or lost. Even without the majority of Emily and Anne Brontë's juvenilia an enormous amount of its total survived: Laura Forsberg has calculated that the writings in these volumes 'are longer than all the Brontë siblings' published manuscripts put together' (Forsberg, 44).

The origins of the Brontës' juvenilia have often been related. Briefly, when Patrick Brontë returned from a clerical meeting in Leeds in June 1826 he brought with him presents for the four surviving Brontë children. The most successful of these gifts was a box of toy soldiers which was presented to the only boy in the family, Branwell Brontë. The following morning each of the children selected one of the toy soldiers and named it after a famous and admired public man. Charlotte and Branwell Brontë chose the Duke of Wellington and Napoleon respectively. Emily and Anne Brontë named their soldiers after two Arctic explorers, Gravey and Waiting Boy, retrospectively. They began to weave stories around these soldiers which they acted out.

There had, however, been previous boxes of soldiers which may have been used in the Brontës' play earlier. Brontë scholar Juliet Barker believes that the 'plays' were in existence before the deaths of the two eldest Brontë sisters in 1825 (*Charlotte Brontë Juvenilia 1829–1835*, ix). Elsewhere, Barker writes that after the deaths of Maria and Elizabeth Brontë the survivors continued 'to make up plays' and 'acted them out with unrestrained enthusiasm' (Barker, 175). In 1829, the Brontës began to write down their imaginary adventures. Drew Lamonica Arms aptly commented: 'If the deaths of Charlotte's two eldest sisters launched a ferment of literary activity in the Brontë household, the deaths of her two younger sisters threatened to silence the lone survivor' (Lamonica Arms, 92).

A marked feature of the Brontë juvenilia is the way it was recorded. The children produced tiny manuscripts. Ostensibly this was because they wanted them to be small enough to be held in the hands of the soldiers. There was also another objective: the miniscule print was too small to be read by the adults in the household. The secrecy further tightened the bonds between the Brontë siblings. They did not even share their literary activities with their own contemporaries. After she had returned from Roe Head School, one of her closest friends asked how Charlotte Brontë spent her days. She replied with an account of 'delightful, though somewhat monotonous' life, which included teaching her younger sisters, walking with them on the moors, sewing, reading, writing and drawing (*L&L1*, no. 5: letter to Ellen Nussey, 21 July 1832, 94). Anne Dinsdale comments: 'What is hidden behind this conventional, lady-like account is the fervid creativity that was going on within the parsonage walls as the Brontës developed their fantasy worlds' (Ann Dinsdale, 21–22).

The Brontës' secrecy concerning their juvenilia meant, however, that since it was confined to the four of them, to the outsider they could be confusing or even bewildering. Laura Forsberg's comment can be taken as typical of this response: 'Writing privately for themselves and for their siblings, Charlotte and Branwell Brontë make no attempt to introduce their characters or to orient the reader in the world of the text. Nor do they explain the strange discontinuities between volumes; characters die and come back to life, change in age and appearance, and morph in personality' (Forsberg, 47). Perhaps the person most famously perplexed about the Brontë juvenilia was Elizabeth Gaskell. Reporting what she had acquired from a visit to the parsonage to gain material for her *Life* Gaskell wrote: 'by far the most extraordinary of all, a packet about the size of a lady's travelling writing case, full of paper books of different sizes . . . they are the wildest & most incoherent things. . . . They give one the idea of creative power carried to the verge of insanity' (Letter no. 297: To George Smith,?25 July 1856, 398). In her *Life,* Gaskell wrote that though she considered her subject's descriptions of real things 'homely, graphic, and forcible', her 'purely imaginative writing', when indulged, led 'her fancy and her language alike [to] run riot, sometimes to the very borders of apparent delirium.' She summed up Charlotte Brontë's juvenilia as 'wild' and 'weird' (*Life,* 89).

The juvenilia of the Stephen children also began with oral transmission between themselves, which in time progressed to their written newspaper. *Hyde Park Gate News: The Stephen Family Newspaper* was established when Virginia was only nine years old. She was not, however, the sole author for, again like the Brontës, the newspaper was a collaborative venture. The authors are stated to be 'Virginia Woolf, Vanessa Bell, Thoby Stephen'. However, Vanessa Bell clarified the question of authorship to some degree, when she wrote of *The Hyde Park Gate News* that 'Virginia wrote most of it' (Bell, 'Notes on Virginia's Childhood' in *Sketches in Pen and Ink,* 64). It was a weekly production and was issued each Monday. The newspaper survived from 1891–1892 and from early 1895; there are sixty-nine extant numbers. There is a marked difference between the narrators in the earlier years and those of 1895. Like the Brontës in their juvenilia, the Stephen children adopted literary role-playing and practised writing using different narrators. This enabled them to subvert Victorian values and attitudes. The world of the Stephen juvenilia was largely that which they experienced in their everyday Victorian family. Unlike the Brontës they did not create an alternative country, world, or universe.

Woolf reflected on her Victorian childhood, of which these juvenilia are a record, shortly before her death in her unfinished memoir, *A Sketch of the Past.* She contrasted the importance the two places most associated with her childhood: London and St Ives. The summer holiday house in Cornwall was preferred to 22 Hyde Park Gate in London, where the other three seasons were spent. Woolf recalled 'dull and monotonous' walks around Kensington Gardens. To make life more interesting they invented stories. They were very long stories and took a serial form, with an episode each day. There was the story of 'Jim Joe and Harry Hoe', which concerned three brothers who appeared to live in the country where they were involved with cattle and had exciting experiences. Looking back fifty years later, Woolf was unable to remember any of the details of these tales. There were also stories invented at St Ives which appear to have been more imaginative and which Woolf thought were superior to the London ones. She recalled the evil spirits, 'Beccage and Hollywinks', who lived in the Talland House garden. Woolf apparently related this story to her mother and an American guest, but she does not recall their reactions to it! (*SP*, 76–77). Unfortunately, there is no detailed account of who or what Beccage and Hollywinks were.

After Thoby Stephen was sent to boarding school, the two sisters, Vanessa and Virginia, continued their storytelling in the nursery. These tales always began with the same invocation of 'Clémont dear child, said Mrs Dilke' (*SP*, 79). According to Vanessa Bell, the spelling of the name varied; she recorded it as 'Cle-mente' or 'Clemente' ('Notes on Virginia's Childhood', 59). That the spelling differed testifies to the fact that at this stage these stories were purely oral. The stories then proceeded with the adventures of their comparatively wealthy neighbours, the Dilkes. Their imaginings of adventures varied between the prosaic (feasting on fried eggs) to the exciting (discovery of treasure under the floorboards). This latter idea would later resurface in Woolf's children's story, *The Widow and the Parrot*, originally written as a contribution to her young nephews' magazine, as Quentin Bell recorded (*The Widow and the Parrot*, no page numbers).

Unlike the Brontës, the Stephen children's juvenilia were not a secret to be kept between themselves. Indeed, they seemed to have been very eager to share it with their parents and to hear their verdict on each number of *The Hyde Park Gate News*. To impress and win adult praise was certainly Virginia's main intention—and her reward when it came. She recorded the extreme pleasure she felt when she heard that her mother had so liked a story Virginia had written that she sent it to Madge Symonds. Her mother had thought it very imaginative as it had dealt with souls choosing the bodies they would be born into. Virginia compared the sense of pleasure by comparing herself to a violin being played upon (*SP*, 95).

Virginia described her excitement when awaiting the Stephen parents' reaction to *Hyde Park Gate News*. Vanessa Bell corroborated this:

> [Virginia] was very sensitive to criticism and the good opinion of the grown-ups. I remember putting the paper on the table by my mother's sofa while they were at dinner and then creeping quietly into the little room to look through the window and hear the criticisms. As we looked, she trembling with excitement, we could see my mother's lamp-lit figure quietly sitting near the fire, my father on the other side with his lamp, both reading. Then she noticed the paper, picked it up, and began to read. We looked and listened hard for some comment. 'Rather clever, I think,' said my mother, putting the paper down without apparent excitement. But it was enough to thrill her daughter—she had had her approval and been called clever and our eavesdropping was rewarded. ('Notes on Virginia's Childhood', 64–65)

The models for the Brontë and Stephen juvenilia were very similar in kind. The Brontës' inspiration for their juvenilia, *Blackwood's Magazine*, and, after 1832, *Fraser's Magazine for Town and Country*, has been copiously commented upon. Joanne Shattock informs us that *Blackwood's* was established by the bookseller William Blackwood in 1817, as a Tory magazine to counter the Whig *Edinburgh Review*. While *Blackwood's* contents were miscellaneous, they were also one of the earliest magazines to publish serial fiction. Its most marked influence on the Brontës' juvenilia was through its political satire and often condemnatory reviews of contemporary fiction and poetry (Shattock, 'Newspapers and Magazines', 270). Christine Alexander further elaborates on the contents of *Blackwood's*: the Brontës enjoyed its 'racy dialogue, reviews, and stories. . . . The colourful accounts of African and Arctic exploration, gothic tales, political, artistic, and philosophical debates, and the witty dialogue of *Blackwood's* fictitious and opinionated narrators . . . all found their way into the early writings of the Brontës ('Nineteenth-Century Juvenilia: A Survey', 21).

It has been established that the Brontë family borrowed *Blackwood's* from a man called Driver who lived in the neighbourhood. Barker has suggested that he might have been a clergyman. When Driver died in 1831, the Brontës no longer had access to *Blackwood's* (Barker, 149). The following year, however, Miss Branwell subscribed to *Fraser's Magazine* (Barker, 179). It bore strong resemblances to *Blackwood's* and, indeed, a regular writer from that magazine became *Fraser's* first editor: it was renowned 'for its harsh satirical assaults on popular contemporary authors.' Yet simultaneously it nurtured young and ambitious writers (Bock, 49–50).

Like the Brontës, the Stephen children were influenced by adult magazines and were permitted to choose their own reading without parental censorship. For the Stephen family it was *Punch* and *Tit-Bits* which were major influences on *Hyde Park Gate News*. *Punch,* or *the London Charivari*, was a radical weekly English illustrated periodical. It was founded in 1841 by Henry Mayhew and during the Victorian era it was famed for its satire and its caricatures. One of its early staff was William Makepeace Thackeray, Leslie Stephen's first father-in-law through his marriage to Thackeray's younger daughter, Harriet Marion ('Minny'). 'From its early years as a campaigner for social justice to its transformation into national icon, *Punch* played a central role in the formation of British identity—and how the rest of the world saw the British nation'. During the nineteenth century it concerned itself with social issues such as the pollution caused by the rapid industrialisation during that period. 'It was imitated, parodied and pirated' throughout the world. (*Punch Historical Archive*, accessed online on 6 March 2023). It was aimed at middle-class families like the Stephens.

In *A Sketch of the Past*, Woolf recalled sitting on the grass in Kensington Gardens with Vanessa, eating chocolate and reading *Tit-Bits* (*SP*, 77). Jackson (to whose article the following discussion is indebted) wrote that it was recognised 'by many historians and contemporaries to be the most popular penny paper of the late-nineteenth century' (Kate Jackson, 203. Accessed 06 March 2023). Like *Blackwood's* and *Fraser's* in the Brontës' time, *Tit-Bits* was a miscellany. Jackson states that it was 'a sixteen-page patchwork of advice, humorous anecdotes, romantic fiction, statistical information, historical explanation, advertisement, legal detail, quips and queries, and reader correspondence' (203). The Stephens' *Hyde Park Gate News* included many of these categories of writing.

In 1889, *Tit-Bits* had introduced the serialisation of fiction in its pages. Its targeted audience included the 'juvenile reader' as well as adults. Newnes also introduced story competitions. According to Vanessa Bell, Virginia, unknown to anybody but her sister, submitted a short story to *Tit-Bits*. The story was not accepted. Vanessa Bell vaguely recalled that Virginia's story was about 'a wildly romantic account of a young woman on a ship' ('Notes on Virginia's Childhood', 65). (Perhaps the annual holidays on the Cornish coast had inspired this story. It is highly improbable that this was the initial dawning of the idea for her first published novel, *The Voyage Out*.)

Of particular interest in view of both the juvenilia and the future Virginia Woolf as an essayist was the function Newnes saw himself as performing. He played the same sort of role as editor to his reader as Virginia Woolf enacted as adult essayist towards her readers. Jackson has explained Newnes' role in the following terms: '*Tit-Bits* constitutes a dynamic process of interaction between editor-proprietor and audience' (Jackson, 206). Newnes did not want to close down discussion; in fact, he promoted the 'more democratic value of equal exchange'. In her adult essays, Woolf asked her readers to see themselves as writers as well. This idea could have been borrowed from *Tit-Bits* in which '[t]he audience of *Tit-Bits* actually became writers, through being contributors, competitors and correspondents' (Jackson, 211).

Alexander has summarised the content of Charlotte and Branwell's juvenilia: 'They wrote editorial notes, contents pages, letters to the editor, advertisements, serialised stories, poems reviews of paintings and books' (Alexander, 'Play and Apprenticeship: The Culture of Family Magazines', 34). Charlotte Brontë experimented with different narrators and perspectives. It is notable that her narrators are, without exception in her juvenilia, men. She practised writing in different genres, styles, and subject matter. She proved herself an equal to her brother, when girls in Victorian Britain were considered inferior to boys. Her projected narrators were often professional writers themselves. She did not identify with her early heroines and the particular challenges they faced in a world which was imaginary, but was also still a patriarchy. The heroines are beautiful but helpless, and they suffer in their relationships with men. Ultimately, they can only die with broken hearts. Charlotte appears to be in love with her own hero, the Duke of Zamorna.

She and Branwell were competitive rivals in the control and direction of the juvenilia. Through her narrator's use of irony, she cut Branwell down to size.

Emily and Anne Brontë's land of Gondal progressed separately from their older brother and sister's imaginary world, though it originated in the same games with the soldiers. The first mention of it occurred in November 1834. Its very landscape is more akin to the moorland area and climate which they inhabited in their own real lives. Because of long periods of separation as adults, Emily and Anne proceeded independently in the creation of Gondal. Two separate books contain Emily Brontë's poems: one is titled 'Gondal Poems' [MSS B], while the other is simply headed with her initials and the dates of writing the poetry in that book [MSS A]. This classification and transcribing into these two books were performed in 1844. Nevertheless, the editors of *The Poems of Emily Brontë* warn against trying to allot rigidly the poems to either the Gondal or non-Gondal categories; MSS B contains sixty-seven poems which are clearly Gondal poems, but also nearly as many which cannot definitely be described as poems belonging to Gondal but which still seem to be fictional rather than autobiographical (Roper with Chitham, 2–4). As with Charlotte and Branwell's juvenilia the situation behind the poetry is on occasion obscure and bewilders the reader. Many are, however, self-contained and complete in themselves and so do not need an intimate knowledge of the whole imaginary kingdom of Gondal.

For these two sisters, as for Charlotte, their fantasy kingdom enabled them to escape the restrictions placed on women as Victorianism became established in England. This may have been particularly applicable to Anne. Emily Brontë appeared not to have felt these limitations so strongly: she did not rely on male narrators through whom she could speak. One of her central female characters is the powerful Augusta Geraldine Almeda (or A.G.A.), whose passion is never curbed as she opposes men in her struggles to gain power. Interestingly, though, Roper and Chitham suggested that the world of Gondal is more 'moral' than those created by Charlotte and Branwell Brontë (Roper and Chitham, 9). The adults at the parsonage would have been likely to disapprove of the sexual licence which is so prominent a feature in the story of Zamorna and the women with whom he associates. In Gondal, erring characters are more likely to get their come-uppance. Early Victorian values of hiding the emotions and passionate sexuality, both inside and outside of marriage, are subverted by the Brontës' novels.

As a child, and later, a female adolescent, Virginia was able, like the Brontë girls, to experience in her juvenilia the same freedoms as her brothers and half-brothers, as she adopted the styles, voices, and subjects of the adult world. Further, this was a world where she would be praised for using her mind. In some ways, the Virginia of *Hyde Park Gate News* used her writing to experiment and explore different voices and personae, in the same way as the Brontës had. Another resemblance between the youthful Brontës and Stephens was that the children were both the writers and the participants in their juvenilia. They referred to themselves in the third person. By also ventriloquising other people's voices, the Stephens like the Brontës subverted conventional attitudes, expectations, and values of the Victorian period. In the *Hyde Park Gate News* there was a persistent satirising of Victorian marriages which were based on wealth and class. There were several series of 'love letters' between young couples. They were constantly in conflict with their parents either because the desired partner lacked sufficient money or because they chose a man or woman who attracted them physically and pushed the question of money out of the equation. Sometimes one or other of the couple recommended deliberately deceiving a mercenary parent (*HPGN*, 22, 25, and 40).

The juveniles also mocked the matrimonial desires of those they were familiar with. For example, Millicent Vaughan's recent trip to Canada to visit her married sister was commented on with a sly wit: the author hoped that Millicent was not envious of her sister's marital situation 'when she herself is searching the wide world in quest of matrimony. But we are wandering from our point like so many old people' (*HPGN*, 42). Similarly, the Victorian views on marriage were satirised in connection with the Stephen children's cousins, Millicent and Emma Vaughan: although they lacked Stella Duckworth's faults, the latter was, nevertheless, likely to 'carry off' as 'good a prize' in the '"matrimony market"' (*HPGN*, 65). When Millicent did marry, from 22 Hyde Park Gate, Virginia expressed some reservation about the rituals of a high-Victorian marriage: the 'stranger can have no idea how much labour and forethought' were involved in such a wedding' (*HPGN*, 171).

The excesses of love, particularly maternal love directed towards male offspring, were mocked throughout *Hyde Park Gate News*. Julia Stephen was observed with a pitiless eye on occasion. It may be significant that both her brothers and her half-brothers received what may have appeared to Virginia to be excessive attention. The female members were not treated in the same way: they did not leave home (except, sometimes, on holiday) and thus did not elicit the same emotional excesses as the males. An example of each of Julia Stephen's exaggerated reception of these returning boys or young men will be quoted. Let us begin with the oldest and work our way down to the youngest. George Duckworth accompanied their mother to visit Thoby at his boarding school. The author reflected: 'It must indeed be sad for the Mother to see her sons growing older and older and then to watch them leave the sweet world of child-hood behind them and enter into the great world of manhood' (*HPGN*, 39). When Gerald Duckworth returned to the family home, we are told, in the third person: 'Our author was much touched to see tears in the maternal eyes' (*HPGN*, 45). Julia Stephen's delight at receiving a short letter from Thoby resulted in the mocking comment: 'we hope all young folks do never forgets [sic] how anxiously the maternal eyes look for some little note or epistle' (*HPGN*, 38). Adrian was definitely a particular favourite of Julia Stephen, which may well have resulted in some jealousy, not only from the other children, but also from Leslie Stephen. There are certainly a number of barbed comments about him (not only made by the juveniles) and no praise of him at all. Critical remarks about Adrian by both Gerald Duckworth and Leslie Stephen were noted. When Adrian had a cold he received extra care from their mother, which Virginia described wittily but with some malice: 'It is indeed a pretty sight to see the Mother holding the spoon between her slim fingers and the uplifted and eager face of the little one whose pretty cherub lips are parted ready to receive the tit-bits from the fond Mother. Oh how like the old bird feeding its young' (*HPGN*, 42). In adult life both Vanessa and Virginia disliked the expression of highly charged emotions. Though they associated it particularly with their maternal aunt, Mary Fisher, they may well also have disliked their mother's lack of emotional restraint as well. Julia Stephen was described as 'really like a "Good Angel" to the poor of St. Ives', for whom she was fundraising to introduce a nurse into their community (*HPGN*, 118). Thinking ahead to Woolf's criticism of the 'Angel in the house', and the female writer's need to kill her, this reference to the angelic nature of her mother sounds ominous.

Like Patrick Brontë, Leslie Stephen was a published author, though unlike the former, he practised as a professional full-time writer. He is described as 'the celebrated author' and there is a picture of him (presumably drawn by Vanessa) (*HPGN*, 18). Later, Stephen is described as possessing 'immense literary powers' (*HPGN*, 144). Twice the young Virginia applauded her father when he was awarded honorary doctorates. Virginia's statement that Julia Stephen was prouder of this honour than her husband was accepted, implied that a woman's academic successes could only be vicariously achieved through her male relatives. This was not commented upon nor resented (*HPGN*, 72 and 75). Nor is there any suggestion of the scorn with which she herself would reject honorary degrees as an adult. It is impossible to identify what changed her view and when it occurred. When she recorded the news that Stephen had delivered a lecture to the 'young ladies' at, Newnham College, Cambridge, on 'The Choice of Books', she certainly could not have anticipated that she would follow in his footsteps in 1928 with a more radical subject for her lecture (*HPGN*, 189).

The comings and goings of the Duckworth half-brothers and her full brothers as they went and returned from school and university were constantly recorded. Twice attendance at the boat race between Oxford and Cambridge was described. In the first account, the whole family support Cambridge rather than Oxford in the annual boat race because of the Stephens' and

Duckworths' association with that university (*HPGN*, 53–54). The familial association in the second description is muted and strikes the reader as being less partial (*HPGN*, 195–98). The Stephen parents receive with 'joy' a good school report about Thoby (*HPGN*, 82). 22 Hyde Park Gate is in a frenzy for a week as its inhabitants wait to see if Thoby has won what his family regarded as an important school prize. Virginia seemed to share the family's pride which was based on the differences in the boys' and girls' education which in turn was dictated purely by gender and not by ability (*HPGN*, 160). All this sits uncomfortably on a girl who in adult life would protest about the iniquitous differences in the education of girls and boys. She particularly resented the same restrictions placed on girls as had existed in period of the Brontës: while girls were taught modern languages, only boys were taught the classical languages. She herself would pursue a classical education after her mother's death. She might have been thought to have a lifelong resentment on this subject, but when did it begin?

There is even a moral tale about a woman's place. Miss Smith has been remarkable and precocious all her life. When she entered society at the age of twenty, she advocated the reform of the world. She wrote an essay on women's rights and condemned men as 'brutes', against whom women must fight. Miss Smith becomes unpopular with both sexes and was embittered. Finally, she allowed herself to be 'only a woman', at which point some 'gallant gentleman' proposed marriage. Accepting that she needed a man who was 'stronger and wiser than herself' Miss Smith marries him. She turned into 'an excellent wife' and then 'a devoted mother' (*HPGN*, 164–66). The reader might hope that this is a satirical story, but actually it seems to be a simple acceptance of her mother's conservative views about women's role. George Duckworth's question as to whether women should have the vote, is not engaged with, but hangs in the air unanswered (*HPGN*, 20). When Woolf's views changed is unknown: we are simply faced with them as a fait accompli in her adult life.

Woolf's later attitude towards her half-sister Laura Makepeace Stephen (1870–1945) underwent an enormous alteration between the Victorian period as she lived it and how she recreated it retrospectively. The opening number of *Hyde Park Gate News* began with the activity of Laura. Here she was simply accepted and then rather cruelly the children played an April fool's prank on her tormenting her about a nonexistent smudge on her face. That this was recorded in the newspaper which was aimed to impress Virginia's parents suggests that Leslie and Julia Stephen saw nothing wrong in this type of bullying (*HPGN*, 3–4). At Christmas 1891, Laura returned, presumably for the festive season, from the Searles who lived in Devon, with whom she spent most of her time from 1886 until she entered Earlswood Asylum in

1893. The newspaper records her arrival: she is greeted with 'joy and delight' by her family' (*HPGN*, 20). During the summer exodus to St Ives, Laura again joins her family, presumably arriving from the Searles'. The newspaper noted her arrival and again claimed she was 'heartily welcomed by all her family' (*HPGN*, 92). In none of these issues is Laura presented as abnormal or threatening in any way.

Yet by the time Woolf wrote her 1922 memoir, 'Old Bloomsbury', Laura was not even viewed as her blood relative (she is 'Thackeray's grand-daughter'), but rather as a severely impaired person mentally who indulged in bizarre and threatening behaviour. Laura became 'a vacant-eyed girl whose idiocy was becoming daily more obvious, who could hardly read, who would throw the scissors into the fire, who was tongue-tied and stammered and yet had to appear at table with the rest of us ('Old Bloomsbury', 182). It is impossible to know when this transformation actually took place.

Hermione Lee sums up the Stephens' juvenilia as 'enchanting, funny and vigorous' (*HPGN*, vii). Although laughter may mark a shared joyful experience, frequently the laughter is jarring, ambiguous and not always positive. When they played an April Fool's joke on their mother, the 'anxious infants' awaited Julia Stephen's laughter. When 'at last it came', the jest was then seen as being successful (*HPGN*, 51). Apparently in the Stephen household what amused the adults was uncertain. In the story sequel 'A Cockney's Farming Experience', the discordant relationship between husband and wife was illustrated by Harriet's reaction to her husband's incompetence when he failed to milk a cow: she 'laughed spitefully' (*HPGN*, 98). The local boys also mocked John's lack of agricultural knowledge; they 'laughed' when he attempted to drive a herd of cows. They laughed at him not with him, leading him to abandon the care of the cow to more experienced hands (*HPGN*, 101). John did not tell Harriet of his fear of cows as she 'would only laugh' (*HPGN*, 102). Later in the serial, when John retired to bed claiming he is dying, he was astonished to hear Harriet 'laughing loudly' (*HPGN*, 113). This was experienced as scornful laughter. Instead of frightening Harriet with his feigned illness he heard Harriet laughing with another man downstairs, who she promised to marry when John was dead. This angered her husband. Eventually, though, he discovered that Harriet was also feigning to find out how much John cared about her. When John and Harriet were able to share a positive laugh rather than a negative ridiculing, it was indicative of their improving relationship.

In the sequel to 'A Cockney's Farming Experiences', 'The Experiences of a Paterfamilias' the laughter used as a weapon does not come from Harriet scorning her husband, but from others. Travelling to their country farm, the cockney shared a carriage with an old man. Having no reading matter, he engaged his fellow-passenger in conversation. John learnt that he hated politics and wished they had never been invented. John laughed at this and replied that that would be the end of the world. The old man received this laughter as hostile, he was 'savage' and ostentatiously returned to reading his newspaper and ignored John (*HPGN*, 127). In the same sequel, John asked his servant James, who was engaged to be married, whether he wanted a honeymoon. James replied that only the gentry have honeymoons and then he dissolved into 'fits of laughter', which John did not understand and found disconcerting (*HPGN*, 154). It is now John who 'laughed' at Harriet's long-term ambitions for their baby son (*HPGN*, 154).

At St. Ives the Stephen children witnessed the loading of a cart of hay. The undiscriminating and inappropriate laughter of an onlooker was noted (*HPGN*, 84). Also at St. Ives, when two guests departed, the author commented on the quietness of the house. One of the guest's laughter was recorded, but not altogether positively, since the cause of it defied understanding: Lily Norton's had had 'sudden and serious fits of laughing whose cause could never be satisfactorily explained' (*HPGN*, 91).

There is frequently a startling divergence between the Virginia who emerges from the juvenilia and the Virginia who wrote of her Victorian upbringing in a series of memoirs as an adult. Several of these later reminiscences she delivered to the Memoir Club where her main aim was to entertain. This cannot be said of her privately written *A Sketch of the Past*. Some of this might be explained by her comment on the past and the present in this unfinished memoir: ''It would be interesting to make the two people, I now, I then, come out in contrast. And further, this past is affected by the present moment. What I write today I should not write in a year's time' (*SP*, 75). Here Woolf seems to be suggesting that our relationship with our pasts changes as we change.

It is highly doubtful that Woolf ever read any of the Brontës' juvenilia. This is explained by the posthumous treatment it received. Arthur Bell Nicholls, Charlotte Brontë's husband, had taken the juvenilia (with other surviving Brontë relics) to Ireland where he returned after Patrick Brontë's death. Clement Shorter bought the juvenilia from Charlotte Brontë's widower for the collector (and forger) Thomas J. Wise, who vandalised these little books. He printed some of them privately in inaccurately transcribed editions which cut out some of the material. In the manuscripts he kept for his own library Wise removed the original covers and had them rebound. He sold other fragments of the juvenilia to book collectors among his own friends and the wider public. Signatures were cut out of the manuscripts and sold. Manuscripts which had been written by Branwell Brontë were falsely ascribed to Charlotte Brontë as her name attracted higher prices. The juvenilia were distributed

over the world. Wise collaborated with John Alexander Symington to produce a very incomplete and inaccurate version of the Brontë juvenilia in
1936–1938. There is no indication anywhere in Woolf's writing that suggests
she had read this edition. That is a great pity: Woolf had shown herself open
to juvenilia in her review of Jane Austen's *Love and Friendship*, which was
written at the age of seventeen. In this essay, Woolf suggested that one of the
fairies who bestow gifts at birth had given Jane Austen an understanding of
the world and its people when she was in her cradle: 'Thus at seventeen she
had few illusions about other people and none about herself. Whatever she
writes is finished and turned and set in its relation to the universe like a work
of art' (*E3*, 334). Given this appreciation, it is to be regretted that Woolf was
unable to read and comment on the Brontës' juvenilia.

Chapter Three

Personal Comments on the Brontës and in Virginia Woolf's Fiction

Virginia Woolf's Personal Comments on the Brontës

Apart from her published critical essays on Charlotte and Emily Brontë, Woolf also made more personal observations about them in her diaries and letters. She made a rare comment on Anne Brontë, who in conformity with her age, she disregarded. The minor novelist, George Moore (1852–1933) expressed the (then) highly heterodox opinion that Anne Brontë 'was the greatest of the Brontës' (*DIII*, 9 March 1926, 67). Not only did Woolf disagree with Moore, but since he had condemned Thomas Hardy, Leo Tolstoy, and Henry James, amongst other writers whose craft she particularly admired, his opinion of Anne Brontë was cited primarily as a proof of his eccentricity.

During the summer of 1897 Woolf was irritable and mentally unstable with the stress of her half-sister's illness and death. It was at this time that Woolf recorded reading Charlotte Brontë's novels. Before Stella's death Woolf recorded that she was reading *Shirley* (*A Passionate Apprentice*, 2 July 1897, 110). Shortly after Stella's death on 19 July 1897, the Stephens and depleted Duckworths went on holiday to Gloucestershire. Whilst away, Woolf was reading *Villette* (*APA*, 30 July 1897, 118) and by the 9 August she was considering reading *Jane Eyre* (*APA*, 121), though she did not actually begin to do so until 7 September (*APA*, 127). The dates she read these Charlotte Brontë novels were baldly stated with no comments on them.

In her epistolary relationships Woolf appeared to associate a particular correspondent, Lady Robert ('Nelly') Cecil with the Brontës. These letters covered a period of decades, beginning in 1909 and continuing into the early 1930s. Whilst she was still publishing only reviews and essays, Woolf wrote of being 'promoted' to being a dinner guest of Reginald Smith, who was the son-in-law of Charlotte Brontë's publisher, George Smith. She had been promised a viewing of 'the Brontë manuscripts' (*L1*, no. 491: To Lady Robert Cecil, 30 May 1909, 397). During the First World War, Woolf revealed a nostalgia for their pre-war relationship which had centred on the Brontës. She wrote that they were geographically separated which made it impossible to continue their discussions of, among other topics, the Brontës (*L6*, no. 1559a: To Lady Cecil, May 1915, 507). Decades later, Woolf recalled how a century ago, she and Lady Cecil had reviewed books for Reginald Smith, 'that long faced old lantern jawed man'. She still remembered his Brontë relics, particularly the socks of Charlotte Brontë which he kept 'in a glass case in his drawing room' (*L5*, no. 2626: To Lady Cecil, 18 August 1932, 96).

The other personal references to one or more of the Brontë sisters tend to be passing remarks and not particularly important, apart from the fact that they reveal a continuing interest in these Victorian writers. They also reveal certain personal and idiosyncratic modes of thinking about the Brontës. Some of these refer to them collectively as a family. Woolf coined a new word for them considered together: 'Stephen Brontëised' was her description of herself while she was staying in Yorkshire and admiring its wild scenery and added that it was 'almost as good as the real thing' (*L1*, no. 266: To Violet Dickinson, 16 April 1906, 221). This phrase reveals how closely Woolf identified with the Brontës; this was far more marked in her youth than in her later life.

Woolf described a visit from Edith Sitwell, whom she had taken to. She compared Sitwell's childhood to that of the Brontës. Woolf seemed to have taken her notion of the latter's childhood from Elizabeth Gaskell's not altogether accurate biography of Charlotte Brontë. Certainly, Woolf's description of Sitwell's childhood does not appear to be very similar (to this reader, at least) to that of the Brontës: Sitwell told her 'awful Brontë stories about being cursed by her mother as a child and made to kill blue bottles in a hot room' (*L3*, no. 1732: To Vanessa Bell, 20 March 1927, 350). Lord Olivier derived from his reading of *To the Lighthouse* that Prue Ramsay was pregnant before her marriage. Woolf cited Charlotte Brontë's death to justify the phraseology she had used about Prue and to reject her correspondent's idea: she argued that Charlotte Brontë 'died in early pregnancy. Isn't that childbirth?' More euphemistically Woolf had written that Prue died of something 'connected with childbirth'. Woolf wrote that she refused to accept responsibility for not having delved into the medical details surrounding Prue's death (Letter no. 1762a: To Lord Olivier, 25 May 1929; Banks Trautmann, 182).

In 1934, Woolf wrote to a relatively recent literary friend and author and demanded who Stella Gibbons was and what her recent book was about. In 1934, Gibbons was awarded the Femina Vie Heureuse Prize for her comic novel *Cold Comfort Farm*. Woolf declared herself 'enraged' by this £40 award being awarded to Gibbons. Woolf apparently did not know that the book's Brontë connection was the character of Mr Meyerburg (whom Flora thinks of as 'Mr Mybug'): an author who wished to marry Flora and insisted that she only refused him because she was sexually repressed and inhibited. In this novel, he was working on a thesis which argued that the works of the Brontë sisters were actually written by Branwell Brontë. Perhaps Woolf would have been even more 'enraged' had she known this! (*L5*, no. 2892: To Elizabeth Bowen, 16 May 1934, 303).

In response to a review of *A Room of One's Own* by Lyn Ll. Irvine of 9 November 1929, Woolf wrote a letter to the *Nation & Athenaeum* which was published on 16 November 1929. Irvine's rather hypothetical perspective on the Brontës was that had they been her contemporaries they would have been employed as teachers and gone abroad under the services provided by the holiday company Thomas Cook and Son. The snag then would have been that there would have been no time to write their novels. Woolf entirely rejected this view. She quoted Florence Nightingale to the effect that Victorian middle-class women had very little time they could call their own. Woolf also argued that Charlotte Brontës would have had more leisure time as a teacher than she had had caring for a demanding father. However, Woolf acknowledged that had Emily travelled abroad in the summer vacations she might never have contracted and died from consumption. But under no circumstances would the Brontë sisters have been typical teachers or travellers, for: 'They remain rare and remarkable women'. Woolf returned to her thesis propounded in *A Room of One's Own*. If more women like the Brontës were to emerge, they would need a room of their own and financial independence: 'One cannot grow fine flowers in a thin soil' (*E4*, 121–22).

A comment Woolf made not on the Brontës but on Jane Austen is surprising and throws into relief Woolf's different approach to these writers. In fact, her judgement reverses traditional nineteenth century wisdom about the attributes of Jane Austen and the Brontë sisters. Writing to a Jane Austen scholar and expert, Woolf wrote that she had 'often thought of writing on the coarseness of J.A'. She expressed her annoyance with people who spoke of Austen 'as if she were a niminy piminy spinster'; but that would be likely to annoy others if she did so (*L6*, no. 3191: To R. W. Chapman, 20 November 1936, 87). Four years earlier Woolf had associated the Brontës with Jane Austen when she expressed her opinion of the relative merits of them. Apparently, Ethel Smyth had implied that 'Bloomsbury' had the highest opinion of Jane Austen and Smyth assumed that Woolf shared this preference. Woolf replied that whatever 'Bloomsbury' might think of Austen, she was not a favourite of her own. She stated that she would sacrifice all of Austen for half of the Brontës' novels. Yet she then qualified this: '—if my reason did not compel me to see that [Austen] is a magnificent artist' (*L5*, no. 2667: To Ethel Smyth, 20 November 1932, 126).

Woolf referred to Charlotte Brontë alone on some occasions. She wrote to Ling Su-Hua who had been the lover of Woolf's late nephew, Julian Bell, when he had taught English at a Chinese University. Ling Su-Hua had asked for recommendations of what books in English she should read. Having stated her preference for biography and autobiography, Woolf recommended, among others in this category, Gaskell's *Life of Charlotte Brontë* (*L6*, no. 3377: To Ling Su-Hua, 5 April 1938, 222). Later in the year, Woolf wrote again to Ling Su-Hua and in this letter elaborated on why she had recommended *The Life of Charlotte Brontë*; the biography would give her correspondent an idea of the lives of Victorian women; their handicaps and how they triumphed over them. She rather vaguely added that it would interest Ling Su-Hua in other ways too (*L6*, no. 3425: To Ling Su-Hua, 27 July 1938, 259).

Curiously, despite her apparent rejection of some conventional terms or labels, Woolf seemed to have a long-lasting fixation on what or who was a lady or ladylike. This first cropped up in her juvenilia. In the serial 'A Cockney's Farming Experiences', the eponymous hero's wife asks him to try to remember 'that she was a lady' (*HPGN*, 98). As an adult she twice distinguished between Charlotte Brontë and Jane Austen along these lines: the former was not a 'lady', while the latter was (*E3*, 211, and *E4*, 561). Woolf drew the same distinction between the characters of these two authoresses: the Elizabeths and Emmas were ladies; Jane Eyre was not. In 1927, Woolf defended Mrs Radcliffe's novels against mockery because she was a 'lady' and until the rot set in around 1850 English ladies knew how to write (*L3*, no. 1802: To Saxon Sydney-Turner, 29 August 1927, 414). This cut-off date excluded Charlotte but comfortably accommodated Austen. Simultaneously, Woolf feared the term 'ladylike' being applied to her own writing, which she would have interpreted as a criticism. This fear was first expressed as early as 1909, when she dreaded her writing being judged as 'ladylike' (*APA*, 395). Nearly a quarter of a century later she was apprehensive that readers of *Flush* would condemn her as a 'ladylike prattler' (*DIV*, 2 October 1933, 181). While in social terms it was a matter of class, in literature it was something intangible. Where she stood overall in the matter of ladies is impossible to determine among these contradictory utterances.

Finally, Woolf made various (and varied), but very small in terms of numbers, comments on Emily Brontë. Clement K. Shorter's understanding of Emily Brontë was nonexistent and had nothing to offer Woolf as she read his *The Brontës: Life and Letters*. The opening sentence of his second volume is the stark sentence: 'Emily Brontë is the sphinx of our modern literature' (*L&L2*, 1). Woolf was free to make of her what she could or would. An early remark occurred within a discussion of Sophocles' *Electra* and may perhaps be considered somewhat cryptic. Having stated that in both Greece and England the 'heroic woman' was very similar, Woolf followed this up with the brief (and cryptic) sentence: 'She is of the type of Emily Brontë' (*D1*, 19 August 1918, 184).

Other remarks passed by Woolf in her letters and diaries never attempted to get inside the mind of Emily Brontë; they were focused on the externalities of this remarkable and complicated character. Woolf described in a letter how, at a party she attended hosted by Lady Londonderry, Buckmaster, 'an aged enlightened Liberal peer', recited Emily Brontë's poem, 'No Coward Soul is Mine, 'word for word, in tones of awful dignity' (*L4*, no. 2133: To Clive Bell, 6 February 1930, 134). Then, however, Woolf proceeded to imply that this story about Buckmaster and Emily Brontë was incidental to what she wished to tell Clive Bell!

The final mention of Emily Brontë in her letters and diaries occurred late in her life. Almost incidentally, Woolf mentioned that she and Leonard Woolf had been given tickets to see the film of *Wuthering Heights* on its premiere night. This was the film in which Laurence Olivier played Heathcliff and Merle Oberon the first Catherine. In fact, this reference brings Woolf close to us, for this film can still be obtained. It was of interest in that it ended with the first generation and did not play out Heathcliff's revenge. However, Woolf did not record her impressions and, indeed, we do not even know whether she and Leonard Woolf actually attended the performance (*L6*, no. 3508: To V. Sackville-West, 25 April 1939, 329).

THE HYDE PARK GATE NEWS

Nineteenth-century novelists were evidently familiar to the Stephen children. Thus, it is perhaps unsurprising that Virginia Stephen's first reference to Charlotte Brontë occurred in the Stephen children's juvenilia, *Hyde Park Gate News,* on 18 March 1895. It was written when Virginia was thirteen years and two months old; and less than two months before her mother's rapid decline and death. It occurred in the section called 'Correspondence'. It is necessary to provide a context for this Charlotte Brontë reference, which revealed both her precocious intelligence and the relationships existing between her and her half-siblings' blood relatives. As so often, Virginia's attitude was not respectful. The fact that her parents were encouraged to read the *Hyde Park Gate News* (unlike the Brontë children's father and aunt), we must assume that they tolerated and were even amused by their children's irreverence.

Virginia was purportedly writing to her cousin (who is not given either a forename or a surname). Virginia was staying with her aunt, not the mother of her cousin, as the aunt was later identified as the spinster Miss Duckworth. After an unsatisfactory meal, Virginia and her aunt visited a Lady Musgrove (a Jane Austen name in *Persuasion*) and her three Irish daughters. Virginia gave an amusing recital of the questions she was asked by them, and also gave her answers, which revealed a failure to communicate in any meaningful way. Virginia was already apparently becoming aware that she did not fit into this conventional Victorian society, where small talk was required. The talk petered out, so Miss Musgrove produced her sketchbook. Every sketch had to be looked at and commented on.

Virginia and Miss Duckworth then paid another visit, this time to Miss March Phillips's room. Virginia gives a very brief and amusing portrait of this lady: 'She is a tall stout lively person with a fatal habit of talking to herself' (*HPGN*, 193). Miss Phillips, it appears, gives lectures. They paid a third visit where they viewed Mr Elgood's pictures, then Virginia and Miss Duckworth returned to the latter's home 'on the top of an omnibus' (*HPGN*, 193).

After dinner Virginia and Miss Duckworth discussed Charlotte Brontë, who, her aunt informed her, 'was a very clever woman'. Virginia did not want to reveal any ignorance on this subject, and so praised Charlotte Brontë's poetry. But her aunt reiterated her initial observation: 'She was a very good *novelist*'. Virginia then mocked Miss Duckworth who praised Charlotte Brontë for having written a couple of 'very pretty poems'. According to Virginia, Miss Duckworth named these poems as *The Spanish Gipsy* and *Aurora Leigh.* Being brought up with a father who was a literary critic, Virginia obviously knew that George Eliot wrote *The Spanish Gypsy* (which she misspelt) and that *Aurora Leigh* was written by Elizabeth Barrett Browning. Virginia refrained from pointing this out, confidently expecting her readership to understand her satirical position vis-à-vis her aunt, whose pretensions to literary knowledge she has exposed (*HPGN*, 194).

THE COMPLETE SHORTER FICTION

Memoirs of a Novelist (1909)

Virginia Stephen had permitted her brother-in-law, Clive Bell, to read her short story, *Memoirs of a Novelist*, and he had evidently been appreciative. Virginia replied to his comments in this letter, she was pleased that Bell had found the story 'imaginative', which mattered more than 'mere cleverness'. She had submitted the story to Reginald Smith, the editor of *The Cornhill Magazine*, suggesting that it should be the first of a series of portraits (L1: no. 510: To Clive Bell, 28 October 1909, 413).

In this story, Virginia mixed her Victorian father's specialism, biography, with her own developing skills as a writer of fiction. It is a putative review of a spoof biography of a fictional minor Victorian novelist called Miss Willatt, who produced three-volume novels in the 1860s and 1870s. She is of interest as she is an inferior imitator of Charlotte Brontë. Her biographer approached the writing of her friend's life in the characteristic way in which Victorian biography was written. The biographer, a Miss Linsett, quoted trivial memories of her surviving brother, and wrote a panegyric on her friend's virtues. Miss Willatt underwent a religious crisis, which Miss Linsett tried to help her through.

Miss Linsett hints at an abortive love affair of Miss Willatt's, with which she dealt 'in the most provoking manner conceivable' (*MN*, 67). Virginia imitated the excessive sentimentality and secrecy of some Victorian biography, which the supposed reviewer quoted from Miss Linsett's biography: 'No one who has read the book (*Life's Crucifix*) can doubt that the heart which conceived the sorrows of Ethel Eden in her unhappy attachment had felt some of the pangs so feelingly described *itself*; so much we may say, more we may not' (*MN*, 67). Virginia, as fictional reviewer, bitterly complains that in this way Miss Linsett's 'nervous prudery' and 'dreary literary conventions' has completely concealed the most significant event of Miss Willatt's life from the reader (*MN*, 67). The reviewer/reader can only speculate what Miss Willatt's experience was.

If the fictional Miss Willatt is a descendant of Charlotte Brontë, there may be here also an allusion to that famous novelist's biography by Elizabeth Gaskell. Although the love letters of Charlotte Brontë were not put into the public domain until 1913, Gaskell had read and suppressed them in her *Life*. The connection between Charlotte Brontë and Miss Willatt is made specifically by the spoof reviewer: she writes that between them George Eliot and Charlotte Brontë were responsible for many of the novels of the time, as they revealed the new subject matter of the familiar domestic and everyday lives of women (*MN*, 69). It is also notable that Woolf also benefited from this 'secret' for many of her interests as a novelist focused on the everyday details of domestic life and everyday events.

Miss Willatt after *her* father's death also made her home in Bloomsbury with *her* brothers, though her job was regarded as being to keep house for her siblings. At this stage, Miss Willatt began to take on a life of her own which was not intended by Miss Linsett, who proceeded to list her friend's propensities and activities; they are those which were expected of mid-Victorian women. Thus, she was benevolent, soft-hearted though upright in her own behaviour; she loved children, the spring, and Wordsworth, whose poetry she kept by her bed (*MN*, 68). She tenderly nursed her father and assisted the poor. But here the fictional reviewer butts in to analyse the various portraits of this descendant of Charlotte Brontë. They revealed Miss Willatt's 'large selfish face', which suggested an intelligence and capacity beyond her biographer's grasp. She was different from the woman her biographer believed her to be (*MN*, 68).

Miss Linsett's portrait of a woman who devoted herself to philanthropy among the poor turned out to be untrue. Having discovered that 'she had "no vocation" for philanthropy', Miss Willatt took up novel writing. Instead, however, of describing what she knew as it was 'indecent', she created romantic Arabian lovers who lived in Orinoco. She believed 'training' was unnecessary to be a novelist and she considered it devious to choose carefully how to express one's thoughts. So, she simply recorded her thoughts and hoped that something relevant would emerge (*MN*, 69).

The irony is delicious and it is evident that Virginia possessed the ability to create and exploit the ironic observation at a very early age. The references to how George Eliot and Charlotte Brontë's influenced Miss Willatt are evidently ironic too; the only thing that these female Victorian greats taught her were that it was possible for a woman to earn money by novel writing. Her subject matter was still completely different and far removed from that of Victorian women's lives.

It is striking that of these early stories, *Memoirs of a Novelist* and also *The Journal of Mistress Joan Martyn*, one was authored by a putative literary reviewer and the other by a supposed historian. Virginia practised writing fiction (a genre to which she eventually dedicated much of her writing) while at the same time she followed in her father's footsteps, for Leslie Stephen was both a critic and reviewer and his biographies for both the *Dictionary of National Biography* were based on just such historical documents. And although Joan's journal was fictional, I have argued elsewhere that she did gain much of her feel for the historical period covered by Joan's diary from the fifteenth-century *Paston Letters*.

A SOCIETY

A Society was first published in Woolf's short story collection, *Monday or Tuesday* (1921). The editor of *The Complete Shorter Fiction of Virginia Woolf*, Susan Dick, suggested that *A Society* might have been written as a fictional response to Arnold Bennett's *Our Women* (1920) (*CSF*, 300). This text needs to be examined closely, as it reveals that many of the sexist attitudes which confronted the Brontë sisters' novels persisted into the twentieth century. The subtitle to Bennett's book was *Chapters on the Sex-Discord*. As well as an 'Introduction', there were nine chapters in Bennett's books, and they covered a wide range: the dangers of writing about women; women in love; slavery; the charm of women; the superiority of men; wage-earning women; wives and finance and the loss of youth; women's social behaviour; the masculine and feminine view of the discord between the sexes. Significantly, Arnold Bennett associated the increase in the discord between men and women with the publication of Coventry Patmore's poem 'The Angel in the House'. As we have seen, Woolf at the outset of her writing career notably wrote how she had to kill the angel in the house or she herself would have been destroyed as a woman writer.

The chapter which no doubt Woolf objected to most, was chapter 4, 'Are Men Superior to Women?' Here, Bennett stated that the 'truth is that intellectually and creatively man is the superior of woman, and that in the region of creative intellect there are things which men almost habitually do but which women have not done and give practically no sign of ever being able to' (*Our Women*, 112). A couple of pages later, Bennett drove home this sexist idea: 'In creation, in synthesis, in criticism, in pure intellect women, even the most exceptional and the most favoured, have never approached the accomplishment of men' (*Our Women*, 114). Less apologetically than Leslie Stephen, who commented with circumspection on the same idea, Bennett claimed: 'Women in the main love to be dominated', which 'is in itself a proof of intellectual inferiority'. He claimed to be a passionate feminist and not to be writing as an 'old-fashioned man'. Furthermore, Bennett stated that this has been true for thousands of years and will probably be true for ever (*Our Women*, 116).

Desmond MacCarthy, Bloomsbury member and friend of the Woolfs', compounded the insult by agreeing with Bennett. MacCarthy who wrote under the name of 'Affable Hawk' in the *New Statesmen* wrote that he agreed with Bennett and quoted his remark with approval: '"no amount of education and liberty of action will sensibly alter" the fact that women are inferior to men in intellectual power, and that women's indisputable "desire to be dominated is . . . a proof of intellectual inferiority"' (*DII*, Appendix III, 339). Although Woolf was prepared to ignore Bennett, perhaps because MacCarthy was a friend, she wrote to the *New Statesman* a letter of protest, which was published under the title of 'The Intellectual Status of Women' (*DII*, 339). Woolf argued that women writers have markedly improved with each passing century, and Charlotte and Emily Brontë were cited, among other female writers, in evidence of this: comparing the Duchess of Newcastle with Jane Austen, Orinda with Emily Brontë, Eliza Heywood with George Eliot, Aphra Behn with Charlotte Brontë, and so on. Woolf argued that these women showed an 'advance in intellectual power', which was 'immense'. She then turned the tables on men: from the 'evidence' of the 'great war and the peace supply', it seemed to women that men's intellectual powers had declined. She ironically stated that women needed more evidence before they proclaimed it as a fact.

'Affable Hawk' returned to the argument, which Woolf's previous letter
had caused him to modify. Woolf provided more proofs of the handicaps
under which women suffered. She ironically concluded with the fact that
women had always 'brought forth the entire population of the universe'
(*DII*, 342). Even more ironically, Woolf's rejoinder actually resembled the
outburst she condemned by Jane Eyre when she demanded a wider lot for
women: 'women should have liberty of experience'. Women should be able
to hold different views from men without fear or favour. If mental activity
were encouraged the result would be that there will always exist a 'nucleus of
women who think, invent, imagine, and create as freely as men do' (*DII*, 342).

Woolf dealt with some of these questions in her deeply ironic short story 'A
Society'. Already, in the short story which would appear in the collection of
early stories published under the title *Monday or Tuesday*, Woolf had touched
on what Charlotte Brontë had called the 'woman question'. In the first story,
'The Mark on the Wall', the narrator had reflected that it is 'the masculine
point of view which governs our lives, which sets the standard' (*CSF*, 80).
Woolf tackled this head on in 'A Society'. It is both amusingly light in tone
and scathing about the patriarchy. One of their number, Poll, has to read all
the books in the London Library as a prerequisite of inheriting her father's
fortune. In the process of fulfilling this condition Poll has become aware that
many of the books written by men are 'rubbish'. The women's society of the
title, state the same fact as Woolf had done in her argument with MacCarthy
in the correspondence pages in the *New Statesmen*: that women were responsible for populating the world while the men civilised it through the arts. But
if this had permitted the male sex to produce only 'rubbish', why had the
young women's mothers 'wasted their youth in bringing them into the world?'
(125). The circle of friends then determined to investigate the world that had
been created solely by men, while women were occupied with procreating.
So, we are told by the first-person narrator: 'we made ourselves into a society
for asking questions. One of us was to visit a man-of-war; another was to hide
herself in a scholar's study; another was to attend a meeting of businessmen;
while all were to read books, look at pictures, go to concerts, keep our eyes
open in the streets, and ask questions perpetually' (*CSF*, 125). Criticism is
disarmed by the unnamed narrator's highly ironic deprecating remarks. Anger
lay behind this tale, but Woolf's case was not characterised by the palpable
anger which she would later claim ruined Charlotte Brontë's novels. Overt
anger was replaced by good-humoured satire. In this story, a group of young
women friends believe the object of life is to 'produce good people and good
books' (*CSF*, 126). They agree not to bear any children before they find
whether the function of women is being rewarded by men's fulfilment of their
part of the division of the labours of the sexes.

The women's research is very funny, but also devastating in their results. The narrator presents Woolf's own experience of the Dreadnought Hoax of 1910 and its aftermath. The masculine concept of honour is revealed to be ridiculous (*CSF*, 126). The Law Courts were revealed to be run either by wooden men or 'large animals', so that the women voted that justice forced them to conclude that the judges were not men (*CSF*, 127). Another of the all-female group went to the Royal Academy. The literary pictures are found to be intolerable. The sententious or sentimental poems these male artists strove to illustrate were found to be 'gibberish' (*CSF*, 127).

Another of the young women went to Oxbridge disguised as a 'charwoman'. The sheer luxury of the male academics' residences astonished Castalia. She examined the professor's research while he was absent and was thunderstruck that so much ink and time was spent in arguing the minutest points between scholars. The professor had edited Sappho and was engaged in defending her chastity. Castalia exclaimed about his ignorance of the subject. Amongst all this, she had forgotten to investigate whether the Oxbridge professors helped the production of 'good people and good books' (*CSF*, 127–8). She is sent back to Oxbridge but returns pregnant! She suddenly reacted to the loss of her female chastity in a way which parodied and ridiculed what Woolf viewed as a male construct which men overvalued in women. The other women dismissed the concept of female chastity as irrelevant.

This circle of female friends had spent five years in their research; now they must conclude and decide whether to bear children. They had submitted profound questions to men to discover whether they were good men but had not received honest answers. The women agreed that men despise women. But, says one of the young women, they themselves have not produced an artist amongst their number, have they? Poll, for whom a condition of her inheritance was that she should read all the books in the London Library, now contributes some women writers' names from the nineteenth century, 'like a man crying muffins in a back street' crying out: 'Jane-Austen-Charlotte-Brontë-George-Eliot' (*CSF*, 132). However, these are all women who are derived from the white, male canon. Whether it was because of this is not clear, the other women damn Poll as 'a bore' (*CSF*, 132). Elizabeth, one of their number, had disguised herself as a man for five years and devoted herself to reviewing fiction. It appeared that there are no great male writers in the present, any more than there are women. Elizabeth had reviewed H. G. Wells and Arnold Bennett and another couple of even less distinguished male writers, Compton Mackenzie and Hugh Walpole. We know that the first two writers were among those Woolf would dub 'Edwardians' and whose novels she would condemn. Elizabeth concluded, 'the truth has nothing to do with literature' (*CSF*, 133).

The narrator admitted: 'It all seemed to us very inconclusive'. About to attempt a summing up of what they have learnt, they are interrupted by a voice of men shouting: war had been declared. Now the women, far too late, realise that they failed to send any of their number to the House of Commons, Poll can inform the group about other earlier wars, but has to admit herself baffled as to the cause of the present 1914 war. At the end of the war, the women are reunited. Now Castalia condemned them all as 'fools' for undertaking such investigations. Their conclusion is now that women were responsible for giving men their conviction of male superiority by educating them to develop their intellects. The spoof suggestion is that they should devise a method to enable men to bear children. Castalia's little daughter is given the accumulation of the society's papers and told she had been chosen to be the president of the Society of the future. On hearing this, she bursts out crying, 'poor little girl' (*CSF*, 136). The fact that little Ann has been playing with that conventional girls' toy—a doll—is not commented upon. Much later in life, Woolf realised that the solution to women's problems would only be found if men changed as well: 'Men too can be emancipated' (*E5*, 647).

Amongst the wreckage of women's failures in achievement when compared to men, only three female nineteenth-century novelists—Jane Austen, Charlotte Brontë, and George Eliot—save women from absolute condemnation. Woolf has to go way back to the Victorian and pre-Victorian eras to find literary foremothers. It was perhaps a comfort to think back into the past and name the period that had contained these inspirational women. For all her modernist credentials, Woolf could not find a woman writer who had excelled, or even equalled the novelists she had discovered as a child reading at 22 Hyde Park Gate. Though they may be mocked in 'A Society', they also offer reassurance as to what women writers could achieve.

NOVELS

The Voyage Out (1915)

In Virginia Woolf's first novel, *The Voyage Out,* it was Emily Brontë and not Charlotte Brontë who is mentioned. The heroine of the novel, the twenty-four-year-old Rachel Vinrace, is surprised in her cabin on board the ship which is taking her, her uncle and aunt, a family friend, and an old servant out to Santa Marina for an extended period of residence there. Temporary passengers are the former Conservative MP Richard Dalloway (who is temporarily out of Parliament) and his wife, Clarissa. Mrs Dalloway seeks Rachel out in her private cabin. Rachel welcomes her and removes from her armchair *Wuthering Heights* and a volume of William Cowper's poems, to accommodate her guest. Both these works of literature had significance for Woolf.

By choosing Emily Brontë's *Wuthering Heights*, Woolf intended to convey to the reader of *The Voyage Out* that her heroine was embarking on a literary adventure in order to discover and define herself. Rachel is amazingly ignorant for a woman of twenty-four. The voyage out is both a literal and metaphorical journey, which is encouraged by her aunt by marriage, Helen Ambrose.

The titles of the novel and the book of Cowper's poems do not escape the notice of Clarissa Dalloway, who exclaims that *Wuthering Heights* 'is more in my line. I really couldn't exist without the Brontës! Don't you love them?' However, Clarissa then contradicts her initial statement by naming another nineteenth-century female novelist who is also part of the literary canon about whom she says: 'Still, on the whole, I'd rather live without them than without Jane Austen' (*VO*, 59). Rachel gains enough confidence from Clarissa's friendly and sympathetic manner to venture her own opinion. It comes out somewhat abruptly: 'Jane Austen? I don't like Jane Austen'. Clarissa reacts by calling her a 'monster' who she can 'only just forgive', but she also wants to know Rachel's reasons for this view. In replying Rachel 'floundered' and can only say that she finds Jane Austen's writing 'so—so—well, so like a tight plait'. Clarissa expresses understanding but not agreement and assures Rachel that she will change her opinion when she is older (*VO*, 59).

Clarissa's choice put her at a distance from her creator, Virginia Woolf, though. It must be said that Charlotte Brontë herself reacted negatively to *Pride and Prejudice*, probably because she and Jane Austen wrote completely different kinds of novels. Woolf had several times stated that in her view the Brontës possessed greater genius than Jane Austen. However, in *A Room of One's Own*, Woolf bracketed Jane Austen with Emily Brontë as the only two female writers in the canon who 'wrote as women write, not as men write' (*AROOO*, 68).

The pompous establishment figure, Richard Dalloway, expresses a desire to be read to. Clarissa has brought with her Jane Austen's *Persuasion*. She tells her husband that this volume is for Rachel, as 'She can't bear our beloved Jane'. Dalloway sententiously tells Rachel this is because she has not read her. He adds that Jane Austen 'is incomparably the greatest female writer we possess'. Strangely enough he explains this by expressing Woolf's opinion about Jane Austen's style: 'She is the greatest . . . and for this reason: she does not attempt to write like a man. Every other woman does; on that account, I don't read 'em' (*VO*, 64). He, too, asks Rachel's reasons for disliking Jane Austen's novels, saying he is ready 'to be converted'. Rachel makes an attempt to defend her view, but this part of the conversation is not given by Woolf. However, Clarissa says that Richard cannot pretend to know Jane Austen's novels by heart, for when one of her novels is read aloud to him, he always falls asleep. Clarissa's words are quickly proved to be true as after she has read for a short time, Dalloway is seen to be soundly sleeping. It seems that Clarissa uses the soporific effect Jane Austen has on her husband to take his mind from politics and to make him relax. This hardly seems to be an adequate response to Jane Austen's novels!

When Woolf's next novel, *Night and Day*, was reviewed, she was stung when Katherine Mansfield compared her to Jane Austen. Mansfield persists throughout her review with this comparison: 'It is impossible to refrain from comparing *Night and Day* with the novels of Jane Austen. There are moments, indeed, when one is almost tempted to cry it Jane Austen up-to-date. . . . As in the case of Miss Austen's novels we fall under a little spell. . . . But whereas Miss Austen's spell is as strong upon us as ever when the novel is finished and laid by, Mrs Woolf's loses something of its potency' (*Collected Works of Katherine Mansfield*, Volume 3, 'A Ship Comes into the Harbour', 532]. Mansfield concludes that *Night and Day* was 'in the tradition of the English novel. In the midst of our admiration it makes us feel old and chill: we had never thought to look upon its like again' (ibid, 534). In her diary, Woolf summarised Mansfield's criticism of *Night and Day* accurately: 'a decorous elderly dullard she describes me; Jane Austen up to date' (*DI*, 28 November 1919, 314). Although she tried to read spitefulness in this review and justify her novel, she was undoubtedly chagrined. She very deliberately moved away from Jane Austen in her next novel, *Jacob's Room*.

Night and Day (1919)

Virginia Woolf wrote her centenary article on Charlotte Brontë in 1916. Although Woolf the Brontës and their novels are not named, it is significant that at this time she was writing her second novel, *Night and Day*, which looks backwards to the eminent Victorian poet Richard Alardyce and also to his daughter, Mrs Hilbery. The latter, with her daughter, Katharine, are occupied with the writing of a seemingly interminable biography of the great poet. It is possible that in writing the centenary article on Charlotte Brontë, Woolf recalled her 1904 visit (and article) to Haworth. Here Woolf had viewed the Brontë relics, and she describes a similar sort of literary shrine for her fictitious nineteenth-century poet.

At the time of Woolf's pilgrimage to Haworth in 1904, the Brontë memorabilia had not found a permanent home and was displayed in a fairly amateur way. Similarly, in *Night and Day*, the relics of Richard Alardyce do not have an official public location but are displayed in the house of his descendants. The Hilbery family show new guests what Mrs Hilbery calls 'our things', by which she means the remnants of her famous father's material effects (*ND*, 7). Ralph Denham in the opening chapter of the novel is led by Katherine into a room which resembles 'something like a chapel in a cathedral, or a grotto of a cave'. The first is felt to be a more accurate simile since 'the little room was crowded with relics' (*ND*, 7). The Hilberys have set up special lighting to illuminate the 'relics'. The nature of these latter items are mostly (like the Brontë relics) personal effects. Thus, such articles as Alardyce's writing table, his pen, his spectacles, and a large pair of shoddy slippers are all on display.

Denham does not want to enter into the sort of ancestor worship which he feels is required of him. He wants to reach an accommodation with modern life. Yet the novel is very backward looking and in constant dialogue with the Victorian period. Mrs Hilbery comments: 'After all, what *is* the present? Half of it's the past, and the better half, too, I should say' (*ND*, 7). Katherine Mansfield would criticise *Night and Day* for ignoring the First World War, and it would be the last novel Woolf wrote in a conventional style. Ralph Denham and Katharine Hilbery would throw off the Victorian past in a way in which Woolf could not do.

Jacob's Room (1922)

In Woolf's third—but first self-consciously experimental and modernist—novel. She wrote of her conviction that in it she had 'found out how to begin (at forty) to say something in my own voice' (*DII*, 26 July 1922, 186). However, she had not turned her back completely on her Victorian past, for the Brontës make an unexpected appearance in a scene in the British

Museum. They are referred to by a minor character, who only makes one fleeting appearance in the novel. She appeared fleetingly in the novel because her research at the British Museum coincided with Jacob's visit there. She contributed one of the many comments on him, which many others, especially women, passed on the enigmatic and elusive central character in an attempt to make a composite portrait of him.

However, Julia Hedge also made reflections which doubtless crossed Woolf's (and many other women's minds) when pursuing research at the British Museum. Julia is described as 'the feminist', which leads the reader to wonder why 'the' instead of 'a' is the word preceding 'feminist'. She seems to be presented as the representative of women, more than simply an individual woman. As she awaited the arrival of the books she had requested, she looked around her. Her attention was caught by the name of Lord Macaulay, which the reader was told on the previous page had recently had the last letter of his name ('y') added in gilt (*Jacob's Room*, 90). Julia Hedge read all the names around the dome, the names of 'great men', but Julia was not impressed. As a feminist she was aware of names which were not, but should have, she felt, been there: "'Oh damn," said Julia Hedge, "why didn't they leave room for an Eliot or a Brontë?"' (*JR*, 91). It is fascinating to note that seven years later, Woolf initially referred to the solely male authors round the dome in the British Museum in an earlier draft of her feminist polemic *A Room of One's Own*. The reader finds the following detail, which Woolf later deleted: 'only the names of men encircle the proud dome' (*Women & Fiction: The Manuscript Versions of 'A Room of One's Own'*, 40).

In *Jacob's Room*, Julia Hedge's thought was directly succeeded with the narrator's remark: 'Unfortunate Julia! wetting her pen in bitterness, and leaving her shoe laces untied' (*JR*, 92). There is no explanation for this perspective on Julia. Why should the reader be expected to feel pity for Julia? Her 'bitterness' may be concerned with her perception of the advantages the male reader has over her. Directly her books arrived, she immediately applied herself to her 'gigantic labours' (surely the tone is ironic). Simultaneously she 'perceived through one of the nerves of her exasperated sensibility how composedly, unconcernedly and with every consideration' the male researchers applied themselves to their own books. She directed this comment against Jacob, who was within her vision. Julia condemned those who read purely for pleasure. She resented Jacob's apparent abundance of leisure to do nothing but 'copy out poetry' (*JR*, 92). She herself was obliged to 'study statistics.' Julia watched a friend enter and carry Jacob off with him; she imagined they will laugh aloud as soon as they have left the library.

All this may be seen as fair feminist comment on the situation then appertaining in the British Museum Library. However, the narrator condemned Julia because of her bitterness: this quality was applied to her twice in one paragraph of twelve lines. The narrator attributed to Julia a ridiculous view of the world of women and work, to which Julia Hedge apparently belonged. Julia believed that women should be allowed to work as men work, but her argument is satirised: 'There are more women than men. Yes; but if you let women work as men work, they'll die off much quicker. They'll become extinct. That was her argument' (*JR*, 92).

Oddly enough, the narrator of *A Room of One's Own* makes the same argument. In this feminist polemic, Woolf's narrator appeared to be making a sensible comment, but it ended up in whimsy. The suggestion was that women should no longer be the protected sex: 'Remove that protection, expose them to the same exertions and activities, make them soldiers and sailors and engine-drivers and dock labourers, and will not women die off so much younger, so much quicker, than men that one will say, "I saw a woman to-day", as one used to say, "I saw an aeroplane"' (*AROO*, 36).

Woolf created a narrator who was similar to, but could not be identified with her—not least because Woolf refused her continuous omniscience. The narrator expressed doubt about whether we know Jacobs's thoughts and described herself as having 'ten years' seniority and a difference of sex' (*JR*, 81). Woolf also wrote that while women may be better or worse than men, the narrator's views in *Jacob's Room* should not be assumed to be hers (*L2*, no. 1330: To Jacques Raverat, 10 December 1922, 592). So, the reader does not know what Woolf thought about this, but can we assume it was intended ironically? Finally, the reader might ask why she named 'the feminist' Julia, the forename of Mrs Stephen, who was definitely not a feminist.

Mrs Dalloway (1925)

In *Mrs Dalloway* it was the most important woman in Clarissa's youth, Sally Seton, who was associated with the Brontës. Sally Seton was prominent in the memories of Clarissa and Peter Walsh on the single June day in which the novel takes place, but she did not appear in person until the party, by which time she had become Lady Rosseter, with five sons. The reader is told that Sally still had the book by Emily Brontë, which Peter Walsh had given her at Bourton, Clarissa's family home. As with Rachel Vinrace in *The Voyage Out*, Emily (not Charlotte) Brontë was associated with a young woman who was determined to break with convention and find her own place in the world. In both these novels, Emily Brontë functions as a symbol of the unconventional and questing young woman.

Sally had briefly swept Clarissa into her vision of the world. Clarissa reflected that Sally had 'made her feel, for the first time, how sheltered the life at Bourton was. She knew nothing about sex—nothing about social problems' (*Mrs Dalloway*, 28). Fired by Sally, they had discussed reforming the world and founding a society to bring about the abolition of private property. They read Plato, William Morris, and P. B. Shelley. Sally shocked her staid elders by running naked along the passage when she had forgotten her sponge. At that time, Clarissa remembers, Sally was 'completely reckless; did the most idiotic things out of bravado, bicycled round the parapet on the terrace: smoked cigars' (*MD*, 29). Sally had given Clarissa the first kiss on her lips, which the latter still regards as 'the most exquisite moment of her whole life' (*MD*, 30), although this hint of lesbian love never developed into anything else between the two young women.

Peter Walsh also remembered Sally Seton's unconventionality. Sally had introduced a subject not usually discussed in mixed society: did the fact that a woman had a child born out of wedlock, affect their attitude towards her? By contrast, Clarissa's response had been 'timid; hard; arrogant; prudish' (*MD*, 50). Peter recalled Sally had had 'the reputation in those days of great daring, and he used to give her cigars, which she smoked in her bedroom' (*MD*, 51). Sally had supported women's suffrage and threatened to denounce at family prayers a young man who had punished her for holding this opinion by kissing her.

Clarissa had always thought that Sally's life would 'end in some awful tragedy; her death; her martyrdom' (*MD*, 154). Instead, Sally had made a marriage to 'a bald man with a large buttonhole who owned, it was said, cotton mills at Manchester' (*MD*, 154). From an impoverished youth, Sally now lived a life of opulence. But she resented the fact that Clarissa had refused all invitations to visit Sally and her husband. Sally believed that at heart Clarissa was a snob whose opinion was that her old friend married beneath her. Sally may have made an unconventional marriage in becoming the wife of a miner, but he had been socially mobile, financially successful and had acquired a title. Ultimately, Sally Seton's youthful association with Emily Brontë must be viewed as a false flag.

The Pargiters: **The Novel-Essay Portion of** *The Years*

The Pargiters is an incomplete work by Woolf. In it, she revealed how she planned to combine the fiction of *The Years,* with a factual analysis of each chapter succeeding each section. Ultimately, however, she failed to achieve what she attempted and ultimately it was abandoned without ever being completed. As its editor, has written: 'The "Novel-Essay" would have been for Virginia Woolf a new and profoundly challenging experiment in form, calling into action both the creative and the analytical faculties almost simultaneously' (*P*, vii). In this fragment Woolf clearly conveyed her interest in the very different educations of men and women. It can be viewed as a sequel to

A Room of One's Own and a prequel of *Three Guineas*, though exploring a different angle of approach to the differences between men and women.

The Years sets up a dichotomy between the south and north of England, which in the latter particularly focuses on Yorkshire, for which Kitty Malone had a 'passion' (*P*, 99). The moors are frequently mentioned, and these are naturally associated in the reader's mind with Brontë country. In the fifth essay which centred on women's lives in 1880, Woolf explained that her novel reflected the mid-Victorian mindset in which the heroines of poetry and novels were not admitted to express any depth of passion (*P*, 110). This was not true of the Brontës' novels; Woolf particularly expressed her awareness of the unusual amount of passion attributed by Charlotte Brontë as something new and revolutionary. Indeed, previously (in the fourth chapter) the reader learns that Kitty Malone was 'forbidden' to read *Jane Eyre* by her mother. It was not considered fitting or 'nice' for a young woman to read so 'immoral' a book. Naturally Kitty obtained a copy of the novel she was told was not she was not old enough to be exposed to; however, she found the novel so tedious that she was perfectly contented to accept Mrs Malone's edict (*P*, 99). Charlotte Brontë and *Jane Eyre* did not, however, make it into the final version of *The Years*.

Chapter Four

Leslie Stephen and Virginia Woolf as Critics and on Charlotte Brontë

It is interesting to compare Stephen and Woolf as writers on Charlotte Brontë. The latter is a particularly interesting example, as she was not only a Victorian novelist, but also a woman—a fact not lost on Woolf. Stephen's criticism of Charlotte Brontë appeared as the first essay in the third of his three-volume *Hours in a Library* in 1885, and in his entry for her in the *Dictionary of National Biography*. The dictionary entry was largely devoted to trying to set the record straight about the Brontë family. Although this was a much-needed task, I will rather be focusing on Stephen's essay on Charlotte Brontë in *Hours in a Library*, since it was dominated by responses to her novels. Stephen also wrote four other essays which illuminate his criticism of Charlotte Brontë. These four essays are 'The Study of English Literature' (henceforth 'SEL'), 'The Essayists' (henceforth 'TE'), 'Biography' (henceforth 'B'), and 'Thoughts on Criticism, by a Critic' (henceforth 'TCC'): all are in S. O.A. Ullman's *Leslie Stephen: Men, Books, and Mountains*. Incidentally, it is worth observing that Leslie Stephen was unusual in writing so much about the works of Charlotte Brontë, as during this period the predominant focus of interest was on the life and character of the novelist rather than on the novels themselves. It is also notable that in *Hours in a Library*, Stephen only wrote about one other woman novelist, and that was George Eliot (on whom he also wrote the full-length 'English Men of Letters' volume).

In *A Sketch of the Past*, which was written towards the end of her life, Virginia Woolf reflected on her father as a literary critic. Although she acknowledged some debt to Leslie Stephen's *Hours in a Library*, she claimed that his mind was incapable of subtlety, imagination, and suggestiveness. While his mind was strong, it was also conventional in its standard of morality and in what constituted masculinity and femininity (115). Stephen had a 'simply constructed view' of the world, which his daughter finds it impossible for her generation to share. Tellingly, though, at this vantage point in time, she admitted she sometimes envied him. Woolf's attitude towards her father's criticism was also ambivalent. Although she had definite reservations about what she saw as his limitations as a critic, she admitted that he had had a lifelong effect on her own criticism. In 'Impressions of Leslie Stephen', Woolf recalled her father reading Walter Scott's Waverley novels to her and her siblings. At the end Stephen would ask each child who was their favourite character and the reason for their preference. He was indignant if any of his children preferred a pasteboard good character to a lifelike villain (*EI*, 128). In the same essay she further recalled how far he had permeated her own mind with the qualities of his own, so that much great literature she could not separate from her father's reading: *'I hear in them not only his voice, but in some sort his teaching and belief'* (*EI*, 129, my italics). Right at the end of her life she also stated his permanent mark on her own critical responses. Although she did not have an instinctive sympathy with him as a critic, she nevertheless always read him on any author she was writing about. She took him as she would a medicine and she responded to his essays with a reader's, not a daughter's affection (*A Sketch of the Past*, 115–16).

Woolf also described her father's intellectual influence on her in a letter. She stated that she was often pleased that she had read English literature when young. This was immediately associated with her memories of her father. She recollected that she would go to his study and ask for another volume. 'Then he would be very pleased and say "Gracious child, how you gobble!" He himself would get up and obtain the volume she wanted. These books tended to be those of eighteenth- and nineteenth-century classics. Of course, though it has often been noted that she was given unfettered access to her father's books, she was still limited to books of Leslie Stephen's choice. Apparently, she was perfectly satisfied with this; years later she wrote, several times that though she did not attend school or college, she had the free run of her father's extensive and unexpurgated library. She also recalled his opinion that if a book was worth reading it merited rereading. Woolf stated her current view of her father in a way which captured her continuing ambivalence: 'I have a great devotion for him—what a disinterested man, how high minded, how tender to me, and fierce and intolerable' (*L4*, no. 2005: To Vita Sackville-West, 19 February 1929, 27). Writing to mark the centenary of her father's birth, Woolf expressed other precepts he had passed on to her as a literary critic: she should read only what she liked and never feign admiration. Her style should be succinct and clear and convey her exact meaning (*EV*, 588). In her contribution to F. W. Maitland's *The Life and Letters of Leslie Stephen*, Woolf wrote that he did not like criticism which concerned itself with the technicalities of books (*E1*, 128). He himself had very catholic tastes and did not limit himself to canonical writers (*E1*, 129).

Stephen's and Woolf's attitudes towards the function of literary critics were sometimes surprisingly similar. Stephen objected to academic critics; he condemned those young university graduates whom he believed composed the vast body of literary critics. These young men thought they were superior to everybody else and, on coming down from university felt they were equipped to pass judgement on anything and everything (*TCC*, 213). Apparently, Stephen believed this had changed since he was young: 'We made orations at the Union Debating Society; but admitted to ourselves, though we did not perhaps state it in public, that we were very young and not competent to instruct the nation at large' (*Some Early Impressions*, 35). Stephen opened his essay 'The Study of English Literature' by stating he did not intend to discuss 'the proper place of English literature in our school and university studies' (*SEL,* 17). However, he did slip in some opinions on this and acknowledged that 'A good education for literary purposes is by no means exclusively an education in literature' (*SEL*, 36). Stephen held the view that life was the best and most important educator. He also warned against the 'exclusive reading of mere criticism on literary history' because it tended 'to make a man a prig', and 'to suppress all spontaneous and independent judgement' (*SEL*, 37).

At the end of his life, Stephen anticipated his daughter as a critic of literature as an academic discipline: 'Happily for us, the doctrine that English language and literature should be made a part of our education had not yet been proclaimed' (*Some Early Impressions*, 38).

Woolf also expressed several times her lack of faith in academic literary criticism. An example of this is her criticism of the young academic 'Peter' (F. L. Lucas), who she thought too judgmental. She was unimpressed by his ordinary mind, and he lacked the charisma necessary to lead the reader. (*D3*, 65). She was by no means circumspect in a letter to Julian Bell in which she criticised George Rylands for becoming a lecturer in English literature at Cambridge University and condemned the teaching of the subject. She agreed with her nephew's view on the futility of academic courses devoted to literature (*L5*, no. 3085: To Julian Bell, 1 December 1935, 450).

Both father and daughter highlighted the importance of emotion in reacting to a book. Stephen spelt this out in his usual accessible way, concluding: 'The fact, however, remains, that after all a criticism is only an expression of individual feeling' (TTC, Ullmann, 221). While we might expect the rationalist Stephen to suggest this feeling should be analysed by the reader, he did not do so. Interestingly, though, his daughter did exactly this. She referred to the 'irrational element' in people's reactions to books. Woolf swiftly added that the emotional response to a book was not the end of reading, and we immediately seek reasons for it. Woolf is almost always more complex in her arguments than her father. She expressed the complex and seemingly contradictory explanation, by hinting that the 'reasons' themselves which the reader found to justify his or her emotional responses to books may be irrational. For her, it was the feeling that was of paramount interest, and she developed this idea by organic natural imagery. The emotion is 'genuine'; it is 'the root and motive of the greater part of our reading, the sap which causes books to go on budding from the trees' (*E3*, 235).

As might be expected, as a practising novelist herself, Woolf was also most interested in Charlotte Brontë's fiction. Later in life, however, Woolf used Charlotte Brontë as an example of what feminist authors needed to put right in their writings. Father and daughter touched on many of the same features in Brontë's novels. These included the importance of place; the predominance of autobiographical elements which implied a certain narrowness and led to a lack of a wider philosophical view, and the place of the individual in society in Stephen, which was transmuted by Woolf into the place of women in society. In this section, the emphasis will be on Leslie Stephen; Woolf's changing attitudes to Charlotte Brontë will be traced in later sections of this book.

Stephen then admits that it is undeniably extremely difficult 'to be alternately witness and judge; to feel strongly, and yet to analyse coolly' (*HL*, 2). By Stephen's admission his own system of criticism begins to break down with such authors as Charlotte Brontë, who rouses almost 'overpowering prejudices' because her character is 'so intense, original, and full of special idiosyncrasy' (*HL*, 2). This in itself testifies to Charlotte Brontë's 'intrinsic force' (*HL*, 2). Stephen did not like having his views on literature and criticism challenged. Thus, in a letter to Anne Thackeray, he told her that 'Julia [Stephen, his wife] has been laughing at me because I am at this moment raging against a review of me in the Spectator wh. I was silly enough to read, contrary to my rule of reading nothing about myself, & wh. I cannot digest. The fool misunderstood everything I have said in the most provoking way conceivable' (Bicknell, Letter to Anne Isabella Ritchie, 29 July 1879, Volume 1: 1864–1882, 241). In a footnote to the letter, Bicknell writes that the main objection of the reviewer in the *Spectator* to *Hours in a Library* was what he 'considered Stephen's theory of the novel to be (which is what he got wrong)'.

It is of interest that in his essay on Charlotte Brontë *Hours in a Library,* Stephen tries to establish some principles for the literary critic by which to evaluate texts. He argues that, though criticism cannot be a science, it should be established on a scientific basis. Stephen envisages the literary critic approaching a text in rather a bizarre way; he 'should endeavour to classify the phenomena with which he is dealing as calmly as if he were ticketing a fossil in a museum' (Stephen, *HL*, 1). Equally startingly he compares the approach to literary criticism as being the same as that of a religious creed; that it 'should rest upon a purely rational ground, and be exposed to logical tests'. However, Stephen insists that 'faith in an author' must initially 'be the product of instinctive sympathy, instead of deliberate reason' (*HL*, 1). Nevertheless, 'when we are seeking to justify our emotions, we must endeavour to get for the time into the position of an independent spectator, applying with rigid impartiality such methods as are best calculated to free us from the influence of personal bias' (*HL*, 2).

Stephen's desire to make literary criticism a science cropped up in several of his essays. Woolf would have been familiar with this preoccupation of her critic father. Therefore, it is surprising that Anne Besnault's analysis of Woolf's review of Percy Lubbock's *The Craft of Fiction* should emphasise that Woolf was thrown by Lubbock's attempt at a scientific approach to literature. Besnault suggested that Woolf's response to Lubbock was to treat it as 'both radically new and radically dangerous . . . the scientist can only fully grasp his subject after he is dead' (199).

In his 'The Study of English Literature', Stephen proposed that literature needed to be studied in a 'scientific spirit', which he defined as an impartial examination and correlating it 'with all the truths known to us' (*SEL*, 25). In his 'The Essayists', he returned to this theme: 'We are greatly exercised in our minds by the claims of the scientific critic; but that only explains why it is so much easier to write about essay-writing than to write an essay oneself' (*TE*, 65). In 'Thoughts on Criticism, by a Critic', Stephen gave his most coherent account of the problem: unlike the historians and scientists, aesthetic critics have 'no available or recognised standard of merit'. The ultimate appeal is to the taste of the individual. Thus far there is no 'science of aesthetics'; though literary critics 'have invented a sounding name and a number of technical phrases', there are still no 'accepted principles' (*TCC*, 217).

Throughout her long writing career, Woolf made a variety of comments on the task of the critic. It is of the utmost importance to stress that Woolf, unlike her father, wrote as a practising novelist. She stressed this position in a letter to her American publisher writing of her *The Common Reader*: 'I think one might describe it as an unprofessional book of criticism, dealing with such lives and books as have chanced to come my way, rather from the point of view of a writer than of a student or a critic. I have often no doubt been interested in a book as a novelist; but as often perhaps have read simply for amusement and without any wish to establish a theory' (quoted in *E5*, 333). She stressed her democratic principles and amateur status as a critic. As an epigraph to the *The Common Reader: Second Series* she quoted from Dr Samuel Johnson's *Life of Gray*: 'I rejoice to concur with the common reader; for by the common sense of readers, uncorrupted by literary prejudices, after all the refinements of subtilty and the dogmatism of learning, must be generally decided all claims to poetical honours'. Her claim to be an amateur is demolished by her 1939 pamphlet 'Reviewing', where she traced the history of the literary critic and reviewer (whose different functions she took care to distinguish). She defined the critic as one who was concerned with past literature and with its principles, while the reviewer evaluated the works produced by his or her contemporaries (*E6*, 196). Woolf was happier practising the former, which included her essays on the Brontë sisters' novels.

Writing about the criticism of contemporary novelists, she wrote that there was general critical agreement among the critics the great critic is 'the rarest of beings' (*E3*, 355). The only advice critics can give is that readers should trust their instincts and check them by repeatedly reading the classics of past eras (*E3,* 354). She was scathing about reviewers' cowardice in refusing to acknowledge that a contemporary writer could produce a work of art (*E4*, 354–55). She acknowledged that there is a wide gulf between writing about a contemporary during their age and writing about the same book fifty years later. Woolf praised Lockhart's criticism of *Jane Eyre*, of which, despite some reservations, he thought highly. The reviewer has to pick out the books of importance from those which will be of ephemeral interest only. Woolf again considered the nature of the critic in her essay 'The Love of Reading'. The reader is not a passive recipient of the critic's views on a book, but rather used the critic's opinion to clarify his or her own attitude towards and evaluation of the book (*E5*, 273).

The swing from awarding the highest powers of the three Brontë sisters to Charlotte, which had been so marked in Gaskell's *Life of Charlotte Brontë*, underwent a change in the early twentieth century. Virginia Woolf came to value Emily Brontë's literary achievements more highly than Charlotte Brontë's. It is therefore interesting to perceive that in the power of creating character, Stephen had already awarded the possession of greater gifts to Emily Brontë, writing that 'Charlotte Brontë, and perhaps her sister Emily in an even higher degree, must have a certain interest for all intelligent observers of character' (*HL*, 3). Stephen also observed, as his daughter after him would too, that Emily Brontë's 'mood of pure passion' was best given expression 'in lyrical poetry' (*HL,* 15). T. Wemyss Reid before him had written that Emily Brontë's poems were the best in the Bells' published book of poetry. Stephen had read Reid's book-length monograph on Charlotte Brontë. He acknowledged several of Reid's critical insights, whilst surreptitiously using others without due acknowledgement. Both Reid and Stephen used the word 'lyrical' to describe a quality in Emily Brontë's poetry. Reid expanded this into a description of Emily Brontë's poems as possessing a 'lyrical beauty which haunts the mind ever after it has become acquainted with them; others have a passionate emphasis, a depth of meaning, an intensity and gravity which are startling' when it is remembered that she also wrote *Wuthering Heights* (Reid, 77–78).

It is hard not to suspect that both these Victorian male critics were unnerved and baffled by *Wuthering Heights* and so preferred to proclaim Emily Brontë's poems as a greater achievement. Woolf appeared to agree; she suggested that possibly Emily's poetry would survive longer than her single novel (*E4*, 168). Reid's attitude to *Wuthering Heights* is decidedly ambivalent. On the one hand, it is 'as marvellous a *tour de force* as *Jane Eyre*' (Reid, 202) and 'Surely nowhere in modern English fiction can more striking proof be found of the possession of "the creative gift" in an extraordinary degree than is to be obtained in *Wuthering Heights*' (Reid, 204). On the other hand, Reid finds Emily Brontë's novel 'repulsive and almost ghastly' (Reid, 202) and 'From the first page to the last there is hardly a redeeming passage in the book' (Reid, 202). This story should never have been written, according to Reid (202). He viewed Emily Brontë's life as sheltered and uneventful and saw *Wuthering Heights* 'as the attempt of an innocent and ignorant child' (Reid, 204). This perplexity, shared by contemporary friends of Branwell Brontë was possibly (combined with the absence of a surviving manuscript for *Wuthering Heights*) the origin of the remarkably tenacious theory that Branwell Brontë wrote at least part of it (not that Reid subscribed to this theory). Yet, Reid, even while regarding the writer as a 'mere child', cannot help exclaiming again about the power of Emily Brontë's novel: 'But how vast was the intellectual greatness displayed in this juvenile work!' He admits that its author 'seizes the reader at the first moment at which they meet, holds him thrilled, entranced, terrified perhaps, in a grasp which never relaxes, and leaves him at last, after a perusal of the story, shaken and exhausted as by some great effort of the mind' (Reid, 204). (Woolf wrote in a similar breathless style, but of *Jane Eyre*.) Reid's final conclusion is that *Wuthering Heights* is a 'wonderful story', and though it has many faults it 'is alone sufficient to prove that a rare and splendid genius was lost to the world when Emily Brontë died' (214).

One cannot imagine that the rationalist Leslie Stephen would endorse Reid's reluctant but irresistible admiration of *Wuthering Heights*. Indeed, writing to accept an article on the Brontës for the *Cornhill Magazine*, Stephen expressed his reservations about *Wuthering Heights*. Here he stated he did not 'admire' this novel as much as the would-be contributor did. In it he saw 'more violence than real strength & more rant than genuine passion'. Stephen fairly concluded though: 'However all this is a matter of taste'. In the *Dictionary of National Biography*, Stephen admitted that some critics have regarded Emily Brontë more highly than Charlotte Brontë. He again appears to be baffled by *Wuthering Heights*, though admitting that other critics have been appreciative of it: 'The novel missed popularity by the general painfulness of the situation, by clumsiness of construction, and by the absence of the astonishing power of realisation manifest in *Jane Eyre*. In point of style it is superior, but it is the nightmare of a recluse, not a direct representation of facts seen by genius. Though enthusiastically admired by good judges, it will hardly be widely appreciated.'

Again, it is difficult not to think that Stephen consciously or unconsciously borrowed from Reid. The latter had compared *Wuthering Heights* to Shakespeare's 'gory' revenge tragedy *Titus Andronicus* (Reid, 202). Similarly, Stephen wrote further of his reservations about *Wuthering Heights*, which he described as 'that strange book', unparalleled except by the 'crude but startling productions of the Elizabethan dramatists' (*HL*, 24). Here Stephen breaks away from Reid's monograph, when he attributed to Emily Brontë a 'feeble grasp of external facts', which creates a book which is a' kind of baseless nightmare, which we read with wonder and with distressing curiosity, but with even more pain than pleasure or profit' (*HL*, 24).

At the same time, Stephen was obviously aware of the shift in favour towards Emily Brontë (and disapproved of it): 'I dont think justice is generally done to C. Brontë now & I shall be glad for that reason to insert your eloquent article' (Bicknell, Letter to George Barnett Smith, 12 May 1873 Volume 1, 123). Nevertheless, he refrained from giving his total agreement to the proposition that Charlotte Brontë 'has been comparatively neglected of late years', prefacing this remark by a qualifying, ''[i]f it be true.' (*HL*, 2). He expressed a further doubt about the position of Charlotte Brontë's neglect on the following page, stating: 'The comparable eclipse, then—if eclipse there be' (*HL*, 3). Certainly, Leslie Stephen never devoted a whole article to Emily Brontë, but then neither did his youngest daughter. However, while accepting some differences, he saw a certain resemblance between Charlotte and Emily Brontë: their natures had been equally moulded, and their characters 'turned inward by the early influence of surrounding circumstances' (*HL*, 15).

Both Leslie Stephen and Virginia Woolf—separately and far apart in time—visited Brontë country and were impressed by it. Yet neither of them ever repeated their visit. This was perhaps odder and less understandable in the case of Virginia Woolf, for the Parsonage was obtained for the Brontë Society and opened as a museum to the public in 1928 and became the permanent home of the Brontë relics. Leslie Stephen stayed in Settle with his first wife, Minny, in April 1870 and recognised (as would his daughter) the significance of the landscape as it appeared in the Brontë novels. His description alludes to Charlotte Brontë's *Shirley*. More surprisingly, considering the relative obscurity of Anne Brontë among the three sisters, Stephen may have read *The Tenant of Wildfell Hall* (though he makes two words of 'Wildfell', 'fell' also being capitalised. This misspelling might suggest that he had heard of the book by word of mouth only, and had never actually read it). He also makes a more generalised allusion to 'the Brontës'.

Stephen was as sensitive as his youngest daughter would be to the Brontëan scenery and atmosphere. He wrote the following description in a letter he sent to his sister-in-law, Anne Thackeray, which included that: 'It is very like Shirley except that there is no heather & the people are all of them of the Yorkshire kind as described by the Brontës'. Stephen then described a visit to a Walter Morrison, a Conservative MP, who lived in an isolated house in which only two rooms were furnished. Morrison's style of living, with only one domestic servant, but 'great kennelfull[s] of dogs', made Stephen opine that Morrison, 'would easily become a kind of tenant of Wild Fell Hall' (Bicknell, Leslie Stephen to Anne Isabella Thackeray, 24 April 1870, volume 1, 80). One wonders whether Stephen might have confused *The Tenant of Wildfell Hall* with *Wuthering Heights* (except that the dogs he met were friendly and, reassuringly, came to be patted, unlike those Lockwood tangled with).

It is noticeable, however, that both Woolf and Stephen described the Brontës' lives as being more circumscribed than they actually were. While both father and daughter thought that *Villette* is Charlotte Brontë's greatest novel, you would not guess from their criticism that much of its action is set abroad, in Belgium. Like Elizabeth Gaskell in her *Life of Charlotte Brontë*, Stephen and Woolf made sure their readers forever associate the Brontës with the Yorkshire moors. This important omission needs commenting on, because the settings of two of Charlotte Brontë's novels—*The Professor* and *Villette*—were set on the Continent. In fact, already within the Victorian period, Belgium—and especially Brussels—had become an alternative Brontë shrine, which drew many American pilgrims like a magnet.

Both Stephen and Woolf thought the region in which so many of the Brontë novels were set, and where they spent most of their lives, were so important because both tended to conflate Charlotte Brontë with her characters. Stephen had some justification for thinking of *Jane Eyre* as an autobiography, for the subtitle was just that: *An Autobiography*. This was high praise as Stephen was enthusiastic about autobiographies, writing in his essay 'Biography': 'The few biographies which give a really instructive account of mental and moral growth are autobiographies' (*B*, 133). In the same essay, he stated that the biographers' 'main purpose' ought to be 'the construction of an autobiography'. Boswell was able to make Johnson talk to the reader (*B*, 138).

But Stephen stressed that in *Jane Eyre* he believed the autobiography presented in it was that of Charlotte Brontë herself: 'Self-evidently, Charlotte Brontë drew on her own experiences in her novels, so that her life and art are closely related life'. Further: 'The scenery and even the incidents are, for the most part, equally directly transcripts from reality . . . the study of her life is the study of her novels' (*HL*, 6). Stephen unequivocally repeated this idea later in his essay, though in a slightly different way: 'We may infer [Charlotte

Brontë's] personality more or less accurately from the mode in which she contemplates her neighbours, but it is directly manifested in various avatars of her own spirit' (*HL*, 20). Stephen argued that while Charlotte Brontë was extremely observant of other people from the outside, her greatest strength lay in her ability to produce characters from the inside. Lucy Snowe and Jane Eyre, Shirley and Rochester are all to a greater or lesser degree 'mouthpieces' of Charlotte Brontë's 'peculiar sentiment'. When we hear them speak, we are actually hearing the disguised voice of Charlotte herself (*HL*, 20).

It is apparent that in her emphasis on the paramount importance of the novelist's creation of character, Woolf was actually in tune with her Victorian father. In their respective fields, that of the biographer and that of the novelist, father and daughter were actually remarkably in unison. In his essay, 'Biography', Stephen stressed repeatedly that it is the character of the subject which is the most important quality, and everything is subservient to this end. Stephen argued that the proper biography is 'the development of the man's own character and fortunes' (*B*, 138). He used a very up-to-date image to describe what the relationship between the biographer and his subject should be: 'to breathe real life' into the 'biographee' (as Stephen dubbed him), the biographer 'must put us into direct communication with the man himself; not tell us simply where he was or what he was seen to do, but put him at one end of a literary telephone and the reader on the other. The author should, as often as possible, be merely the conducting wire' ('*B*', 140).

This essay also anticipated, in the biographical art, what Woolf would conclude about the novelist's creation of character. Stephen wrote, using the image of a painter's portrait, that the biography should:

> be a portrait in which not a single touch should be admitted which is not relevant to the purpose of producing a speaking likeness. . . . The book should be the man himself speaking or acting, and nothing but the man. It should be such a portrait as reveals the essence of character; and the writer who gives anything that does not tell upon the general effect is like the portrait-painter who allows the chairs and tables, or even the coat or cravat, to distract attention from the face. (*B*, 141–22)

Earlier in the essay, Stephen had written: 'Our aim should be to present the human soul, not all its irrelevant bodily trappings' (*B*, 141). Woolf's innovation in her novels can be seen in terms comparable to Stephen's genre of biography: both aimed at conveying the essence of a character. His ideas were also echoed by Woolf in her criticism of the Edwardian novelists and their emphasis on the external and material, at the expense of the inner and spiritual. Woolf's position was that the novelist is obsessed with capturing and conveying character (*E3*, 422). The Edwardians were also preoccupied by character, but they used the wrong methods. In an earlier essay, Woolf had summed up the Edwardian novelists in one word: they were 'materialists' (*E3*, 32). In 'Modern Novels', Woolf defined the approach to writing fiction the Georgian writers embraced, as represented by James Joyce who was concerned with the 'spiritual' and revealed 'the flickerings of that innermost flame which flashes its myriad messages through the brain', following his imagination and disregarding everything external (*E3*, 34).

It is ironic that Woolf, who intellectually rejected the Victorians, should have shared some of her apparently Victorian father's ideas about biography, and followed him in trying to apply his paradigms to capture character in her experimental and modernist novels. The difference between them was the problem of *how* a character should be conveyed to the reader. Much of Woolf's writing, fiction and nonfiction were directed towards solving this problem. This led directly to her development of the modernist novel. Woolf, however, makes a crucial distinction between biography and fiction, which does not appear to have been observed by her father. A general perspective which emerges from her vast body of criticism, that while she acknowledged that both biography and fiction stand or fall on the presentation of character, Woolf implied that while biography *interprets* character, fiction *creates* character (*E1*, 112).

Numerous examples from Woolf's early reviews express her conception of the novel as a vehicle for character creation which was, for her, the touchstone of great novels. Woolf's consideration of character creation became increasingly complex as her writing career progressed. Further, as a novice reviewer, she already sees as one of her tasks the separating of the permanent landmarks of literature from the ephemeral (*E1*, 11). This view was shared by her father: 'To anticipate the verdict of posterity is the great task of the true critic,' to which he added that this task was only 'accomplished by about one man in a generation' (*TCC*, 219).

Stephen himself was arguably condemning Charlotte Brontë's characterisation for not doing what she never intended to do. By contrast, Woolf perceived that Charlotte Brontë's character creation was dedicated to producing a different sort of protagonist. Charlotte Brontë herself explained to W. S. Williams: 'The standard heroes and heroines of novels, are personages in whom I could never, from childhood upwards, take an interest, believe to be natural, or wish to imitate: were I obliged to copy these characters, I would simply—not write at all' (*CBL2* Early September 1848, 118. Shorter did not include this letter, which makes Woolf's perceptiveness about Charlotte Brontë's heroines even more impressive). Woolf recognised that Charlotte Brontë was revolutionising the nature of the female character and Jane Eyre who was 'very uncompromising' was a catalyst for change (*E3*, 193).

Not as perceptive as his daughter, Stephen implicitly raised doubts about whether Charlotte Brontë possessed a creative imagination at all. This does not invalidate Charlotte Brontë's novel for Stephen, who found that the 'specific peculiarity' of her novels 'seems to be the power of revealing to us the potentiality of intense passions lurking behind the scenery of everyday life' (*HL*, 8). Strangely, and coincidentally, this use of the ordinary, everyday, and domestic were to be among Virginia Woolf's greatest achievements in her fiction and a marked feature of the modernist literature that Stephen would not live to see. A later comment in this essay seems to be prophetic about his daughter's writing achievements: 'All people seem to be commonplace to the commonplace observer. Genius reveals the difference; it does not invent it' (*HL*, 12).

It is perhaps ironic that while Stephen doubted whether Charlotte Brontë actually had any imagination, Woolf asserted the same doubt as to her father himself; she reported having frequent arguments about this with her paternal aunt, Caroline Emilia Stephen (*L1*, no. 348: To Violet Dickinson, 17 February 1907, 285). Five years later, Woolf returned to the subject of Stephen's imagination. She wrote to her sister that she had been giving a lot of thought to their father and had concluded that he had 'practically no imagination' (*L1* no. 503, To Vanessa Bell, 16 August 1909, 408). Ten years later, she professed an interest in Bernard Holland because she believed he had imagination, the quality she found most admirable and which, she claimed, her father and his agnostic circle of friends lacked (*DIII*, 21 August 1929, 246). Woolf reaffirmed this perception of her father towards the end of her life: Stephen did not possess 'an imaginative mind' (*A Sketch of the Past*, 115).

Stephen regarded *Villette* as 'this masterpiece of Miss Brontë's art' and compares Paul Emanuel with other great characters in literature. Woolf agreed with this assessment, describing *Villette* as Charlotte Brontë's 'finest novel' (*E4*, 168). Stephen claimed of Paul Emanuel, that '[a] more charming hero was never drawn', or one whose 'reality is more vivid and unmistakable' (*HL*, 16). Stephen made the perceptive guess that 'Perhaps we might venture to add that it is hardly explicable, except as a portrait drawn by a skilful hand guided by love, and by love intensified by the consciousness of some impassable barrier' (*HL*, 16). Stephen returned to this theme, stating that Paul Emanuel is 'so real that we feel at once that he must have been drawn from a living model. . . . He is a real human being who gave lectures at a particular date in a *pension* at Brussels We are as much convinced of the fact as we are of the reality of Miss Brontë herself' (*HL*, 16–17). Stephen died nine years before the letters from Charlotte Brontë to M. Heger were published in full in *The Times* in 1913. Although Woolf knew about these letters, she did not directly quote from them, or even allude to them. An obscure remark here and there does, nonetheless, imply she was fully aware of these letters.

The literalness of the portraits for Stephen meant that ultimately Paul Emanuel was not a character to be put beside other great literary creations of characters. Stephen viewed Paul Emanuel as basically 'a true woman, simple, pure heroic and loving', as were, he believed, all heroes created by women writers (*HL*, 18). As for Rochester, he exists only 'as a reflection of a certain side of his creator; really he is the personification of a true woman's longing (may one say it now?) for a strong master' (*HL*, 21). These quotations possibly say more about Stephen's perception of Victorian womanhood than about Charlotte Brontë's character creation.

Stephen also passed a conventional and quintessentially Victorian judgement on Rochester, whose behaviour to Jane Eyre was 'abominable'. If he had openly explained his marital position to Jane and asked her to live with him outside marriage he would 'have acted like a rake, but not like a sneak' (*HL*, 21). It is hard to forgive Rochester's 'treachery' (*HL*, 21). In 'Charlotte Brontë' Stephen urged that her inclusion of this was due to 'inexperience' and not because of an innate lack of 'true purity and moral elevation' (*HL*, 22). But in a letter, Stephen had expressed rather a different view:

> I think there is some excuse for the charge of coarseness, as, e.g., the scene where Jane Eyre is half inclined to go to Rochester's bedroom. I dont mean coarseness in the sense of prurience; for I fully agree that Miss Brontë writes as a thoroughly pureminded woman; but she is more close to the physical side of passion than young ladies are expected to be. Perhaps we are too squeamish about young ladies; but the critics were, I think, excusable. There is also some coarseness in the artistic sense in Jane Eyre. The mad wife is I fancy, unnecessarily bestial. (Bicknell, Leslie Stephen to George Barnett Smith, 12 May 1873, volume 1, 123)

From almost the beginning of her reviewing career, Woolf stated her disagreement with the nineteenth-century critics whom, she believed, were more interested in morals than aesthetics.

Arising from Charlotte Brontë's tendency to write from her own experiences, both Stephen and Woolf felt that Charlotte Brontë's creativity was limited. Stephen commented on 'The amazing vividness of her portrait-painting', which he argued 'makes her work unique among modern fiction.' He carried on to qualify this praise by remarking on the limitations of her vision: while she had a 'mind of extraordinary activity', it functioned 'within a narrow sphere' and brooded 'constantly upon a small stock of materials' (*HL*, 7–8). Unlike her father, Woolf perceived that the very narrowness of Charlotte Brontë's life conduced much to her power as a writer; her intensely passionate novels were produced from inner conflict. Had she been happy and sociable she would have produced different books (*E2*, 194). Woolf reiterated this perspective in another essay, '*Jane Eyre* and *Wuthering Heights*' (*E4*, 167).

In both instances—the using of autobiographical material and the narrowness of Charlotte Brontë's experience—father and daughter are in agreement. But, as we have seen, they evaluate both these matters differently. Considering the use of autobiography, Woolf did so primarily as a novelist herself, who looked for novelistic material. This idea surfaces strongly in 1920, when she commented on Marjorie Strachey's autobiographical novel *The Counterfeits* and questioned whether she herself wrote autobiography which masqueraded as fiction (*DII*, 14 January 1920, 7). She, like Charlotte Brontë before her, was equally disingenuous: 'I think one's readers tend to identify one's characters more than one does oneself.' She admitted 'Of course there are touches of Lady Ritchie in Mrs Hilbery; but in writing one gets more and more away from reality, and Mrs Hilbery became to me quite different from any one in the flesh' (*VW L2,* no. 1103: To C. P. Sanger, 2? December 1919, 406). Yet only six months later she wrote gleefully that *Night and Day* had outraged the Ritchies (*L2,* no. 1182: To Vanessa Bell, June 1921, 474). In a letter, Vita Sackville-West made a comment on Woolf's novels which clearly stung the latter. Sackville-West believed Woolf copied people from life and her appreciation of them was intellectual rather than emotional (*L3,* no. 1502: To Vita Sackville-West, 4 October 1924, 138).

Stephen appeared not to attribute to the literary artist—in this case Charlotte Brontë—any *creative* ability. What the great writer does with the bare bones of any person is to transmit that actual and real person into a fully realised character in a novel. Stephen does not give any credit to Charlotte Brontë for this transformative power.

Stephen distinguished between the 'scientific' and the 'poetic mind'. The poetic mind 'sees intuitively, prefers synthesis to analysis, and embodies ideas in concrete symbols instead of proceeding by rule and measure, and constructing diagrams in preference to drawing pictures' (*HL*, 4). Stephen suggested, however, that the two qualities were 'not mutually exclusive'; in fact, the greatest writers combine them: 'The most analytic mind has some spark of creative power, and the great creators are capable of deliberate dissection' (*HL*, 4). He proceeded to say that Charlotte Brontë, viewed even under the most favourable conditions, was not 'a philosophical thinker'. While saying this might not matter, he undercut this when he referred to her 'comparative poverty of thought' and her limited number of ideas (*HL*, 5). Woolf agreed.

Similarly, Woolf divided writers into two divisions: those who thought and those who felt. She went on to say that if this division is accepted, Charlotte Brontë first and most importantly investigated feelings rather than thoughts

(*E2*, 28). She argued that Charlotte Brontë, unlike Thomas Hardy, lacked all 'speculative curiosity'. Further, she later stated that we do not read Charlotte Brontë's novels for a philosophy of life; her view remained that of 'a country parson's daughter' (*E4*, 168). Nevertheless, Woolf perceived that this lack of intellectual content resulted in a positive outcome—one which Stephen had failed to grasp—that we read Charlotte Brontë's novels for their poetry (*E4*, 168).

If Charlotte Brontë had no philosophy, she did have certain ideas which arose from the urgent and immediate experiences of the heroes and heroines of the novels. Stephen perceived conflicts between emotion and duty and the individual and society. He dealt with these dichotomies at some length and his treatment of them revealed a good deal of thoughtful and sensitive consideration. He referred to the preface to the second edition of *Jane Eyre*, in which Charlotte Brontë had explained that her novel was 'a protest against conventionality'. However, Stephen commented:

> But the protest is combined with a most unflinching adherence to the proper conventions of society; and we are left in great doubt as to where the line ought to be drawn. Where does the unlawful pressure of society upon the individual begin, and what are the demands which it might rightfully make upon our respect? At one moment in *Jane Eyre* we seem to be drifting towards the solution that strong passion is the one really good thing in the world, and that all human conventions which oppose it should be disregarded. This was the tendency which shocked the respectable reviewers of the time. Of course they should have seen that the strongest sympathy of the author goes with the heroic self-conquest of the heroine under temptation. . . . Yet it is also true that we are left with the sense of an unresolved discord. (*HL*, 23–24)

Stephen concluded that Charlotte Brontë was caught between 'the opposite poles of duty and happiness' (*HL*, 26). Charlotte Brontë had not reconciled these opposing claims or even articulated the problem distinctly. Stephen proposed that Charlotte Brontë's 'position speaks of a mind diseased', and that a 'more powerful intellect would even under her conditions have worked out some more comprehensive and harmonious solution' (*HL*, 26).

At times Stephen appeared to take a superior and patronising attitude towards Charlotte Brontë's dilemma as presented in the predicaments of her heroines. He saw this as a failure for which she, as novelist, was to blame. Woolf regarded the situation rather differently: she blamed society for the limitations and faults of Charlotte Brontë's vision and those of her fictional heroines. Woolf's attitude was more interesting than her father's, for, as we shall see, it evolved and changed throughout her writing on Charlotte Brontë. Unlike Stephen, she stressed the importance of the fact that Charlotte Brontë was a female writer and woman in the patriarchal age of the nineteenth century.

Both Stephen and Woolf were familiar with Elizabeth Gaskell's *Life of Charlotte Brontë,* and it deeply influenced their views of the Brontës, particularly of Charlotte Brontë. Stephen referred to Gaskell's *Life* as 'touching' and, despite some 'minor faults' it is 'one of the most pathetic records of a melancholy life in our literature' (*HL*, 8). There were, of course, several 'buts'. In view of the fact that Gaskell was writing so soon after Charlotte Brontë's death, she was forced to suppress certain facts.

Woolf appeared to have thought about the subject far more profoundly than her father about biography, which evolved and developed over many years. By 1920, Woolf was actively considering the radical idea that possibly it was impossible to write biographies. In reviewing Constance Hill's biography of a minor Victorian writer, Woolf questioned whether we can really know other people. Even our friends are elusive, how much more difficult it is to portray the dead. Her friend Lytton Strachey had revolutionised Victorian biography with his lean spare and iconoclastic biographies of prominent nineteenth-century (*E3*, 220). His *Eminent Victorians* (1918) had begun a trend away from vast hagiographic tomes. Woolf subsequently argued that in the twentieth century the biographer changed his relationship to his subject. He became the latter's equal, he was free and independent, so that 'he has ceased to be the chronicler; he has become an artist' (*E4*, 475).

Strachey's example as a biographer has been followed by others, including Harold Nicolson. Woolf's review of his *Some People* began with some remarks about the development of biography from the eighteenth century. Boswell's *Life of Johnson* was the first revolution in biography and ensured that it focused on the personality and not merely on the 'action and works' of its subject (*E4*, 474). Nineteenth-century biographers then tried to combine the outer and inner lives of their subjects. However, much Victorian biography was unsuccessful; it was 'a parti-coloured, hybrid, monstrous birth' (*E4*, 474). Victorian biographers were handicapped by the belief that their subjects should be praiseworthy, possessing all the good qualities which the period approved and upheld (*E4*, 474–75).

However, in *Some People*, Nicolson also took an independent approach on his own initiative; he combined fiction and reality. Woolf was particularly thinking about biography in 1927 when she reviewed Harold Nicolson's *Some People*. In an author's note to his book, Nicolson said people had often asked him if its characters were 'imaginary' or 'accurate portraits'. His answer is that for his characters, he 'drew largely on my imagination, mingling fact with fiction'. He added that the portraits are 'mostly composite'. Ultimately, Woolf had her reservations about *Some People*: she wanted either fact or fiction, not a combination (*E4*, 478).

Harold Nicolson also gave further consideration to the art of biography in *The Development of Biography*, which was published by the Hogarth Press in 1928. Interestingly, Nicolson praises Leslie Stephen's *Dictionary of National Biography* and the 'English Men of Letters' Series. Nicolson deliberately excluded Elizabeth Gaskell's *Life of Charlotte Brontë*, ironically enough, because he viewed it is a work of fiction: in his view Gaskell's *Life* 'is a story, but it is not history' (*The Development of English Biography*, 128). This idea seemed to have been circulated a fair amount during this period. There is no evidence that Woolf herself ever criticised Elizabeth Gaskell's biography of Charlotte Brontë for being based more on fiction than fact. Indeed, a year after her review of Nicolson's *Some People*, and in the same year as the Hogarth Press published his book on *The Development of Biography*, Woolf published a fictional biography of Vita called *Orlando*. In this funny fantasy life, she drew attention to and sent up all the formal properties and manoeuvres of nineteenth-century biographers. Moreover, in 1933 she produced another fictional biography, this time of Elizabeth Barrett Browning's dog, Flush. In these works, she may be said to have achieved what she had thought no biographer could achieve: she combined 'that queer amalgamation of dream and reality, that perpetual marriage of granite and rainbow' (*E4*, 478).

As a critic of Charlotte Brontë's novels, Stephen found Charlotte Brontë's letters 'disappointing' (*HL*, 10). This is of interest because Gaskell's made a conscious decision to include a large number of Charlotte Brontë's letters as the most powerful way to create a portrait of her subject (*LMG*, no. 304: To George Smith, 19 August 1856, 404–405). Leslie Stephen offered a somewhat patronising explanation for his view on the letters; they are 'young-ladyish . . . Miss Brontë, with all her genius, was still a young lady. Her mind, with its exceptional powers in certain directions, never broke the fetters by which the parson's daughter of the last generation was restricted' (*HL*, 10). Strikingly, Woolf's view was the exact opposite of her father's: she thought that unlike Jane Austen, Charlotte Brontë was not a lady, and she stated this several times.

Attempting to summarise the meaning of one of Charlotte Brontë's heroines, 'or, in other words, of Charlotte Brontë', Leslie Stephen had recourse to fire imagery: 'such utterances always give us the impression of a fiery soul. . . . The fire is pure and intense. It is kindled in a nature intensely emotional' but one which also had a strong sense of duty (*HL*, 23). *Jane Eyre* is, of course, permeated by fire imagery; so too is Virginia Woolf's language in discussing Charlotte Brontë's novels. For example, Woolf wrote of *Jane Eyre*: 'it is the red and fitful glow of the heart's fire which illumines her page' (*E4*, 168).

Both Stephen and his daughter commented on Charlotte Brontë's style in her fiction, which evidently struck them both as individual and not altogether successful. Stephen commented that:

> There is a certain feverish disquiet which is marked by the peculiar mannerism of the style. At its best, we have admirable flashes of vivid expression, where the material of language is the incarnation of keen intuitive thought. At its worst, it is strangely contorted, crowded by rather awkward personifications, and degenerates towards a rather unpleasant Ossianesque. More severity of taste would increase the power by restraining the abuse. We feel an aspiration after more than can be accomplished, an unsatisfied yearning for potent excitement, which is sometimes more fretful than forcible. (*HL*, 23)

As we shall see, Woolf's comments on the style of Charlotte Brontë again differed from her father's, because of her feminist perspective (although she did not like the word 'feminist'). Her different opinion also arose from the fact that she considered Charlotte Brontë's style over a long period and during that time her opinion altered (*E2*, 30).

Stephen concurred with Gaskell's very negative picture of Branwell Brontë, but he blamed the sisters themselves:

> The scamp Branwell Brontë took the unluckily commonplace path of escape from a too frigid code of external morality which leads to the public-house. His sisters followed the more characteristically feminine method. They learnt to be proud of the fetters by which they were bound. Instead of fretting against the stern law of repression, they identified it with the eternal code of duty, and rejoiced in trampling on their own weakness. (*HL*, 14)

In his entry for Branwell Brontë in the *Dictionary of National Biography*, Stephen's language about his subject was emotional and judgmental. Stephen detailed the deterioration of Branwell Brontë. Branwell Brontë's was dismissed by the Robinsons when his behaviour became 'openly offensive'. He is described as bragging to his friends and behaving like 'a village Don Juan'. Stephen states that the only evidence of this affair 'rests solely upon the testimony of the pothouse brags of a degraded creature'. Now that all Branwell Brontë's assertions have been investigated and disproved, 'The whole may be dismissed as a shameful lie, possibly based in part on real delusion'. This is hardly disinterested criticism; it is based solely on Stephen's morality. He was equally dismissive of Branwell Brontë's putative authorship of *Wuthering Heights*, though this was far from a dead issue and cropped up again in Woolf's maturity. Her only interest in Branwell Brontë was to reject the idea, expressed by several critics, that he had partly written *Wuthering Heights*. Through the Hogarth Press, during the 1930s, Woolf would publish works on the Brontës by which she thought the putative authorship of Branwell Brontë of *Wuthering Heights* would be most effectively challenged.

Even as a novelist (a form in which her father had not attempted to write and which she could therefore strike out on alone, without being intimidated by paternal precedence), Woolf retained an ambivalent attitude towards Leslie Stephen. Probably unconsciously, she accepted some of his values, which she believed she had rejected and freed herself from. When writing her first novel (which would become *The Voyage Out*), Woolf wrote to her brother-in-law: 'I dreamt last night that I was showing father the manuscript of my novel; and he snorted, and dropped it on to a table, and I was very melancholy, and read it this morning, and thought it bad' (*L1*, no. 406: To Clive Bell, 15 April 1908, 325).

Much later in her life, Woolf still referred to her father's view of her. This time it was based on their common ground as critics of literature. The Master of Trinity College, Cambridge, had written to Woolf to invite her to deliver the Clark Lectures in 1933. Leslie Stephen had given the first Clark Lectures, on eighteenth-century literature, fifty years before in 1883, when Virginia was a baby. Woolf reflected that it is the first time a woman had been invited to give the Clark Lectures, consisting of six lectures. Although Woolf declined the invitation, she was pleased to have been asked. Part of this pleasure was derived from how she thought Leslie Stephen would have reacted: 'father would have blushed with pleasure could I have told him 30 years ago, that his daughter—my poor little Ginny—was to be asked to succeed him: the sort of compliment he would have liked' (*DIV*, 29 February 1932, 79). Moreover, she accepted the Victorian canon, particularly of women writers.

Whereas, like his subject, Leslie Stephen was a Victorian, his youngest daughter's adult life was mostly lived out in another era. She and her contemporaries—and especially Lytton Strachey in *Eminent Victorians*—reacted against what they believed were the values and beliefs of the Victorians. It would seem that while, intellectually, she identified herself with the Modernists (or Georgians as she called them), she was emotionally attached to her Victorian past. Woolf's ambivalence about her Victorian childhood, also applied to her attitude towards her Victorian father. Stating that on 28 November 1928 her father would have been ninety-six, she thinks it is a mercy he did not attain that great age: 'His life would have entirely ended mine. What would have happened? No writing, no books; —inconceivable' (*DIII*, 28 November 1928, 208).

Moreover, Woolf was still faced with the sexism and misogyny to which the Brontës had been exposed. Woolf fought back with her pen, but it must have been discouraging and demoralising. What is utterly astonishing is that Stephen appeared to have believed that the inequalities between male and female writers had been sufficiently reformed:

Johnson's famous comparison of the preaching women to the dancing dogs
gives the general sentiment. They were not admired for writing well, but for
writing at all.

We have changed all this, and there is something pathetic in the tentative
and modest approaches of our grandmothers to the pursuits in which their
granddaughters have achieved the rights and responsibilities of equal treatment. (*TE,* 58)

There are two further aspects of the criticism of father and daughter which
should be noticed. Stephen had received no formal training for his role as a
literary critic, as it was not then studied as an academic university subject. His
preparation for his task was the same as his daughter's: both read intensively
and critically. Secondly, it is a surprise that despite the criticism that has been
directed to him as a markedly 'masculine' critic, he hinted at Woolf's later
idea androgyny, writing to his mother-in-law in 1877: 'Every man ought to
be feminine, *i.e.,* to have quick and delicate feelings; but no man ought to be
effeminate, *i.e.,* to let his feelings get the better of his intellect' (Maitland,
314). Of course, his interpretation of the 'feminine' and 'effeminate' may be
challenged, but this seems a remarkable thought for a Victorian and a man
produced by this epoch who his daughter thought so conventional.

Finally, as a coda to the story of Leslie Stephen's and Virginia Stephen
Woolf's approach to the Brontës, there was a *third* generation of the Stephen
family who was involved in the Brontë story: Leslie Stephen's father and
Virginia's grandfather, Sir James Stephen (1789–1859). Leslie Stephen wrote
the article on his father for the *Dictionary of National Biography.* His account
is rather arid and uninspiring; but we emerge from reading it with a sense of
a man who had distinguished himself both as a lawyer and as a civil servant
in the colonial office, but who was prone to the mental illness which would
be inherited by some of his descendants, including both Leslie and Virginia.

It was as a lawyer rather than as a literary critic that Sir James Stephen
became involved in the Brontë story. Sir James Stephen became embroiled
in the arguments about Branwell Brontë's involvement with Mrs Robinson,
as presented by Elizabeth Gaskell. Tom Winnifrith explained that Sir James
responded to Gaskell's condemnation of Mrs Robinson as the seducer of
Branwell Brontë with 'an indignant letter' which contained 'threats of legal
action'. As Leslie Stephen informed us in his *Dictionary* account of his father,
his father was made a K.C.B. and a privy councillor in 1847. By the time
the *Life* appeared, Winnifrith described Sir James as being 'near the end of
his life', by which time he was 'a representative of the real establishment'
(Winnifrith, 'The Background to Sir James Stephen's Letter', *BST,* 21:4,
151–53). By the time of Gaskell's *Life,* the former Mrs Robinson had become

a titled lady and occupied a secure place in high society. Both George Smith and Elizabeth Gaskell were less secure in their social positions and felt unable to stand out against such a powerful and influential member of society as Sir James Stephen and so were obliged to retract the account of her adultery with Branwell Brontë. As we have seen, Leslie Stephen apparently adopted his father's position completely on the matter and wrote harshly of Branwell Brontë and defended Lydia Robinson. The Brontë scholar, C. K. Shorter (who will appear again) wrote of Virginia Stephen-Woolf's father and grandfather: 'I was assured by the late Sir Leslie Stephen that his father, Sir James Stephen, was employed at the time to make careful inquiry, and that he and other eminent lawyers came to the conclusion that it was one long tissue of lies or hallucinations' (*L&L1*, 14).

If this chapter began with her negative criticism of Stephen's writing, it is appropriate to end it with the positive picture she had of her father. She wrote nostalgically of her adolescent relationship with Stephen: she pictured him tramping home from the London Library with the volumes of her favourite Elizabethan prose writer, Hakluyt (*D3*, 8 December 1929, 271). Nearly ten years later she had a correspondence with a young woman called Elizabeth E. Nielsen, who was considering writing a PhD dissertation on Leslie Stephen. Woolf expressed delight at this news and curiosity as to what Nielsen would make of him (Letter no. 3462: To Elizabeth E. Nielsen, 28 October 1938, Banks Trautmann, 198). In another letter to the same correspondent, Woolf thanked Nielsen for having sent her an essay on Stephen. Woolf wrote that she was unable to read her father 'critically' herself, but Nielsen has succeeded in presenting his whole character. She expresses her gladness that Stephen is still considered 'a figure of such importance'. She now recognises that her father was primarily a philosopher, whose work she is not competent to judge. She pays tribute to his qualities, which are also at the basis of her own work: he was 'extremely truthful, serious, and aware of the lasting side of life' (Letter no. 3484a: To Elizabeth E. Nielsen, 1 February 1939, Banks Trautmann, 199). Between these early, mid, and late quotations, Virginia Woolf's ambivalence to her father is contained. Here we see both her emotional enthrallment to the Victorian period and her modified intellectual and modernist rejection of that time.

Chapter Five

Virginia Woolf's Essays on the Brontës

It is of interest to examine how far her criticism converged with, or differed from, those of her contemporaries. Woolf was particularly fascinated by the Brontës as *women* writers, as we will see in her reviews of W. L. Courtney's *The Feminine Note in Fiction* (1905) and R. Brimley Johnson's *The Women Novelists* (1918). Many of the ideas discussed in these reviews were taken up again in *A Room of One's Own*. This chapter will begin with some general critical comments about novels, which are applicable both to those of the Brontës and her own, which are scattered throughout Woolf's essays. It will then move on to consider those devoted solely to the Brontës. It is important to remember that Woolf's literary career began with literary criticism, only later moving to novel writing.

In the 1920s, Woolf did her best to distance herself from the Victorian critics and their modern counterparts. She argued that the nineteenth-century critics wrote for a cultured and leisured public while contemporary critics had to appeal to a wider, less cultivated audience. She admitted that the modern essay had some advantages over the old one (*E3*, 219–20). In the same essay, Woolf stressed that they were written with the sole aim of giving the reader pleasure.

The fact that she published two volumes of *The Common Reader* (published in 1925 and 1932) reveals her increasing desire to be a critic. The writers she focused on in these books were, without exception, all dead, and the only recent one was Joseph Conrad who had died in 1924. Many nineteenth-century critics were hostile and aggressive to the books they were reviewing.

REFERENCES TO THE BRONTËS IN
VIRGINIA WOOLF'S ESSAYS

On the whole, though, the Bloomsbury Group, including Virginia Woolf, were hostile to the Victorian period, at least on an intellectual level. She commented on this era (in which her unhappy adolescence and young adulthood had passed) when she reviewed the *Reminiscences and Reflexions of a Mid and Late Victorian* by Ernest Belfont Bax. She observed that the Victorian period already seemed remote and separate from the modern world (*E2*, 261). Similarly, when she reviewed Arthur Haywood's *The Days of Dickens. A Glance at Some Aspects of Early Victorian Life in London*, she felt a need to escape this remote era, which struck her as intolerable (*E4*, 339–400).

Neither was Woolf generally favourable in her opinion of the majority of lesser female Victorian novelists, such as Margaret Oliphant, Lucy Clifford, and Mrs Humphry Ward. Whilst she admired Elizabeth Gaskell's *Life of Charlotte Brontë* (which substantially shaped her own view of its subject), her novels aroused impatience in Woolf; she was provoked by Mrs Ellis Chadwick's suggestion that anyone would be sufficiently impressed by Gaskell's fiction to wish to make pilgrimages to places she had lived in. She thought even the despised Edwardian novelist, John Galsworthy had treated social unrest more convincingly than Gaskell. Woolf condemned her as an amateur, rather than a professional, in her approach to authorship. Woolf conceded that her irritation arose partly because of the methods of the mid-Victorian novelists. They wrote too copiously and indiscriminately, whereas the moderns aimed to exclude everything that was extraneous (*E1*, 341).

However, generally speaking, Woolf never deviated from her positive assessment of—selected—classic Victorian novels; she was impressed by their ability to habitually produce masterpieces which were instantly recognised for what they were. As an example of such novels, which Woolf cited under her title, 'A Born Writer', was *Jane Eyre* (*E3*, 250). She also wrote that good novelists, living or dead, continued to be relevant and always had something to contribute, even if not in a direct way, to different people at different periods (*E*, 44). She championed four major Victorian female novelists whom she believed had produced literary classics: Charlotte and Emily Brontë, Jane Austen and George Eliot. In her centenary article on George Eliot, *Jane Eyre* was preferred to *The Sad Fortunes of the Rev. Amos Barton* (*E4*, 174).

Writing on the future of fiction, Woolf opined that the form of the novel needed to evolve. (She herself repeatedly denied that her long prose fictions were 'novels' and sought for another name for them.) Yet she acknowledged that some earlier great novelists were experimental and even 'daring'. Among these novels Woolf included *Villette*. Woolf will sometimes express the same preoccupation with a certain aspect of the novel in two or more essays written in close proximity to each other in time. Two months after the essay discussed immediately above, Woolf wrote that the novelist should display more boldness in developing the form (*E4*, 463).

Woolf could be defensive about the Brontës and on such occasions demanded their rights to be acknowledged as great writers. Such was the case when she reviewed Logan Pearsall Smith's edition of *A Treasury of English Prose* in 1920. She criticised the shortcomings of his selection: he had devoted eleven pages to Emerson, about whose claims as a prose writer she had 'considerable doubt', while omitting anything from any of the English classics, among whom, she named the Brontës (*E3*, 172–73).

Early on in her career as a reviewer Woolf wrote several essays which considered the problem of the presentation of character in the novels she was reviewing. She admitted in her 1924 essay, 'Character in Fiction' that people greatly differed about what made a novelist's character real. If, however, the reader took a longer time period he or she would recollect some character in the 'great' Victorian novels who strike him or her as real and through whom their particular world vision was conveyed. One of her examples was *Villette* (*E3*, 426). Interestingly, though, in the typescript of this essay Woolf had cited *Jane Eyre* (*E3*, 509).

Although she had not yet begun her parallel career as a novelist, she was evidently learning her trade through the study of the novels of others. She condemned many of the novels, (which proved to be ephemeral), for their failure to convey character in a meaningful way. Many of Woolf's ideas about character in fiction have been described in the chapter comparing Leslie Stephen and Virginia Woolf as critics of Charlotte Brontë and need not be repeated here. Nevertheless, certain aspects of characterisation in the Brontës' novels still remain and should be discussed.

Woolf was familiar with Charlotte Brontë's thoughtful approach to her characters, for the latter made several remarks on the subject which were published in Clement K. Shorter's two volume *Life and Letters* (1908), which makes it clear that Charlotte was aware that her heroes and heroines were a new departure. Charlotte rejected her publisher's invitation to illustrate *Jane Eyre* and described earlier novelists' heroines and heroes as being in the main either good-looking or handsome; 'but my personages are mostly unattractive in look, and therefore ill-adapted to figure in ideal portraits' (*L&L1*, letter no. 276: To W. S. Williams, 11 March 1848, 402).

Charlotte Brontë touched on the matter in her letter declining Henry Nussey's proposal of marriage: 'It has always been my habit to study the characters of those amongst whom I chance to be thrown' (*L&L1*, no. 48: To the Rev. Henry Nussey, 5 March, 1839, 153). She also stressed that she was slow to judge characters: 'I have not the faculty of telling an individual's disposition at first sight. Before I can venture to pronounce on a character I must see it first under various lights and from various points of view' (*L&L1*, no. 82: To Ellen Nussey, 3 March 1841, 203–204).

Once Charlotte Brontë was established as a successful novelist, she wrote on her techniques for creating character. Shorter quoted a rather disingenuous letter to Ellen Nussey: 'You are not to suppose any of the characters in *Shirley* intended as literal portraits. It would not suit the rules of art, nor my own feelings, to write in that style. We only suffer reality to *suggest*, never to *dictate*' (*L&L2*, no. 391: To Ellen Nussey, 16 November 1849, 84). Resembling Woolf, Charlotte Brontë's touchstone for a book's success or failure was its characterisation. She criticised Alexander Harris's *The Emigrant Family* (lent by Williams) on this ground: 'I should say he scarcely possesses the creative faculty in sufficient vigour to excel as a writer of fiction. He *creates* nothing—he only copies. His characters are portraits—servilely accurate; whatever is at all ideal is not original' (*L&L2*, no. 343: To W. S. Williams, 5 April 1849, 40).

It is notable that neither Charlotte Brontë nor Woolf were confident about their creation of male characters in their fiction. The former replied to a criticism of *Shirley* which was shared by W. S. Williams and James Taylor (who both worked for her publisher George Smith) that she lacked 'distinctness and impressiveness in my heroes'. She accepted that they were very likely to be right since '[i]n delineating male character I labour under disadvantages: intuition and theory will not always adequately supply the place of observation and experience'. She admitted that although she was certain of her portraits of women, she was less sure about her creation of men (*L&2L*, no. 332: To James Taylor, 1 March 1849, 30). Similarly, when Woolf turned on her portrayal of men in *Night and Day,* she was anxious to know whether they convinced the reader (*L2*, letter no. 1087: To Lytton Strachey, 28 October 1919, 394).

In July 1922 Woolf welcomed the timely publication of new editions of the novels of the Brontës and Jane Austen. Both those who have already read these novels and new readers would benefit. She viewed her contemporary Georgians (among whom she included herself), as more in touch with the Victorians than with their immediate predecessors, the Edwardians. She used a metaphor of family relationships between generations to express her perceptions (*E3*, 336).

Perhaps surprisingly, the opening up of hitherto male employments to women only occurred during Woolf's lifetime. Shorter included a letter from Charlotte to Emily Brontë, in which she described the available work for women as summarised by her feminist friend, Mary Taylor: a woman could be only 'a governess, a teacher, a milliner, a bonnet-maker' or a 'housemaid'

(*L&L1*, no. 85, To Emily J. Brontë, 2 April 1841, 208). Later Mary Taylor narrowed the possible occupations for women further: in Victorian Britain the only work open to them was 'teaching, sewing or washing'. She added that the last was paid the best, was the healthiest and gave the greatest freedom. But it did not enable a woman to be self-supporting and was only open to women who were 'born to this position' (*L&L2*, no. 330: Mary Taylor to Ellen Nussey, 9 February 1849, 25–26).

Seventy years later, employment for women had not much improved, though this period witnessed the beginning of a widening of work open to women. Woolf's narrator in *A Room of One's Own*, described the 'chief occupations that were open to women before 1918': she earned her living 'by cadging odd jobs from newspapers'; by reporting on minor and local events such as a donkey show or a wedding. She supplemented her income 'by addressing envelopes, reading to old ladies, making artificial flowers, teaching the alphabet to small children in kindergarten' (*AROOO*, 37).

Both Charlotte Brontë and Virginia Woolf shared the view that novelists should not have a moralistic or didactic intent in writing fiction. The former wrote emphatically: 'I am no teacher; to look on me in that light is to mistake me. To teach is not my vocation' (*L&L2*, no. 395: To Ellen Nussey, 22 November 1849, 89). She repeated this point in a letter to her publisher, in which she stated she could not 'write a book for its moral' (*L&L2*, no. 592: To George Smith, 30 October 1852, 283). The highly intelligent friend from their schooldays, Mary Taylor, commented on this aspect of *Jane Eyre* (disapprovingly): 'Your novel surprised me by being so perfect a work of art. . . . You are very different from me in having no doctrine to preach. It is impossible to squeeze a moral out of your production' (*L&L1*, no. 296: Mary Taylor to Charlotte Brontë, 24 July 1848, 431–32). Mary Jean Corbett has convincingly suggested that Woolf never mentioned the New Women novels of the last two decades of the nineteenth century because they were devoted to the didactic message that men and women should be equals (Corbett, 26).

The subject of didacticism in the novel also cropped up in Woolf's letters. She maintained her original perspective in her maturity: when she was nearly fifty, she wrote hotly about John Middleton Murry's life of D. H. Lawrence, *Son of Woman*. She declared that she did not believe in preaching, causes, and attempts to convert: they were 'blasphemy' (*L4*, no. 2372: To Ethel Smyth, 12 May 1931, 329). Six days later, and to the same correspondent, Woolf stated the horror she felt when people tried to promote causes; the desire to convert and interfere with other people's beliefs seemed to her 'impertinent, insolent, corrupt beyond measure' (*L4*, no. 2374: To Ethel Smyth, 18 May 1931, 333).

Much of Woolf's subject matter in her novels was inherited by her from such nineteenth-century novelists as the Brontës, in particular, personal relationships. What is noticeable here is the different attitudes of the two novelists to their material. Charlotte Brontë appeared (whether consciously or unconsciously) to have accepted the male view of subject matter. Of *Jane Eyre* she wrote: 'It has no learning, no research, it discusses no subject of public interest. A mere domestic novel will, I fear, seem trivial to men of large views and solid attainments' (*L&L1*, no. 239: To W. S. Williams, 28 October 1847, 363). Similarly, she was abjectly willingly to give publishing precedence to the socially conscious novel *Ruth*, over *Villette* because Gaskell's subject matter contributed to a public debate, which her own did not (*L&L2*, no. 606: To Mrs Gaskell, 12 January 1853, 300).

By contrast, Woolf not only accepted but promoted the different subject matter of male and female novelists. She clearly saw the consequences affected every other aspect of the novel: the manner of its composition, its plotting and incidents and style (*E2*, 316). In 'Modern Novels', Woolf boldly restated her position on the novelist's subject matter—though here she only implicitly suggests this is the woman writer's perspective—when she challenged the idea that life and literature existed solely in what was generally assumed to be big rather than in what was generally considered small (*E3*, 34).

Looking at the social history of different epochs (a critical approach to the literary text inherited from Leslie Stephen), Woolf's commented on the limitations placed on women's activities in society. Unlike her father, though, she recognised that history was largely about men and written by men (*E5*, 28). Socially and economically, as late as the nineteenth century few women had occupations outside the domestic role in their homes. Merely on account of their sex, even the greatest authoresses were limited to what they could observe in their middle-class homes (*E5*, 30, 30–31). In an earlier essay, Woolf argued that the sexes were distinguished not so much by different experiences, but by the fact that they wrote about their own sex (*E2*, 316).

Woolf was familiar with Charlotte Brontë's frustration with her very limited horizon, which she expressed several times (as well as ascribing such feelings to her eponymous heroine, Jane Eyre). Charlotte Brontë's longing for experience was so intense that it affected her physically and her account leaves a painful impression on the reader. Charlotte Brontë described her reaction to her friend Mary Taylor's descriptions of her sight-seeing on the continent:

Mary's letters spoke of some of the pictures and cathedrals she had seen— pictures the most exquisite, cathedrals the most venerable. I hardly know what swelled to my throat as I read her letter: such a vehement impatience of restraint and steady work; such a strong wish for wings—wings such as wealth

can furnish; such an earnest thirst to see, to know, to learn; something internal
seemed to expand boldly for a minute. I was tantalised with the consciousness
of faculties unexercised; then all collapsed, and I despaired. (*L&L1*, no. 91: To
Ellen Nussey, 7 August 1841, 218)

Charlotte Brontë wrote the enduring result had been that 'a fire was kindled
in my very heart, which I could not quench' (*L&L1*, no. 94: To Ellen Nussey,
2 November 1841, 223). The only available response to this powerful desire
was to arrange to become a pupil at a continental school.

After the publication of *Jane Eyre*, Charlotte Brontë corresponded for a
time with G. H. Lewes. He warned her that her very limited experience of
a wider world was a handicap for a novelist, and that she would soon have
exhausted her possibilities of subject matter for creating new books. Charlotte
Brontë does not straightforwardly contradict Lewes but suggests that an individual's experience is necessarily circumscribed. If 'he' limited 'himself' to
his own experience, 'he' would be in danger of repeating himself and becoming an egotist to boot. She put this to him as a question. The rest of the paragraph has multiple question marks as if she were challenging him about the
accuracy of her own views. Despite this apparent deference, she was actually
questioning *his* views. Then she played her trump card:

> Then, too, imagination is a strong, restless faculty, which claims to be heard
> and exercised: are we to be quite deaf to her cry, and insensate to her struggles?
> When she shows us bright pictures, are we never to look at them, and try to
> reproduce them? And when she is eloquent, and speaks rapidly and urgently
> in our ear, are we not to write to her dictation? (*L&L1*: To G. H. Lewes,
> 6 November 1847, 366)

Charlotte Brontë emphasised what can only be described as inspiration or
genius taking over from the writer's conscious efforts. For then:

> an influence seems to waken in them, which becomes their master—which will
> have its own way—putting out of view all behests but its own, dictating certain
> words, and insisting on their being used, whether vehement or measured in their
> nature; new-moulding characters, giving unthought-of turns to incidents, reject-
> ing carefully elaborated old ideas, and suddenly creating and adopting new ones.
> (*L&L1*, Letter no. 263: To George Henry Lewes: 12 January 1848, 386)

Certainly, Woolf would have perfectly understood this creative process as
described by Charlotte Brontë, for finishing writing *The Waves* she had
a similar experience which she described in her diary (*DIV*, 7 February
1931, 10–11).

It is also worth noting here that Charlotte Brontë defended *Wuthering Heights*, and particularly the creation of the character of Heathcliff on the same grounds of the unconscious inspiration of genius:

> the writer who possesses the creative gift owns something of which he is not always master—something that at times strangely wills and works for itself. . . . Be the work grim or glorious, dread or divine, you have little choice left but quiescent adoption. As for you—the nominal artist—your share in it has been to work passively under dictates you neither delivered nor could question—that would not be uttered at your prayer, nor suppressed nor changed at your caprice. (Currer Bell, 'Editor's Preface to the New Edition of *Wuthering Heights*', appendix 1, *Wuthering Heights*, 310)

Nevertheless, if Charlotte Brontë defended her writing to a critical reader, she uneasily confessed to W. S. Williams on the subject of *Shirley*'s characters, which she feared could lead to her recognition as its author. Simultaneously though she insisted her protagonists were not drawn from life: 'the book is far less founded on the Real than perhaps appears. It would be difficult to explain to you how little actual experience I have had of life, how few persons I have known, and how very few have known me' (*L&L2*, no. 378: To W. S. Williams, 21 September 1849, 73).

In Woolf's long essay, 'Phases of Fiction', Charlotte Brontë was not mentioned at all, but Emily Brontë was considered in some detail under the sub-heading 'The Poets'. Woolf was now proposing that one of the characteristics of the novel was that it included its own poetic prose, derived from the prevailing 'mood and temper' of the work. Over a quarter of a century after her father's death, Woolf rejected Stephen's condemnation of *Wuthering Heights* and expressed her own high opinion of it. She took the scene of Catherine Linton (née Earnshaw) in semi-delirium pulling out the feathers from her pillow and describes it as 'a master stroke of vision' which harmoniously combined 'people and scenery and atmosphere'. Even more seldomly achieved by the novelist and yet 'more impressive' is that we glimpse through the atmosphere created by Emily Brontë 'other symbols and significances' (*E5*, 78). The poetry of *Wuthering Heights* is expressed through Catherine and Heathcliff (*E5*, 78–79).

Woolf reviewed W. L. Courtney's *The Feminine Note in Fiction* in 1905 and R. Brimley Johnson's *The Women Novelists* in 1918. W. L. Courtney's four great women novelists of the nineteenth century differed from those suggested by both Woolf and Johnson. Like Johnson and Woolf, Courtney included Jane Austen, Charlotte Brontë, and George Eliot. But both male critics exclude Emily Brontë (selected by Woolf). Courtney's fourth great woman novelist is Elizabeth Gaskell, while Johnson's is Frances Burney.

In his introduction W. L. Courtney stated his central thesis: 'The assumption is that when women write novels they introduce a particular point of view of their own, attack the problems of life from their own angle of vision, and arrive at conclusions not always the same as those which appeal to male novelists' (Courtney, vii). Woolf was disappointed that Courtney was unsuccessful in discovering the nature and explanation of the feminine elements. She believed that the time was not yet right for such a classification, and that this task would be best undertaken by a woman (*E1*, 15). Moreover, later in his introduction Courtney contradicted and undermined his essential assumption when he stated that it was 'absurd' to divide novelists according to their sex between whom there should be no distinction (Courtney, xiv). Woolf did not pick him up on this inconsistency. (*A Room of One's Own* would present the same contradictory arguments about whether men and women were different or the same, and similarly fail to reach a conclusion.)

Woolf found Courtney's division of his great four nineteenth-century writers into two schools or traditions unhelpful. The first of these derived from Charlotte Brontë and George Eliot, the second from Jane Austen and Mrs Gaskell. In this brief review Woolf was more interested in the general characteristics of women writers than in particular women writers. She referred to Courtney's claim that women novelists were not artists since their love of detail skewed the correct artistic proportions of their fiction (*E1*, 16). She omitted Courtney's stated opinion that both Charlotte Brontë and George Eliot extended these boundaries, and that after their first heavily autobiographical fictions, their subsequent ones 'were in the real sense creative and original' (Courtney, xi).

It is likely that at this early date (1905) Woolf had not yet developed her ideas on women and fiction, though they came to increasingly occupy her thoughts as she herself began her career as a novel writer. It must also be acknowledged that Courtney failed to state many general principles of female novelists; instead, he got bogged down in the detailed discussion of particular female novelists, both major and minor. If Woolf's response to Courtney's book on female novelists was one of disappointment, in 1918 she published an essay on the same subject, with which she engaged in the question of women writers in a much more characteristic way.

According to Woolf's 1918 review, R. Brimley Johnson's *The Women Novelists* not only made pertinent remarks about literature generally but, what interested her even more, 'about the peculiar qualities of literature' authored by women. She generously acknowledged his credentials for this task by claiming that he has read more fiction by women than most people had heard of (*E2*, 314).

Johnson wrote that originally women authors imitated men's novels. However, contemporary women 'assume that their powers are as great' as men's and 'their right to express themselves equally varied' (Johnson, 1). As Woolf would do, Johnson considered women novelists from the beginning of a female literary tradition which resulted in women finding themselves as writers during the century between 1778 and 1876. Woolf would borrow Johnson's championing of Aphra Behn as the first woman to earn her living by her pen (Johnson, 2).

He described Charlotte Brontë as a 'genius' whose originality separated her from earlier women novelists. Paramount among these was her 'so powerful an expression of passion as felt by women', who generally do not 'admit the power of such stormy emotions'. Her novels are also outstanding in 'being mainly inspired by memory' and by the fact that she depicted '*mutual* passion as it has been seldom revealed elsewhere' (Johnson, 164–65).

Unlike Woolf, Johnson explicitly referred to the 1913 publication of Charlotte Brontë's letters to Heger in *The Times*. For him, this explained most, but not all, of her genius: in *Jane Eyre* and *Villette* 'we have discovered the tragedy which fired her imagination, the utter loneliness which taught her to dwell on the aching void of unreturned affection, to idealise so romantically the rapture of marriage' (Johnson, 165–66). He argued that 'the emotional power of her work is entirely imaginative', because she had very limited experience and could not write about many aspects of the human condition with which she had had no contact and 'she had little interest about the trivialities of the tea-table' (Johnson, 166, 275). Like other critics, then, he was conscious of her limited material (Johnson, 169). Woolf repeated his awareness of Charlotte Brontë's experience and vision in her 1916 essay: 'to be always in love and always a governess is to go through the world with blinkers on one's eyes' (*E2*, 29).

Johnson argued that Charlotte Brontë's 'feminine ideal' differed from that of her predecessors: 'The hero, the ideal lover, is always "the Master" of the heroine' (Johnson, 171). He developed this idea further: the heroines are '"doormats"' who 'delight in *serving* the Beloved: they expect him to be a superior being, with more control over his emotions; less dependent on emotion or even on domestic comfort, appropriately concerned with matters not suited to feminine intellects, and accustomed to "keep his own counsel" about the important decisions in his life' (Johnson, 171). This line of criticism is not commented on by Woolf; neither has it been accepted by subsequent critics. Aside from *Jane Eyre* the only novel by Charlotte Brontë analysed at any length by Johnson was *Shirley*. He related it to social conditions and the position and role of women in society in a way that he did rarely. Woolf would make good these defects in *A Room of One's Own*.

Johnson and Woolf agreed about the sheer power of Charlotte Brontë's narrative. He described her powerful style: 'It bears no impress of being written at all, but is poured out rather in the heat and flurry of an instinct which flows ungovernably on to its object, indifferent by what means it reaches it, and unconscious too' (Johnson, 175). Woolf was equally enthusiastic in her description of the heady experience of reading *Jane Eyre* (*E4*, 166).

The Women Novelists also, but more briefly, commented on Emily and Anne Brontë. While he stated that many of the Brontë fans thought Emily Brontë a greater writer than her elder sister, Johnson neither endorsed nor challenged this opinion. However, several times he makes the same point using different language: Emily Brontë's *Wuthering Heights* is 'unique' in its presentation of passion (Johnson, 179): she 'stands alone for all time' (Johnson, 179). Clearly, Johnson believed that Emily Brontë's uniqueness meant that she fitted into no tradition of women writers, nor had she any literary successors.

In discussing both Emily and Anne Brontë, Johnson relied heavily on Charlotte Brontë's preface to the posthumous edition of their works. He expresses the verdict of his age (also, seemingly uncritically, accepted by Woolf) that Anne Brontë 'sheds but a pale glimmer beside her fiery sisters' (Johnson, 184). Both her novels were autobiographical in content. Johnson dismissed her achievements with a damning sentence: 'She worked quietly, but with mild resolution; reproducing exactly her own observations on life, never straying beyond what she believed to be literally true' (Johnson, 184–85).

While Woolf agreed with some of Johnson's comments about Charlotte and Emily Brontë, in her review she focused on women writers and their difficulties more generally from an angle largely derived from her father's criticism. She felt questions needed to be asked about women's lives in previous centuries: from where did eighteenth-century authoresses come and what made them challenge the view of women inherited from their predominantly male contemporary novelists? (*E2*, 314). Woolf dwelt more on the problems facing early women novelists than on their achievements as Johnson had done, who had discussed them mainly in a social vacuum. Thus, she cited Frances Burney ('the mother of English fiction') whose stepmother had her manuscripts burnt and condemned her to needlework as a penance. Likewise, Jane Austen concealed her manuscript when visitors entered the room and Charlotte Brontë 'stopped in the middle of her work to pare the potatoes' (*E2*, 315). Woolf, however, argued that these 'repressions' impacted negatively on their works. Society's opinion of women writers forced them either 'to conciliate' or to 'outrage' public opinion. She suggested that Charlotte Brontë's use of a pseudonym was not only aimed at receiving unbiased criticism, but additionally to liberate her mind from the tyrannical expectations of men from women (*E2*, 315). Woolf stressed the awareness of the woman writer of her sex is disastrous for her literary work.

To conclude this section, it is plain that the Brontës' novels remained a touchstone for the successful novel for Woolf, who cited them in a review of Olive Schreiner's letters. These epistles provided Woolf with a reason of Schreiner's failure to become 'the equal of our greatest novelists'. Her *The Story of an African Farm* was 'inevitably' compared to the novels of the Brontë sisters but Woolf felt that Schreiner's novel did not have their strength and was not a 'masterpiece' (*E4*, 5).

FULL-LENGTH ARTICLES ON THE BRONTËS

There has been a recent nascent interest in literary pilgrimages. Before exploring Woolf's account of the visit to Haworth, there will be a wider look at her attitudes to such pilgrimages and their possible derivations. She developed her own attitudes towards the subject partly by reviewing her contemporary writers' accounts of literary pilgrimages. This section will examine three books about such visits which Woolf reviewed: *The Thackeray Country* by Lewis Melville, *The Dickens Country* by Frederic George Kitton (both published in 1905), and Edward Thomas's *A Literary Pilgrimage in England* (1917). The first two books dealt with Victorian novelists, arguably the period in literature with which Woolf felt most at home. Later literary pilgrimages Woolf made (and about which she wrote) were to Thomas Carlyle and John Keats's houses in her essay 'Great Men's Houses'. Another pilgrimage she made was to their childhood holiday home in St Ives, Cornwall. As with her essays on literary pilgrimages, Virginia Stephen's journey (which she herself called a 'pilgrimage') with her siblings to Talland House was a return (and a very emotional one for her) to her Victorian childhood. First, the Brontës' own attitude towards Haworth will be considered.

Barker aimed to dispel what she called Gaskell's 'popular legend' or 'mythology' about Haworth and the Brontës: Gaskell created a 'wonderfully evocative picture of a family of genius, growing up in physical and social isolation, excluded from all the normal preoccupations of ordinary life, let alone genteel society' (Barker, 92). Barker challenged this view: 'in reality, Haworth was a busy, industrial township not some remote rural village of Brigadoon-style fantasy' (Barker, 92). It is strange that though no doubt Barker is correct, the *impression* Haworth made on the Brontës was more akin to Gaskell's description. In a letter to her brother Charlotte wrote of 'the little wide, moorland village where we reside' (*L&L1*, no. 3: To Branwell Brontë, 17 May 1831, 84). While Charlotte Brontë envisaged Ellen Nussey 'surrounded by society and friends', she emphasised that she herself did not have the same resources in Haworth, but lived 'in the solitude of our wild little hill village' (*L&L1*, no. 11: To Ellen Nussey, 11 February 1834, 107).

To the same correspondent, Charlotte wrote five years later of Haworth being 'such an out-of-the way place, one should have a month's warning before they stir from it' (*L&L1*, no. 56: To Ellen Nussey, 9 August 1839, 166). A few months later that both Patrick Brontë and his curate had lectured at the Keighley Mechanics' Institute and that the newspaper 'mentioned as a matter of wonder that such displays of intellect should emanate from the village of Haworth, situated amongst the bogs and mountains, and, until very lately, supposed to be in a state of semi-barbarism' (*L&L1*, no. 64: To Ellen Nussey, 9 April 1840, 178). While it is evident that Charlotte Brontë's tone was ironic, this report surely shows that this was a view that was held generally at the time, if not by the villagers themselves, at least by some outsiders. Further, how long was 'until very lately'? Was it until the reporter had actually heard the lectures by two men from Haworth? In a letter not included by Shorter, Charlotte Brontë wrote of her own life in Haworth as being that of 'anchorite seclusion', among 'our rude hills and rugged neighbourhood' which 'shuts out all bearers of tidings'. Nevertheless, a couple of 'curiosity-hunters' have materialised in Haworth, but she believes 'our rude hills and rugged neighbourhood' will deter others. (This letter was not used by Shorter, but appears in Smith, *LCB2*, To W. S. Williams, 22 February 1850, 350). Charlotte Brontë's final comment on Haworth was made less than a year before her death, when she agreed with Miss Wooler that it was 'as you say—a very quiet place; it is also difficult of access . . . few take courage to penetrate to so remote a nook' (Again, Shorter does not include this letter, but Smith did: *LCB3*, 19 September 1854, 290). Even without access to the last two letters just quoted, Woolf had imbibed Gaskell's view of Haworth: but it may have been a literary construct rather than the reality. It has to be concluded that while Charlotte Brontë took an entirely unromantic view of Haworth; later writers, including Woolf, romanticised the village.

Nicola J. Watson explained that 'During the eighteenth and nineteenth centuries the practice of making pilgrimages to places associated with particular authors or books developed into a phenomenon which also gave rise to an economic industry' (Watson, 1). Melville's book on Thackeray and Kitton's on Dickens belonged to a particular genre, being in the 'Pilgrimage' series. *The Dickens Country* refers to 'literary pilgrims' who visited 'literary shrines' (Kitton, xvii). This is an application of religious terminology to a secular object of worship. This was perhaps important in an era of declining religious practice when people looked for meaningful substitutes. In her reviews of them, Woolf engaged with these books, although privately she dismissed then as 'trashy books' (*L1*, no. 217: To Violet Dickinson, mid-February 1905, 178).

Melville admitted that there was not a 'Thackeray Country' in the same way as there were a Scott Country or Burns Country (and he might have added a Brontë Country) (Melville, 8). Nevertheless, Melville lists five previous authors on literary pilgrimages to places visited or lived in by Thackeray alone. Although Thackeray was well-travelled both at home and abroad, Melville argued that he was more interested in people than places. Interestingly, he visited Brussels, which was 'the scene of many incidents in Thackeray's writings' (Melville, 196). As he outlived Charlotte Brontë by eight years, it would be fascinating to know whether he ever tried to follow the footsteps of the heroine of *Villette* in Brussels.

In her 1904 Haworth essay, Woolf had expressed doubt about the validity of such journeys to the 'shrines' of great writers' houses. Are they undertaken from 'sentimental' motives? She dismissed the idea of visiting Carlyle's house with its 'sound-proof rooms', and carefully preserved manuscripts. She poked fun and suggested that instead of being charged an entrance fee, visitors should rather be required to sit an examination on Carlyle's biography of Frederick the Great. But she concluded, would-be visitors would no longer come, resulting in the closure of the house.

Woolf was ambivalent about the type of person who undertakes literary pilgrimages and their motive. She believed that it was snobbery that made people turn the typical pilgrim into a badly dressed man with 'an anaemic and docile brain' gazing at Dr Johnson's house and trying to imagine the great man. For, indeed, Woolf herself has done this, but secretly, so as not to be discovered by these writers' ghosts. Yet, the pilgrim might enjoy and learn from such an activity. We feel that we can attain a personal impression of his voice and that seeing relics of the writer's life comes as a 'revelation' (*E2*, 161). Despite some reservations and ambivalence, in her 1904 essay on Haworth and in her review of Edward Thomas's book, Woolf concluded that literary pilgrimages can have a legitimate purpose if they lead us to a better understanding of the writer's works (*E1*, 5). In her view, this justified her journey to Haworth. Kitton also raised the question of the preservation of such literary shrines. This was particularly relevant to the Brontës and Woolf alerted us to changes in Haworth.

Kitton, writing about Dickens's arrival in London in 1823, explained how much a person's geographical environment affected their writing, particularly in the creation of certain sorts of characters: Kitton had argued that London had exercised 'a fascination' over Dickens, who populated his fiction with the characters he observed in 'its various types' (Kitton, 23). Gaskell had made the same argument as Kitton made a generation later, and Woolf had absorbed from Gaskell's *Life;* the idea that Haworth and the Brontës were inseparable and that each expressed the other (*E1*, 5).

Edward Thomas devoted a section to Haworth and Emily Brontë in his *A Literary Pilgrim in England.* Thomas displayed a novel approach to literary pilgrimages. He divided the country into different areas, under which he grouped writers who had lived within that region: 'London and the home counties' considered William Blake, Charles Lamb, John Keats, and George Meredith; in 'The Thames' part were Shelley, Matthew Arnold, and William Morris; 'The Downs and the South Coast' dealt with John Aubrey, Gilbert White, William Cobbett, William Hazlitt, Richard Jefferies, Thomas Hardy, and Hilaire Belloc; 'The West Country' featured Herrick, Samuel Taylor Coleridge, and W. H. Hudson; under the title 'The East Coast and Midlands' were Cowper, George Crabbe, John Clare, Fitzgerald, George Borrow, Tennyson, and Swinburne; the 'North' was represented by Wordsworth and Emily Brontë; finally the 'Scotland' section dwelt on Burns, Scott, and R. L. Stevenson (Thomas, 7–8). I have listed these writers for three reasons: firstly, because it is noticeable that the only woman writer included is a Brontë; secondly, because it is unusual for the time in focusing not on Charlotte but Emily Brontë; and thirdly, because it implicitly implies the limitations placed on the woman writer who wanted to travel. During the nineteenth century it would not have been permissible for middle-class women to travel unaccompanied. A few women such as Marianne North broke with this convention, but the majority of Victorian women complied with it.

It is easy to be misled into thinking it was Gaskell's *Life* which first made the association of the Brontës with Haworth. Indeed, Thomas alluded to Gaskell's *Life* in his opening sentence of the section dedicated to Emily Brontë: her 'country is that tract of the West Riding of Yorkshire which is the scene of *Wuthering Heights* and of Mrs. Gaskell's *Life of Charlotte Brontë*' (Thomas, 283). What Thomas showed by including a substantial quotation from '[*Currer Bell:*]: *Preparatory Note to 'Selections [of Poems by Ellis Bell]*', was that it was Charlotte Brontë herself who identified Emily Brontë with Haworth for ever in the minds of readers; it has come to be viewed as an almost symbiotic relationship. As a poet himself, Thomas strongly related to Emily Brontë as the greatest poet among the three sisters. Also authorised by Charlotte's account of her sister, Thomas confidently asserted that Emily 'fits into the moorland—she is part of it—like the curlew and the heather, and she herself knew it. The moorland was a necessity to her, but it was also her chief pleasure and joy. Her poems always imply it, and often express it' (Thomas, 286).

Woolf does however challenge the assumption of Kitton and Gaskell about how far and how radically a place can affect its inhabitants' minds. She questions whether a London slum would have had led to the same type of novel as the Yorkshire moors. For example, in a 1905 review of two Irish novels, which were viewed as regional novels by their creators, Woolf wrote that both these authors agreed that their shared geography was 'all important' since it produced such original writers (*E1*, 77). But she undercut this when she remarked that the same place could produce writers who created completely different types of characters (*E1*, 78).

In her essay, 'Haworth, November, 1904', Woolf and her companion approached in the weather she associates with the moors of *Wuthering Heights*, being stormy and snowy. They had decided against awaiting fine weather, perhaps feeling it would have been less authentic under such conditions. Resembling Gaskell's *Life of Charlotte Brontë*, Woolf dwells on their gradual approach to the Haworth parsonage from Keighley (which, she helpfully tells the reader, it is pronounced 'Keethly'). This town, though it was largely unchanged since the Brontës' time, produced no emotion. They could imagine Charlotte Brontë, a small figure 'trotting' along and being elbowed into the gutter by a larger passer-by (*E1*, 6). This creates a rather ridiculous picture, but Woolf admitted to a growing excitement as though she was going to meet a friend who may have altered in the interval. In the village itself Woolf recorded that the church tower was a sign they had nearly reached the destined 'shrine' at which they were to worship. The village was found to be disappointing, being 'gloomy', 'dingy', and 'commonplace'. Their interest mounted again as they approached the top of the village.

They discovered that all the Brontë sites are close together: the church, the parsonage, and the Black Bull public house. The churchyard remained and Woolf referred to Gaskell's *Life* again, as she recalled its title page whose print established the tone of the whole: 'it seemed to be all graves'. (This was possibly a false memory. The Haworth edition of Gaskell's *Life of Charlotte Brontë* provides a facsimile of the original title page but there was no illustration at all on it. Woolf may, however, have attributed the illustration of 'Haworth old church as the Brontë family knew it', which was opposite page 8 in the Haworth edition of the Brontës' novels.) It is true that during the Brontës' occupancy of the parsonage their small garden was barely separate from the graveyard. The family's successors had planted a hedge and trees so that death—of which the gravestones were a daily reminder—did not so urgently and continuously intrude into their lives.

At the time of Woolf's visit the Brontë Museum was situated above Haworth's Yorkshire Penny Bank. (The Parsonage would not become the property of the Brontë Society until 1928.) The place of the Brontë relics when Woolf visited was disappointing; yet simultaneously she recognised that it offered a safe place where the memorabilia will not be destroyed. She never returned to Haworth to see the relics when they had acquired a permanent home.

In her 1904 visit, Woolf could not help being moved by the case containing the small surviving items which had belonged to Charlotte Brontë. Her shoes and dresses have long outlasted her and this transformed Woolf's attitude towards her. These relics brought Charlotte Brontë to life so that she was perceived as a woman rather than as a great writer (*E1*, 7). Here Woolf conformed to the dichotomy first established by Gaskell's *Life of Charlotte*

Brontë: 'Henceforth Charlotte Brontë's became divided into two parallel currents—her life as Currer Bell, the author; her life as Charlotte Brontë the woman' (Gaskell, *Life*, 348). This dichotomy was very important to Gaskell who reiterated this division again later when she wrote that she distinguished between the 'literary opinions of the author' and 'the domestic interests of the woman' (*Life*, 507). This is, of course, a completely false dichotomy, but perhaps one that Woolf accepted too readily. The other object that thrilled Woolf was the little stool that Emily Brontë took out with her on to the moors so that she could sit and think or plan her works. Woolf's opinion was that these contemplative acts of Emily Brontë were probably greater than anything she wrote (*E1*, 7). Woolf may have proposed this view in the light of her own experience which led her often to think that her books were better at the planning stage than when written down.

In common with the church and garden, Patrick Brontë's successor as perpetual curate, John Wade, had changed the parsonage itself by extending the building. Woolf found she could visualise the original parsonage and was not impressed by it. She disliked the colour of the building materials and altogether condemned it as 'ugly' and like a square box. They were fortunate in being admitted by the present incumbent who allowed them to satisfy their curiosity by looking round the building. Woolf thought that the small kitchen was the room in which the sisters perambulated as they composed and discussed their novels. It is ironic that this mistake led her to declare that the kitchen was the only room of any interest to her. She also was grimly interested in the recess to the left of the stairs where Emily Brontë famously chastised her bulldog Keeper when he transgressed once too often in his habit of lying on the beds' white counterpanes (*E1*, 8).

Woolf was aware that the church (apart from the tower) had been rebuilt since the Brontës' period. This was where Charlotte Brontë had worshipped and been married. Finally, she was laid to rest in it with the majority of her family. Woolf observed the slab on which were recorded the dates of seven of the Brontës. Woolf apparently was unaware that the single exception was Anne Brontë had been buried in Scarborough where she died. Woolf praised the slab's inscription from Corinthians xv, 56–57, which she quoted: 'The sting of death is sin, and the strength of sin is the law, but thanks be to God which giveth us the victory through our Lord Jesus Christ'. Woolf added her own secular tribute to Corinthians: 'however harsh the struggle, Emily and Charlotte above all, fought to victory' (*E1*, 8).

Woolf (like her father) commented on how narrow the boundaries of Charlotte Brontë's life were. In this connection it is strange that Woolf identified Haworth with Charlotte Brontë so strongly for *The Professor* (posthumously published, although the first novel she wrote) and *Villette* (1853) were mainly set abroad. Had Charlotte Brontë never been to Brussels, we would have been deprived of what Virginia Woolf regarded as her 'masterpiece'— *Villette*. Although she and Leonard Woolf were quite often on the Continent, she never expressed any interest in visiting Brussels. While the Brussels experience was so fraught with consequences for Charlotte Brontë's literary existence, it made no evident impact upon Emily Brontë or her novel.

Beth C. Rosenberg commented on 'Haworth, November, 1904' that this was among several of Woolf's early essays which takes 'the tone of her later more personal and occasional essays'. Rosenberg characterises these essays as being distinct from her reviews on more ephemeral writing of her contemporaries (Rosenberg, 278). Woolf also recognised this distinction (*E6*, 196). Rosenberg's justified praise, however, renders Woolf's own assessment of her essay somewhat ironic: she wrote it in less than two hours and doubted its worth (*L1*, no. 194: To Violet Dickinson, 26 November 1904, 158). Perhaps most important is the way in which in this essay Woolf engaged in dialogue with the Victorian period by frequently referring to Gaskell's *Life of Charlotte Brontë* and the Haworth tourism it created.

After she had written up her 1904 article on her pilgrimage to Haworth, Woolf did not devote an entire essay to Charlotte until the centenary of her birth in 1916. Seven years earlier she had reviewed another centenary essay on the American Oliver Wendell Holmes. In this, among other topics, she clearly stated the perceived value of marking such anniversaries, or 'celebrations': she argued that it enabled communications between different generations. Also, the retrospective critic offered an insight denied to writers' contemporaries (*E1*, 296). In 1916, Woolf was doubly involved in celebrating Charlotte Brontë's centenary year. In April 1916 she wrote 'Charlotte Brontë' for the *Times Literary Supplement*. Slightly confusingly, the centenary was additionally marked by a book of essays on her, which Woolf reviewed in 1917, also under the identical title of 'Charlotte Brontë'.

The 1916 essay 'Charlotte Brontë' was, despite some minor reservations, highly commendatory, so much so, that it more or less constituted a panegyric. Woolf's appreciation of Charlotte Brontë had slowly evolved and matured since her 1904 pilgrimage to Haworth. This might have been expected for she had finally completed and published *The Voyage Out* in 1915. She was now a novelist writing about another female novelist from the loved and hated Victorian period. Woolf made several interesting new points about Charlotte Brontë. She repeatedly used the editorial 'we' in this essay, thus completely drawing in and involving the reader in her appreciation of the earlier novelist. We are assumed to partake of Woolf's enthusiasm.

It occurred to Woolf that had Charlotte Brontë survived into old age, she might have overlapped with her own life. There were now very few living people who had talked with or seen her. Charlotte Brontë's reputation has not been promoted by surviving friends. Because of the brevity of her subject's life, Woolf saw her as remote from the present: she had to be imagined as 'someone who had no lot in our modern world'; instead, she had to be recreated as a figure from the 1850s, whom Woolf therefore saw as belonging to the high Victorian world (*E2*, 26). She was also remote in terms of geographical location, so Woolf suggested we viewed her as a figure who had lived in a remote parsonage on the 'wild Yorkshire Moors' (*E2*, 26).

Nevertheless, despite their temporal and geographical distance, Woolf claimed that when Charlotte Brontë's name was mentioned, we envisaged her with the same sharpness as we see that of a living contemporary and still aroused greater interest than nearly any other subject. But Woolf wondered what can be added to the knowledge of educated people about 'so strange and famous a being?' She used the editorial 'we' again and suggested that we have all made our pilgrimage to Haworth or seen pictures of it. The longevity of Elizabeth Gaskell's *Life of Charlotte Brontë* is attested to by the fact that it was this first biography which had 'stamped our minds with an ineffaceable impression' (*E2*, 27). Nevertheless, not contented with this alone, later generations of students have gathered every surviving scrap, however insignificant, that has made possible the re-creation of Charlotte Brontë's brief and fairly narrow life.

Woolf ascribed to Charlotte Brontë's novels the 'peculiarity' only possessed by 'real works of art': She created organic works (Woolf used a natural image of tree and the sap in leaves), which grow with the reader, and so comprise the reader's autobiography (*E2,* 27). Charlotte Brontë's ability to have created 'changing and living creations' in her novels is compared with the same quality which Shakespeare possessed. These achievements will be continued for future and as yet unborn generations. Despite this comparison, Woolf denied that she aimed to establish Charlotte Brontë's final literary status. All she desired to do was to offer her own observations for other readers to set beside their own.

At this stage Woolf drew back: possibly readers might outgrow Charlotte Brontë's novels and discover she has ceased to be relevant to their lives. Further, she did not desire to be pulled backwards in time into the mid-Victorian age of the Brontës or breathe fresh life into it. So, she opened *Jane Eyre* with some trepidation. She is immediately reassured and drawn into the novel as one is suddenly drawn into a 'heightened existence'. Everything is as eternal as the moors themselves. Woolf compares the reading of *Jane Eyre* to the chance meeting with 'a most singular and eloquent woman' in Yorkshire who has related her autobiography. Woolf attempted to analyse this impression which is so strong that any disturbance in the reading of the novel appears to be a disturbance *in* the novel (*E2*, 28).

Woolf explains these effects in two ways. Firstly, Charlotte Brontë 'is herself the heroine of her own novels'. Secondly, in the possible dichotomy in novelists between those who think and those who feel, Charlotte Brontë recorded emotions and not thoughts. Her characters are connected by their explosive passions. Whenever Jane Eyre or Lucy Snowe described a new place or person, the reader was certain to respond. The heroine is surrounded by 'characters of extreme individuality and intensity', who are forever marked with how she has perceived them. Other great writers, such as Tolstoy or Jane Austen, create characters whose complexity is conveyed by their effects on other characters in the novel. But in *Jane Eyre*, even when Rochester interacts with other characters he is seen from the perspective of Jane Eyre. He has no independent existence (*E2*, 29).

Woolf's pendulum swings back and forth between the successes and limitations of Charlotte Brontë. As a writer, Woolf was not surprised that Charlotte Brontë had no pleasure in writing her books. Yet, simultaneously, writing was the only employment that could liberate her from the 'burden of shame and sorrow which life laid on her weighted her to the ground'. (This seems to be the only reference to Charlotte Brontë's love letters to Heger; and it is an obscure one.) Each one of her books, Woolf argued, defied her 'torturers' as her imagination soared. Resembling a military commander, Charlotte Brontë had gathered her forces and 'proudly annihilated' her foe (*E2*, 29).

Although it is often said Charlotte Brontë described actual incidents and characters taken from her own life, Woolf probed the matter further: her uncommon and heightened sensibility vividly caught each character and scene so they formed a pattern. She was also so tenacious and tough that she persistently followed and investigated her impressions to their conclusions (*E2*, 29). Woolf believed that it was through Charlotte Brontë's style that she achieved her effects. She forged her own style and it was not derived from literary theory or from the reading of other authors. Though she was not sophisticated, she was sufficiently powerful and forceful of creating her own individual diction and rhythm. These abilities developed until they resulted in her mature and greatest achievement—*Villette* (*E2*, 30).

Woolf also attributed to Charlotte Brontë's early endeavours to make herself an artist the 'rare gift' of communicating 'the colour and of texture in words', which invested her scenes 'with a curious brilliance and solidity' (*E2*, 30). The following year (1917), Woolf defended Charlotte Brontë's style to refute Alice Meynell's criticism of particular words and phrases used by the Victorian novelist. Woolf objected to Meynell's attempt to interfere with the freedom of the writer's instinctive choice of her own language and grammar. Meynell cited examples of the words she objected to, of which Woolf gives some examples. However, while she accepted that Meynell's criticism might be true, she also found it irrelevant, since it did not adversely affect our reading experience of Charlotte's novels (*E2*, 177–78).

In her 1904 essay she had described her visit to Haworth in pursuit of a greater understanding and appreciation of the Brontës. Woolf now suggested (1916) we do not need to know her biography or to visit the parsonage. Without these external aids, we can still experience her honest and courageous integrity and perceive that she loved freedom, independence and the uncultivated country which she populated with passionate and truthful characters. Everything she wrote is the embodiment of her intellect and personality, so that Woolf ended the essay with a tribute: readers should 'rise and salute her not only as a writer of genius, but as a very noble human being' (*E2*, 31). Was this comment an acceptance of Gaskell's dichotomy of Charlotte as woman and Charlotte as writer, or has Woolf managed to unify the woman and the writer into a single Charlotte Brontë?

The other centenary essay by Woolf was a review of a celebratory book of essays devoted to the works of Charlotte Brontë to mark the hundredth anniversary of her birth. The book was called *Charlotte Brontë 1816–1916: A Centenary Memorial*. In 1916 Woolf was not yet the distinguished woman of letters she would later become, so she was not solicited to contribute an essay herself. The essays were mainly the work of an earlier generation of Brontë critics and scholars. Indeed, several of them, including the editor, Mrs Humphry Ward, were friends or acquaintances of Woolf's parents.

The contents of this centenary volume were composed of an introduction and foreword, followed by the following thirteen chapters:

*Some Thoughts on Charlotte Brontë. By Mrs Humphry Ward.
*A Word on Charlotte Brontë. By Edmund Gosse.
*Charlotte Brontë as a Romantic. By G. K. Chesterton.
Charlotte Brontë. A Personal Sketch. By Arthur Benson.
*Centenary Address at Haworth. By the Right Rev. Bishop Welldon.
Charlotte Brontë in Brussels. By M. H. Spielmann.
Story of the Brontë Society. By H. E. Wroot.
*The Place of Charlotte Brontë in Nineteenth Century Fiction. By the late
    Dr Richard Garnett.
*Charlotte and Emily Brontë: A Comparison and a Contrast. By Professor
    C. E. Vaughan, M.A.
Charlotte Brontë in London. By Sir Sidney Lee, LL.D.
The Spirit of the Moors. By Halliwell Sutcliffe.
The Brontës as Artists and Prophets. By J. K. Snowden.
A Brontë Itinerary. By Butler Wood.
[* = Essayists in this collection of essays discussed by Woolf in her review.]

Woolf first commented on the sheer diversity of the opinions held by the thirteen contributors of essays to the book. She remarked that few writers after the lapse of a hundred years would still be able to provoke a lively discussion (*E2*, 193). In Woolf's opinion Mrs Humphry Ward's essay was overall the most complete, not only because it was the opening essay, but also owing to the fact that she was herself a practising novelist and, she further gained authority because she was an experienced and widely read person (*E2*, 193). This statement surprises when compared with Woolf's views on Mrs Humphry Ward, as expressed in her letters and diaries which were totally hostile to the older writer. One example from each will suffice. In a letter Woolf wrote that reading Ward's *Eltham House* had been morally deleterious to her, and snobbishly added that her nurse was thoroughly enjoying it (*L2*, no. 733: To Lady Robert Cecil, 25 October 1915, 68). In her diary Woolf wrote that Ward's novels had the same effect on the body as influenza had on the mind (*D1*, 30 October 1918, 211). Perhaps she considered Mrs Humphry Ward a better critic than novelist. Alternatively, the difference between Woolf's public and private response may also have been personal. Corbett quoted Octavia Hill's biographer's revelation that Julia Stephen recommended Mrs Humphry Ward to her daughters as a role model (Corbett, 144). Mrs Humphry Ward also referred in her centenary essay to Leslie Stephen as one of George Smith's authors. It is impossible to speculate as to what thoughts this reference might have created in his daughter. But it is clear that Woolf's response to Mrs Humphry Ward was shot through by associations with both her Victorian parents.

Nevertheless, there was some critical agreement between the two writers; the older novelist, like the younger one, believed that Emily Brontë was greater 'by far' than Charlotte Brontë (*CBACM*, 37). Strangely enough, what Woolf took the greatest issue with was Mrs Humphry Ward's dislike of the three curates in *Shirley*; in Woolf's view these same curates proved that Charlotte Brontë had a sense of humour. Nevertheless, Woolf agreed with some of Mrs Humphry Ward's statements, particularly that the pre-eminent quality in Charlotte and Emily Brontë's novels is their 'poetry' (*CBACM*, 24). Overall, Woolf approved of Mrs Humphry Ward's essay, and praised her as a good critic whose criticism was 'subtly suggestive' (*E2,* 193).

The second essay in the centenary book was by Edmund Gosse. Woolf was interested in his imagining a talk with Charlotte Brontë, by which (she thought) he would probably have been greatly disconcerted (*E2*, 193). Woolf may have remembered this essay, for when she wrote an article on 'Mr Gosse and His Friends', she repeated this point. She shrewdly observed that Gosse was fascinated by genius, except when it was 'prudish and provincial', and this may have alienated him from the Brontës (*E3*, 106–107). In his centenary essay on Charlotte Brontë Gosse considered (as many before him and many after would do) that happiness might have benefited her.

Woolf then skipped to the fifth essay by Bishop Welldon. As was appropriate to his professional calling he wished to consider Charlotte Brontë's religion. He adopted the opposite point of view from Gosse. For Welldon, in a sentence which Woolf quoted in her own review, wrote: 'If Charlotte Brontë owed much to her own life, most of all did she owe to its sadness' (*CBACM*, 74). Woolf expressed her own agreement with Bishop Welldon. She urged that Charlotte Brontë's passion resulted from her inner conflict; lacking this she would have been a different person and writer (*E2*, 194).

Woolf had not approached writing the review with an intention of plodding through the essays in the order they appeared in the book. She bracketed essays together for the effect of producing opposing or contradictory opinions as to Charlotte Brontë's achievements. Woolf then attempted to reconcile the three essays she had just mentioned. She found that the different views were not incompatible and that they performed a useful function. She then proceeded to discuss 'more general questions' which the book raised. As with so many critics of Charlotte Brontë's novels the question of how far they were autobiographical cropped up in this book. In the eighth essay Richard Garnett found Charlotte Brontë's novels limited by her creation of her characters through her own biography. According to Garnett, her protagonists were not created by 'sheer force of imagination.' The consequence was that her material, which was all subjective, had been 'exhausted' (*CBACM*, 167). For Woolf the disagreement arose from a use of insufficiently defined terms: 'what is meant by "sheer force of imagination"', and she confessed herself puzzled by Garnett's division of writers into 'the old subjective and objective' (*E2*, 194). Woolf turned to the ninth essay by Professor C. E. Vaughan, which she noted contradicted Richard Garnett and reversed his conclusion. Vaughan described Charlotte and Emily Brontë as 'above all, great imaginative writers' (*CBACM*, 182).

After reading these five essays Woolf concluded that the general consensus was that Charlotte Brontë 'is the novelist of passion, of intensity, of revolt' (*E2*, 194). However, only one of the critics in this volume of essays made 'an unexpected contribution.' This was G. K. Chesterton's essay, the third in the book. It is difficult to decide how seriously she really took Chesterton's anecdote about an Irish friend living in Yorkshire. This friend, he wrote, 'once made to me the suggestive remark that the towering and over-masculine barbarians and lunatics, who dominate the Brontë novels, simply represent the impression produced by the rather boastful Yorkshire manners upon the more civilised and sensitive Irish temperament' (*CBACM*, 52). Woolf quoted this long sentence verbatim. She proceeded to find this 'all the more suggestive' if one considered the Celtic influence on the Brontë. (This was a pet theme of Mrs Humphry Ward, but neither Chesterton nor Woolf acknowledged their debt to her.)

Readers of the Brontës and their critics still had 'much to ponder and to guess', yet in Charlotte Brontë's centenary year, despite differences, all agreed that they were regarding a 'star' (*E2*, 194–95). Woolf closed her review with a long sentence from Gosse's essay, which included a phrase quoted from *Villette*: Charlotte Brontë was, '"furnace-tried by pain, stamped by constancy," and out of her fires she rose, a Phoenix of poetic fancy, crude yet without a rival, and now, in spite of all imperfections, to live for ever in the forefront of creative English genius' (*CBACM*, 45; *E2*, 195). Lucy Snowe thus described what she mistakenly believed Emanuel's mental attitude to his first dead love to be (*Villette*, 585).

Evidently, *Villette* was so real to Woolf that she referred to a scene in the novel while writing a review of Francis Gribble's *Rachel. Her Stage Life and Her Real Life* (1911). Charlotte Brontë had described an actress called Vashti in *Villette* based on the actress Rachel, whom she had seen in a play on a London visit. Woolf questioned whether Rachel was real off stage, or during the performance Charlotte saw. Woolf quoted Lucy Snowe's fascinated and horrified description of Vashti/Rachel's acting:

> I had seen acting before, but never anything like this: never anything which astonished Hope and hushed Desire; which outstripped Impulse and paled Conception; which, instead of merely irritating Imagination with the thought of what *might* be done, at the same time fevering the nerves because it was *not* done, disclosed power like a deep, swollen, winter river, thundering in cataract, and bearing the soul, like a leaf, on the steep and steel sweep of its descent. (*EI*, 353; *Villette*, 323–24)

It is our misfortune that Woolf never devoted a full-length essay to *Villette*. Nevertheless, Woolf's full-length essays on Charlotte Brontë were so perceptive that she received an unexpected and unwanted response from some of her more conventional older women friends, who did not appreciate her modernist experiments in her novels. (It is now impossible to determine whether they read the 1916 or 1917 essay on Charlotte Brontë. The editors of Woolf's diaries think it was 'probably' the earlier essay, as among Janet Case's papers a copy of it was found.) Woolf described this conversation in her diary. Margaret Llewelyn Davies and Janet Case had a shared response to these essays. Llewelyn Davies said they much preferred Woolf's criticism to her novels (*DI*, 15 November 1919, 313). Woolf's response was curiously aggressive: she lost her temper and attacked what she believed to be the inadequacies of Margaret Llewelyn's character. This suggested that Woolf sometimes desired to look forward not backward and to escape from her Victorian past and its writers in order to pursue her experiments in the contemporary modernist novel. But in her essays, Woolf never really escaped the influence of that past, and particularly her father's. It is worth mentioning that during her own lifetime Woolf was famed as much for her essays as her novels, and that the two pulled her in opposite directions. Her essays tugged at her emotions and frequently look back to the Victorian age and are largely conventional in form. By contrast, her novels were consciously written as experimental modernist endeavours, deriving from her intellect. However, here again there was a dichotomy: often the content of Woolf's fiction derives from emotions and events she had experienced during her Victorian family period, though she strove to embody them in a modernist form.

Emily Brontë did not have an essay solely devoted to a discussion of her work. However, the 1916 essay on Charlotte Brontë was revised and a discussion of her younger sister was added to it for its publication in *The Common Reader First Series*. This increased scope was indicated in the essay's title, '*Jane Eyre* and *Wuthering Heights*'. The material which Woolf had used in her earlier essay will be silently passed over, and only the new content will be discussed here.

In the earlier essay Woolf had compared Charlotte Brontë's achievements to those of Shakespeare. The later essay dropped this comparison in favour of a more modest claim. Thomas Hardy's *Jude the Obscure* had been referred to in the 1916 essay. Here the comparison is worked out more fully. These two writers are alike characterised by their powerful personalities and their narrow vision (*E4*, 167). Although Hardy and Charlotte Brontë's selves were limited, they achieved more in their novels than novelists whose focus was less concentrated and who did not dwell on themselves (*E4*, 167). Woolf was now more critical of Charlotte Brontë's style of writing, which she had praised in 1916: and again, she aligned her with Thomas Hardy and his style: both appeared to have based their style on a 'stiff and decorous journalism' (*E4*, 167).

Woolf qualified and modified the appreciation of Charlotte Brontë that had characterised her praise of her in the 1916 essay. Although she continued to be impressed with 'the red and fitful glow of the heart's fire which illumines her page', Woolf also reversed her opinion of certain aspects of Charlotte Brontë's novels, although there was beauty in her creation of her characters, they remained 'vigorous and elementary'. Where she had argued against Mrs Humphry Ward's condemnation of the curates in *Shirley*, which she saw as evidence of Charlotte Brontë's sense of humour, she now found her comic touch to be 'grim and crude'. She breathed new life into her father's opinion that Charlotte Brontë lacked 'a philosophic view of life' and added rather dismissively that her view of life 'is that of a country parson's daughter' *E4*, 168). Despite this attempt to arrive at a detached criticism, Woolf was still captivated by the poetic quality of the novels and the strength of Charlotte Brontë's personality.

It was Charlotte and Emily Brontë's expression of 'their more inarticulate passions' which made them poets, though they ostensibly wrote in prose. Both of them invoked nature to convey the passion of their characters, although they were not concerned with its minutiae: instead, they succeeded in carrying on the emotion and illuminating the meaning of their novels (*E4*, 168). Because they wrote as poets, Charlotte and Emily Brontë employed a language which was inseparably combined with this poetic quality. As poets, they created a mood rather than detailed observations. Elsewhere, Woolf argued that the reader's first response must be emotional. But if, in fiction, a wallowing in emotion was encouraged, it was as destructive as it would be in life. Nevertheless, this pleasure can be safely enjoyed from the experience of the 'intoxicating' effects derived from the reading of great nineteenth-century novelists, among whom she cited Charlotte Brontë (*E3*, 340).

Woolf argued that *Wuthering Heights* is more difficult to understand than *Jane Eyre*, because Emily Brontë was 'a greater poet' than Charlotte Brontë. This was because in *Wuthering Heights* Emily Brontë saw beyond her own individuality and did not speak at all in her own character, nor treated her protagonists as alter egos of herself. She had a wider and more general conception of the world than her older sister and seemed to be breaking out of the traditional nineteenth-century form of the novel. It almost suggested that Woolf saw Emily Brontë as an exploder of the nineteenth-century novel, who was therefore endowed with her own endeavours. Woolf struggled with language to express this (*E4*, 169). For all these perceived qualities in *Wuthering Heights*, to Woolf it was not wholly successful; she agreed with her father's opinion that it would be the poetry of Emily Brontë that would last the longest. Nevertheless, Woolf attributed to Emily Brontë 'the rarest of all powers': she abolished the need for facts and with a few sketches indicated the spirit behind a face without the necessity of a body; by writing of the moors, she made 'the wind blow and the thunder roar' (*E4*, 169–70).

Chapter Six

A Room of One's Own
and Three Guineas

A ROOM OF ONE'S OWN

Woolf had been invited to give a lecture at Newnham and Girton, two women's colleges in Cambridge on the subject of 'women and fiction' in October 1928. She revised and expanded it into a feminist polemic which was published a year later as *A Room of One's Own*. When it first appeared, fellow writer Rebecca West immediately recognised its uniqueness and importance when she described it as 'an uncompromising piece of feminist propaganda: I think the ablest yet written' (*VWCA*, volume II, 169). Ellen Bayuk Rosenman confirmed this when over sixty years later she wrote of *A Room of One's Own*: 'The importance of the work itself is difficult to overestimate. It was the first literary history of women writers and the first theory of literary inheritance in which gender was the central category' (Rosenman, 11). In this polemic, Woolf picks up all the ideas about female writers that had previously featured, albeit briefly, across the broad range of her literary essays. All these ideas combine into a convincing conclusion that women need financial independence and a private space of their own if they are to develop their writerly skills. Additionally, I consider *Virginia Woolf and Fiction: The Manuscript Versions of* 'A Room of One's Own', edited by S. P. Rosenbaum. This is particularly relevant as we see the creative mind of Woolf at work.

It is tempting to assume that the Brontës were integral to the lecture on women and fiction from the first paragraph of *A Room of One's Own* in which Woolf attempts to tease out the exact interpretation of the subject of 'women and fiction'. Indeed, the reader may feel that the completely different opening of *Women and Fiction* is 'a sort of sacrilege', as Woolf herself feels when she considers that Milton's *Lycidas* had been revised.

Although Woolf probably agrees with the views expressed in the polemic, she creates a fictitious narrator: '"I" is only a convenient term for somebody who has no real being' (*AROOO*, 6). She suggests several names for her fictitious narrator; the surnames differ but the forename is always 'Mary', so I will refer to the narrator as Mary. In the manuscript version, Woolf develops the nature of her narrator in more detail: '<I am not a lecturer—a professor. I am a writer a> strolling ~~Mendicant~~ peddler; the kind of person who, in medieval times travelled round the villages selling lace & ballads to women at their cottage doors, & passing on gossip of doubtful veracity. what I offer is <a hidden basket of odds & ends for you to buy, or reject> (*WF*, 3–4). Woolf's first creation of a literary itinerant peddler was in *The Mistress of Mistress Joan Martyn'*, written in 1906, but only posthumously published.

After several revisions, Woolf did place the Brontës in the opening paragraph of *A Room of One's Own*. She offers various possibilities as to how she might tackle the subject of 'women and fiction'. Firstly, she could make a few remarks about past female writers. It is notable that all these authoresses are taken from the past; there are no contemporaries, although nearly three decades of the twentieth century have passed by the time *A Room of One's Own* was published in 1929. In her list of prominent women writers only the physical environment of the Brontës is described. Secondly, Mary states that she could have talked about 'women and what they are like'; thirdly, 'women and the fiction they write'; fourthly, 'women and the fiction that is written about them'. The fifth option was the one Mary adopts: she combines all these interpretations in her exploration of 'women and fiction' (*AROOO*, 5).

Mary adopts an approach to women's fiction in a socially aware way that had been defined and practised by Leslie Stephen in his literary criticism. He described it in the following way: the writer expressed his own individuality, but that individual is also 'a constituent part of society. . . . He utters his own thoughts, but he is also the organ through which the spirit of the age utters its thoughts. He looks upon the world, but he is also, in part at least, a product of its development'. Stephen argued that for a genuine knowledge the literary critic should also know about the social history of an author's time (*SEL*, 24–25). Similarly, Mary is interested in what social conditions prevail at different times which account for the production (or lack of it) of fiction by women (*AROOO*, 26). To discover the answers to these questions, Mary turns to the historians for facts. She is aware that to obtain such information history needs to be radically rewritten—and she suggests one of the young women in her audience might do this. If Mary and her contemporaries think back through their mothers, so too did nineteenth-century women novelists; without this tradition masterpieces could not be written (*AROOO*, 62–63).

The idea of women writers thinking back through their mothers is not entirely original to Virginia Woolf, as she was probably aware. In *The*

Library of Leonard and Virginia Woolf: A Short Catalog is listed *The Letters of Elizabeth Browning*, edited by Frederic G. Kenyon. It was published by Charlotte Brontë's own publisher, Smith, Elder. Woolf's copy was the third edition published in 1898. In a letter of 7 January 1845, Barrett Browning lamented the same lack of a woman's tradition in terms of the metaphor of direct female ancestors. She felt the lack of 'the faculty of poetry. . . . England has had many learned women, not merely readers but writers of the learned languages, in Elizabeth's time and afterwards . . . and yet where were the poetesses?' Like Woolf she realised the immense achievement of Elizabethan literary poetry, but asked 'why did it never pass, even in the lyrical form, over the lips of a woman? How strange! And can we deny that it was so? I look everywhere for grandmothers and see none' (Volume I, 231–32).

Woolf develops this further in the manuscript versions of *Women and Fiction*: she distinguishes what looking back through our mothers as opposed to our fathers actually means. If we look back through our fathers, we consider ourselves as the inheritors of civilisation. By contrast, modern civilisation is not the creation of our mothers, and a woman is at least partially an alien and a critic of male civilisation. She contrasts a man in Whitehall with a woman sitting in a tree in a primeval jungle (*Women and Fiction: The Manuscript Versions of* A Room of One's Own (142–43). 'Thinking back through our mothers', Woolf is aware that if contemporary women had remained content to be shut up in sitting rooms embroidering bags' and occasionally 'taking a walk on the leads and looking at the view', men would not have felt compelled to assert their masculinity. This is presumably a reference to *Jane Eyre*. Interestingly, Woolf here sees Jane Eyre taking a walk on the leads as uncontroversial and not subversive of men's sense of their own virility (*WFMV*, 191).

There is undeniably a great deal of anger in *A Room of One's Own*, and it is not confined to Charlotte Brontë and/or Jane Eyre. In this feminist polemic the incidence of the word 'anger', 'angry', or 'rage' is twenty-four. Woolf or her narrator are most interested in understanding the emotion of anger in both herself and others, male and female. It is enlightening to trace anger in *A Room of One's Own*. The reader will be presented by a series of verbal snapshots of reactions to anger in this text; the material presented will enable him or her to decide which of the reaction(s) over the decades seem most convincing.

The anger of the narrator is first aroused only three pages into the text. She describes being refused entry to the university library because she is neither accompanied by a fellow, nor possesses a letter of introduction. She curses the library and 'descended the steps in anger' (*AROOO*, 7). Her anger is reported in a matter-of-fact manner, being neither condemned nor justified.

Researching her subject in the British Museum Library, the narrator finds herself drawing an unflattering sketch of the misogynistic Professor von X who is engaged in writing 'his monumental work' whose title is *The Mental, Moral, and Physical Inferiority of the Female Sex* (*AROOO*, 28). The sketch makes the Professor look 'very angry'. From this emerges 'the submerged truth' that the drawing of the professor had been done in anger. While she was daydreaming, her pencil had independently sketched this portrait. She asks why she was angry. She describes this anger metaphorically as a lurking 'black snake'. She freely acknowledges her emotion as anger. She explains her instinctive anger which she sees as 'nothing specially remarkable'. She explains and then dismisses her anger: she did not like to be told she was inherently the inferior of the ugly and angry professor.

The narrator is interested in why the professors (collectively) are angry. Her conclusion is that 'it was anger that had gone underground and mixed itself with all kinds of other emotions. To judge from its odd effects, it was anger disguised and complex, not anger simple and open' (*AROOO*, 28–29). Their books about women were written 'in the red light of emotion and not in the white light of truth' (*AROOO*, 30). Over lunch, Mary ruminates over the professors' anger. A glance at a newspaper reveals that England is a patriarchy; men possess all the 'power and the money and the influence'. They control practically everything, yet they reveal their anger when they write about women. Mary perceives that their subject is actually themselves, not women. The latter function like mirrors for men which enlarge men's images of themselves. Napoleon and Mussolini have to insist women are inferior, or they would cease to enlarge men (*AROOO*, 32–33).

Mary devotes a considerable number of pages to a discussion of 'the famous four' nineteenth-century women novelists. Mary believes that Jane Austen was satisfied with her circumscribed existence; however, the same was not true of Charlotte Brontë. Mary proceeds to attack Charlotte Brontë for allowing her anger to distort *Jane Eyre*. Opening chapter 12 the narrator reads 'Anybody may blame me who likes'. Mary immediately equates Charlotte Brontë with her character and asks what she was being blamed for. A long passage from *Jane Eyre* is quoted in which the eponymous heroine surveys the countryside from the roof of Thornfield Hall and longs to live out her existence in a wider world where she could have a greater variety of experiences. Jane complains that women have the same feelings as their male relatives and men should not confine their sisters to so-called feminine tasks at home. Men should not condemn or laugh at women if they harbour greater ambitions (*AROOO*, 65–66). Mary then finds a jerk is caused in the narrative by the return to Jane's actual story, with the abrupt description of Grace Poole's laugh: it is 'an awkward break' in the narrative and disturbs the continuity of *Jane Eyre*. Though Charlotte Brontë had more 'genius' than Jane

Austen, her 'indignation' was disruptive and interfered with the complete expression of her genius. Mary uses an image taken from the male's military profession: Charlotte Brontë was 'at war with her lot' (*AROOO*, 66–67).

As in other features which seem almost inherent in *A Room of One's Own*, so effective are they, that it is surprising that the phrase 'an awkward break' and the reference to Grace Poole are not in the manuscript versions of *A Room of One's Own*. In these earlier versions we see Woolf struggling towards the memorable phrase; this makes the relevant passage worth quoting at some length (though Woolf often heavily revises passages, so the number of deletions does not, alone, enable us to draw definite inferences):

> <Heavens>Heavens, What power – what indignation! I had opened at Chapter 13, <12> where Jane Eyre climbed<s> onto the roof & looked out afar & my eye was caught by the phrase "Anybody may blame me who likes". And what are they blaming Charlotte Brontë for, I asked. It was for going now & then for a walk by myself in the grounds; it was for this terrible sin; she used to climb <up> onto the roof & look out over the fields & hills & the dim sky-line & when Mrs Fairfax was making jellies & she used to gaze at the distant view & long "for a power of vision etc. That she used to long & then she used to long

> 'Who blames me? Many no doubt.' (105)

Various critics discuss the passage and its treatment of women's anger as it appears in the final version. Broadly speaking, the evaluation of anger in *A Room of One's Own* has changed with the different waves of the feminist movement. For another woman writer, a feminist of the 1970s, Adrienne Rich, Woolf's anger is the emotion that she was most aware of in *AROOO*:

> In rereading Virginia Woolf's, *A Room of One's Own* (1929) for the first time in some years, I was astonished at the sense of effort, of pain taken, of dogged tentativeness, in the tone of that essay. And I recognised that tone. I had heard it often enough, in myself and in other women. It is the tone of a woman almost in touch with her anger, who is determined not to appear angry, who is *willing* herself to be calm, detached, and even charming in a roomful of men where things have been said which are attacks on her very integrity. Virginia Woolf is addressing an audience of women, but she is acutely conscious—as she always was—of being overheard by men. . . . She drew the language out into an exacerbated thread in her determination to have her own sensibility yet protect it from those masculine presences. Only at rare moments in that essay do you hear the passion in her voice; she was trying to sound as cool as Jane Austen, as Olympian as Shakespeare, because that is the way the men of culture thought a writer should sound. ('When We Dead Awaken', Rich, 37)

Rich believes that women need to express that anger. If women try to be objective and detached, as Woolf is, 'we will betray our own reality'. Women should not try to sound like Jane Austen or Shakespeare: our lives are more complex than Austen's, and being women, we know more about ourselves than Shakespeare did (48–49). Rich argues that the victimisation and the anger women experience are real, and 'have real sources, everywhere in the environment, built into society, language, the structures of thought' (49).

In another essay, '*Jane Eyre*: The Temptation of a Motherless Women', written three years later, Rich critiques Woolf's comments on Charlotte Brontë. Rich criticises Woolf's remarks about Charlotte Brontë on several grounds. The passage from chapter 12 which Woolf had seen as Charlotte Brontë's inartistic intrusion into the text, which undermines its 'integrity'; for Rich constitutes Brontë's 'feminist manifesto'. Further, Rich views its message as equally relevant in the 1970s, and still 'unacceptable to many'. In voicing these sentiments, Rich believes that they still lay one 'open to blame and to entrenched resistance' (97). While Woolf complains about Brontë sacrificing her artistic integrity, Rich reverses the judgement, while employing the same word: 'As a child, she rejects the sacredness of adult authority; as a woman, she insists on regulating her conduct by the pulse of her own integrity' (106).

In the late 1990s, Jean Long convincingly argues that 'Woolf's understanding of [Charlotte] Brontë is not straightforward' (*WSA,* volume 3, 1977, 80). Long argues that this may be accounted for by their different backgrounds— although, as we have seen, they also had much in common. Long, however, persuasively suggests that Woolf's response to 'strong personal emotion in literature was an aesthetic one'. Nevertheless, it is possible that Woolf is expressing the common Victorian opinion of Charlotte Brontë's novel as coarse (Long, 80–81). Long states that the Victorians were much preoccupied with the association of anger with the feminine, a combination which disturbed them. In the manuscript version of *A Room of One's Own*, however, where Charlotte Brontë is contrasted with Florence Nightingale, the former gains approval because she thinks 'passionately' (184). Presumably these 'passionate' thoughts might contain anger?

In 1986, Mary Jacobus also implies that Woolf (rather than simply her narrator) was herself ambivalent about the expression of anger by women (Jacobus, 35). Quoting Jane's complaints, she suggests is a covert way of expressing Woolf's own resentments at the reception authoresses have received and continued to receive without having to put herself forward to utter these grievances in her own voice. There remains the central ambivalence though at the heart of *A Room of One's Own*: Jane's anger may distort *Jane Eyre*; at the same time this emotion is justified and needs to be expressed by women writers.

As we approach nearer our own time, Eleanor McNees, writing in 2015, expresses attitudes towards Woolf on *Jane Eyre* which reveal further modifications. McNees expresses doubt about whether the Victorian and modern age could really be distinguished (*The Cambridge Quarterly*, 119). Criticism of Woolf by this time had begun to concentrate on Woolf's troubled relationship with her Victorian past.

Finally, a 2018 article is an indicator of present criticism on Woolf and Brontë's anger. Margaret Kotler tries to look beyond the personal emotion of anger as it was expressed by Brontë and criticised by Woolf. Kotler maintained that Woolf views anger as being impersonal and objective: 'A project grounded in negative, but impersonal, affect does not conceptualise anger as a personally exhausting emotion to overcome, but as a critical methodology that supports a more sustainable feminist politics' (*WSA*, volume 24, 2018, 53).

Many women readers who were Woolf's contemporaries responded to *A Room of One's Own* with their own anger about the position of women, as some of their letters to Woolf reveal. One correspondent went out of her way to praise Woolf's approach, adopting a neologism to convey her appreciation of how 'un-angrily' Woolf had crystallised the current position of women. But the writer then bitterly complains: 'Our approach to work & to relationships is made extraordinarily confused & difficult because women (apparently) aren't people; they are suspicious strangers, or pets or performing animals' (*WSA*, volume 12, 2006, 71 and 72). Another woman who has been repressing her anger burst out to Woolf that her polemic expresses 'directly all my hidden rebellions' (*WSA*, volume 12, 2006, 87). Another woman expresses anger and resentment: 'I am greatly hindered by the fact that my work is inextricably mixed with a sense of rebellion. It poisons my outlook' (*WSA*, volume 12, 2006, 74).

By contrast, some women took inspiration from the polemic to take startling and positive steps. For example, one woman wrote to say after having read *A Room of One's Own,* she decided to devote a property she owned in France to the establishment of a woman's college, modelled on Girton College in Cambridge (*WSA*, volume 12, 2006, 86). Yet another correspondent also found inspiration. Although she earns a salary, she often feels too tired to write at the end of a day's work. Nevertheless, Woolf has 'excited me with the thought that I may in some minute degree help to give Shakespeare's sister the opportunity she has been waiting for all these centuries' (*WSA*, volume 12, 2006, 68).

Woolf knew about the financial remuneration Charlotte Brontë received for her novels from Shorter, who writes that it did not raise the household above 'comparative penury' (Shorter, *L&L2*, 75). He compares what she was paid with what contemporary (1908) novelists would receive. By his calculations,

Jane Eyre for which its author received £500, would have, in 1908, been paid £5,000 which would have enabled the family to live in comfort. For the copyright for the three novels published in her lifetime Charlotte Brontë received £1,500. Shorter writes that the manuscript, still extant, would have now fetched £1,000. He thinks that this was nobody's fault, but in Woolf's first polemic her narrator berates Charlotte Brontë as a 'foolish woman' for not having extorted more from her publishers (*AROOO*, 67). It is highly significant that Shorter apparently decided not to publish a letter from Charlotte Brontë in which she haggled for greater financial remuneration from her publisher. It suggests that he wanted to present her in a certain way which such bargaining might clash with or contradict. Shorter was strongly influenced by Gaskell's *Life of Charlotte Brontë* and was himself protective of the latter's posthumous reputation. The letter he omits reveals that, contrary to what Woolf thought, Charlotte Brontë knew the value of her books. The letter in question was published by Margaret Smith in the first volume of her edition of *The Letters of Charlotte Brontë* and reads: 'One hundred pounds is a small sum for a year's intellectual labour, nor would circumstances justify me in devoting my time and attention to literary pursuits with so narrow a prospect of advantage'. She expresses the conviction (which was her way of suggesting a course of action to her publisher) that they would make further payments to her if *Jane Eyre* sold better than anticipated (*LCB1*: To Messrs Smith, Elder and Co, 12 September 1847, 540). This omission distorts Woolf's estimate of the Brontës as *professional* writers and Charlotte's shrewd knowledge of her worth to her publisher. It is noteworthy, though, that there is none of this harsh judgement and condemnation of Charlotte for having sold her copyrights outright in the manuscript version of *A Room of One's Own*.

Mary devotes considerable space to a discussion of 'the famous four' nineteenth-century women writers, whom she named as Jane Austen, and George Eliot, as well as Charlotte and Emily Brontë. She wonders why all these women wrote novels, for they had very little else in common. The only 'possibly relevant fact' is their childlessness. Woolf had much earlier criticised a novelist whose novel conveys the belief that woman's 'real task of living' is 'marriage and motherhood'. Woolf's expresses her contempt for this view with the acid observation: 'The prosaic mind may be tempted to suggest that the world might, perhaps be considerably poorer if the great writers had exchanged their books for children of flesh and blood' (*EI*, 40). Mary suggests that not all of the four great nineteenth-century women novelists had found their best genre for their talents: she opines that Emily Brontë's powers would have been best expressed in 'poetic plays' (*AROOO*, 64).

By 1929, Woolf had reversed her 1904 description of Charlotte Brontë's style. She now believes that women need to develop a style of their own and she accuses Charlotte Brontë of having imitated the sentence men had evolved for themselves; but she 'stumbled and fell with that clumsy weapon in her hands'. Jane Austen had mockingly rejected this masculine sentence and invented her own. The consequence was that although she was less of a genius than Charlotte Brontë, she achieved more. Woolf's narrator regards the core of art to be a full and free expression; lacking a long tradition of authoresses make this difficult for women writers and impact women's writing negatively. (The influence of this, Woolf judges, still affects her own female contemporaries. Despite some unresolved ambivalence towards the modernist writer Dorothy Richardson's multi-volume *Pilgrimage*, she credits her with the creation of the feminine sentence.)

Woolf claims great nineteenth-century authoresses were both inheritors and originators who came 'into existence because women have come to have the habit of writing naturally' (*AROOO*, 104). Nevertheless, Woolf recognises significant changes which had occurred since the Brontë sisters wrote and admonishes the female student audience that they no longer had excuses for not working to create the environment for a female Shakespeare to be born. The peroration was optimistic and appreciative. She had returned to the quest of the young women in 'A Society' when she declares her conviction, or instinctively feels, that 'good books are desirable and that good writers . . . are still good human beings' (*AROOO*, 104). These alterations in Woolf's opinions perhaps illustrate her theory that the greatest organic novels change as a reader progressed through life and understands more than hitherto, owing to a larger range of experiences.

In *A Room of One's Own* Woolf discerns the fundamental difference between Charlotte and Emily Brontë. In *Jane Eyre*, the reader is aware of the authoress intruding herself into her novel to complain about the bad way women are treated in comparison with men. This expression of a personal grievance interferes with the artistic unity of *Jane Eyre*. By contrast, Emily Brontë kept herself out of *Wuthering Heights* and did not distort it by any expression of anger.

Woolf, however, seems to negate her previous argument of male and female sentences being distinct and different; she proposes the necessity of androgyny for both sexes: 'Some marriage of opposites has to be consummated' in the minds of both male and female writers. Michelle Barrett argues that Woolf's attitude towards 'the "equality/difference" debate' moves from androgyny to differences between the sexes between *A Room of One's Own* and *Three Guineas* (*A Room of One's Own/Three Guineas*, x). From what has been said above, it is clear that the transition is not as neat or as orderly as Barrett claims. Further, this could have been Woolf's intention: to stimulate debate and not to close down any particular argument or option. Indeed, Woolf mocks the academic lecturer by having her narrator state at the beginning that she realises she would be able to reach a conclusion, ending with a golden nugget of truth to hand to her audience at the end of her lecture. She returns to this theme at the end. The narrator says that her audience will have been making deductions about her character and how that may have influenced her ideas. They will all the time have been rejecting or adding their own views, and she thoroughly approves of this. Lecturer and audience must work co-operatively. She will not deliver the peroration that convention expects; she will leave that to men.

THREE GUINEAS (1938)

The tone of *Three Guineas* (1938) is often viewed as being much darker and more pessimistic than her 1929 polemic had been. In this polemic the words 'anger', 'angry', or 'rage' occur only four times, but the whole book is shot through with an a more strident tone than *A Room of One's Own*. As a signed essay in the *Atlantic Monthly*, which appeared in May and June 1938, Woolf published an abridged version of *Three Guineas*, under the title 'Women must Weep—Or Unite Against War'. As the subtitle suggests, Woolf's focus was no longer on female writers but on how *all* 'daughters of educated men' can prevent war. One woman manages to clearly express her own sense of how women themselves collude in preserving the status quo by marrying 'members of the "Procession". Though they have been invisible in it, they have been its bearers.' She had felt helpless and irrelevant, but now she has and will continue to act (she does not say how). She describes *Three Guineas* as 'very dangerous stuff. Inflammable material.' (*WSA*, volume 6, 2000, 73). Another reader of *Three Guineas* predicts that it will 'infuriate' some of its readers (*WSA*, volume 6, 2000, 57).

Some contemporary correspondents did not comment on its strident and angry tone; indeed, they stressed the opposite. One correspondent writes that *Three Guineas* is written 'without a trace of the acrimony and acerbity which so often weaken feminine discussion of the roles which men have imposed on women' (*WSA*, volume 6, 2000, 85). Another praises *Three Guineas* for being written with a 'lack of heat' (*WSA*, volume 6, 2000, 86). Older women friends react differently again to the polemic. Ruth Fry writes that she is having it read aloud to her and 'we are chortling with delight and entertainment, on top of deep satisfaction at your effective telling' (*WSA*, volume 6, 2000, 26). Philippa Strachey also rejoices in the skilful way in which it was written: it is 'swollen by all sorts of extraneous currents including the joys of a vent to evil feelings. You don't display these yourself but the exposition of the case for them is extraordinarily comforting to the restrained furies' (*WSA*, volume 6, 2000, 20).

Woolf frequently turns to her father's area of expertise to gain evidence for the case she is making in *Three Guineas*: the biographies and autobiographies of nineteenth-century women. Woolf repeatedly connects the domestic and public worlds. She recognises that the profession most intimately connected with war is politics. Having consulted memoirs written by women in the nineteenth century, she finds they are dominated by men who hold the most powerful political offices. She finds that a glaring omission in such memoirs are the greatest nineteenth-century novelists, among whom she names Charlotte but not Emily Brontë.

Woolf discovers that while most of the professions fought against admitting women, literature is exceptional in that it does not have to undertake 'a fierce battle' to get women accepted within it (*TG*, 188). She discusses some of the lives of these great writers and the education (or lack of it) that they received. One of these women writers, Emily Brontë, despite an unpaid for education, had received benefits as well as defects from such an education. Such writers had not been educated in the way males were, but they were nonetheless civilised women. If they practise four things: 'poverty, chastity, derision and freedom from unreal loyalties' they would have had a better education than their male peers (*Three Guineas*, 204).

In part 3, Woolf turns to an examination of how to promote culture and intellectual liberty. She believes that the education given to boys and young men fails to promote either. Woolf limits her study of culture and intellectual liberty to literature. Culture, Woolf defines as 'the disinterested pursuit of reading and writing the English language'. Intellectual liberty is 'the right way to say or write what you think in your own words, and in your own way' (*TG*, 216). Women promote both culture and intellectual freedom simply by pursuing their own methods of reading and writing. Woolf suggests that literature is different from the other professions, here she develops this idea further. It has no 'head' and no official body, with the power to lay down rules and to compel readers and writers to follow them. Unlike other professions, women can use male pseudonyms and nobody knows their sex or marital status.

Woolf admits that there are women writers who do not promote culture and intellectual liberty. She is particularly scathing about Margaret Oliphant (1828–1897). Although Oliphant had an 'admirable brain', she prostituted culture and rejected her intellectual freedom in order to earn enough money to provide a home for, raise, and educate her children. Woolf writes that as culture and intellectual freedom can conflict with the need to earn a living and support a family, she limits the promoters of culture and intellectual freedom to those daughters of educated men who possess a sufficient income to live upon and do not depend on writing to be self-supporting. (This surely greatly limits the number of possible authoresses). While selling her body is bad,

committing 'adultery of the brain' is worse. It is 'writing what I do not want
to write for the sake of money' (*TG*, 218). This applies not only to writing
imaginative literature but to the writing of lectures, publishers and editors.
Such writing infects, corrupts and sows the seed of disease in those who are
subjected to it, in any of its forms.

The women she views as the great four of the nineteenth century did not
commit adultery of the brain. Woolf does not write about all these women writers. Her emphasis falls on Charlotte Brontë, not as an author but as a Victorian
daughter of a father who has 'infantile fixation'. The Nolloth Professor of the
Philosophy of the Christian Religion at Oxford University had used this term
to explain the exclusion of women from the ministry. 'Infantile fixation' is a
Freudian term which described early patterns of behaviour or emotions which
persists later in life. Professor Grensted described these emotions as rational
and unconscious. They reveal their persistence by manifesting themselves
strongly and intensely.

Woolf applies the concept of 'infantile fixation' much more widely; in
her view, it manifests itself both in the domestic and in the public spheres.
Since it is all-pervasive it is a matter which should be urgently addressed.
Once again, Woolf turns to Victorian biography, and two of her examples are
nineteenth-century women writers. The one who concerns us here is Charlotte
Brontë. Woolf quotes from Elizabeth Gaskell's *Life of Charlotte Brontë*, in
which Gaskell had quoted a letter from her subject detailing an account of
Arthur Bell Nicholl's proposal of marriage. The passage with which Woolf
concerns herself is when Charlotte asked Nicholls whether he had spoken
to her father, and he replied that he 'dared not' (*Life*, 590). Woolf probes
this phrase which she finds incomprehensible. She cannot understand why
Nicholls 'dared not': he was 'strong and young and passionately in love; the
father was old' (*TG*, 259). Woolf finds the answer easy to discover: the Rev.
Patrick Brontë had long disapproved of marriages and he was unable to bear
the idea of Charlotte being married to Nicholls. Anxious about the effect of
the proposal on her father, Charlotte rejected Nicholls who left Haworth for a
time. Woolf comments that Charlotte's life as a wife was brief and was further
shortened by her father's opposition.

The conflict between Charlotte and her father is returned to several pages
later. Again, Woolf quotes from Gaskell, though certainly not echoing
Gaskell's praise of her subject's 'unselfishness' (*Life*, 591); she clearly disap-
proves of it (*TG*, 262). In the following paragraphs Woolf is more outspoken
and savages these self-deluded and selfish Victorian fathers. The 'infantile
fixation' could fight the strongest of loves between men and women because
it was sanctioned by society. It was excused and excused by 'nature, law
and property' (*TG*, 263). If Victorian fathers thought their daughters should
remain at home, society supported them. A woman who put her own interests

before her father's was considered 'unnatural' and her 'womanhood was suspect'. The law threw its weight behind the father and a daughter had not means of financing an independent life. If the woman resorted to the only job open to her—prostitution—she 'unsexed herself'. Thus the Rev. Mr Brontë was openly able to cause pain to his only surviving child for several months and his form of tyranny was never criticised (*TG*, 263). She concludes that society 'it seems, was a father, and afflicted with an infantile fixation too' (*TG*, 263).

Though Charlotte Brontë and an increasing number of later Victorian women defeated the 'infantile fixation' within their homes, Woolf thinks it still persists in the public world in her own time. Men want women to retire back into the private domestic sphere after the war and the men's 'infantile fixation' causes a deafening row among the men (*TG*, 269).

As we have seen, Emily Brontë's unpaid but positive education had been commented on by Woolf earlier. Unlike her sister, Charlotte, Emily Brontë's writing is referred to. Woolf saw a connection between early religion and literature. Woolf suggests that originally religion was open to all, male or female, when they were gifted with prophecy. Like literature, early religion was not taught; the only necessity was a 'voice, and a market-place, a pen and paper'. But later, in the nineteenth century, although Emily Brontë had written 'No Coward Soul is Mine' (from which Woolf quotes the first two stanzas), she was 'not worthy to be a priest in England'. Woolf traces Emily Brontë's spiritual descent from 'some ancient prophetess' who had prophesied when the activity was unpaid and voluntary. When the church turned into a profession, men were accepted into the ministry, while even such women as Emily Brontë were excluded (*TG*, 251–52). Woolf's accumulated references to Emily Brontë reveal how much male authorship of *Wuthering Heights* would undermine much of her argument in *A Room of One's Own* and *Three Guineas*.

Chapter Seven

Brontë Critics Published
by the Hogarth Press

Virginia Woolf read past and contemporary critics on the Brontë sisters' novels and their lives, as well as publishing some of this material by the Hogarth Press which she with her husband, Leonard Woolf, had founded in 1917. It is helpful to look at some of the books the Woolfs published to determine what may have influenced and shaped her responses to Charlotte and Emily Brontë's writings. The Hogarth Press might be expected to have reflected some of the Woolfs' interests in its publications. It is unsurprising, therefore, to discover that there were a number of books and essays published by the Press in the 1920s and 1930s on the Brontë family and their novels.

C. P. SANGER

Sanger was originally a friend and fellow Apostle of Leonard Woolf at Cambridge, though nine years senior to Woolf. Sanger kept abreast of Virginia Woolf's development as a novelist. From *Night and Day* (1919) to *To the Lighthouse* (1927) he never failed to produce an epistolary response to each novel as it was published. Virginia Woolf took his comments seriously. Sanger's *The Structure of Wuthering Heights* was a twenty-four-page essay that appeared as Hogarth Press publication number 108, and number 19 in the Hogarth Essays, first series. The number of copies is unknown (Woolmer, 44).

C. P. Sanger's 1926 essay bolstered Woolf's arguments for Emily Brontë's artistic control exceeding that of Charlotte Brontë, by proving that *Wuthering Heights* was painstakingly constructed and not, as some nineteenth-century critics believed, 'chaotic'. However, the first part of Sanger's second sentence, 'I do not propose to discuss its literary merits' (5), indicates a very different approach to and interest in *Wuthering Heights* from those of Woolf. Sanger stressed the orderly structure of the novel with its symmetrical characterisation between the three generations (9). Sanger also made the discovery of the consistency of the dating of events and the ages of the characters at all stages of the novel. Although these are unobtrusive, the reader receives extensive help in keeping their bearings:

> There are a considerable number (perhaps nearly a hundred) indications of various kinds to help us—intervals of time, ages of characters, the months, the harvest moon, the last grouse, and so forth. . . . Taking all these indications, it is, I think, possible to ascertain the year, and, in most cases, the month of the year in which every event takes place—also the ages of the various characters. (11–12)

(Sanger exempted Heathcliff from this, since his exact age was unknown when he was found in Liverpool by Mr Earnshaw.) Sanger also noted the preciseness of the topography and the correctness of the botany in *Wuthering Heights*.

Sanger's specialist knowledge of the law, as a barrister, also came into play. Heathcliff planned to gain possession of all the property of the Earnshaws and Lintons. Emily Brontë's knowledge of the law and the legal facts behind the story impressed Sanger, though it is not impossible to ascertain where she acquired this specialist knowledge. Sanger comments:

> What is remarkable about *Wuthering Heights* is that the ten or twelve legal references are, I think, sufficient to enable us to ascertain the various legal processes by which Heathcliff obtained the property. It is not a simple matter. There was a fundamental difference between the law of land (real property) and that of money and goods (personal property). (15)

Sanger explained these legal concepts in a lucid and succinct way.

He concluded by praising Emily Brontë's detailed planning undertaken to ensure that all the details in *Wuthering Heights* are correct, especially the ages of the characters. These features are not only 'unusual' characteristics of a novel, but also a demonstration of the writer's 'imagination' (20). He ended his essay by an impressively detailed chronology of *Wuthering Heights,* which he added as an appendix (21).

Regrettably, Virginia Woolf does not appear to have recorded her response to Sanger's essay on *The Structure of Wuthering Heights*. It is likely that they had discussed the Brontës at some of their meetings. Certainly, Lytton Strachey wrote from Nottingham in 1926, three months after the publication of the essay, that 'Sanger chatted about the Brontës, which was all that Nottingham could desire' (*The Letters of Lytton Strachey*, 557–58). Yet, despite Woolf's affection and respect for Sanger, it is likely that she had some reservations about *The Structure of Wuthering Heights*. Woolf probably felt that Sanger was too preoccupied with facts. In 1917, after a visit from Sanger,

Woolf wrote that barristers seemed to find the world 'so definite . . . —so full of information' (*L2*, no. 828: To Lady Robert Cecil, 14 April 1917, 148). By the end of 1920, Woolf was wryly admitting her inattention to facts, which littered her essays as well as novels: 'Oh dear! I've been writing an article and getting all my dates wrong, and a furious old gentleman has written to wring my neck' (*L2*, no. 1150: To Janet Case, 4 November 1920, 446). In another letter to Janet Case, Woolf writes of facts, 'there's nothing that bores me more' (*L2,* no. 1228: To Janet Case, 20 March 1922, 514).

Woolf did not really think such errors were of importance, but she felt obliged to tell Sanger they were there. After *The Structure of Wuthering Heights*, Woolf continued to be unconcerned with facts. Perhaps most damning of *The Structure of Wuthering Heights* was a comment to Sanger's daughter Daphne that seems dismissive of his greatest achievements in the piece, that is, the working out of the facts (including the dates of events and the ages of the characters) underpinning *Wuthering Heights*. Woolf wrote that she was fairly indifferent to facts in her own novels whose purpose was 'something else'. She added, however, that she would have objected had Jane Austen disregarded facts in her novels (*L3*, no. 1785: To Daphne Sanger, 18 July 1927, 398–99).

On a professional level, Woolf may have been indebted to Sanger's legal knowledge for parts of *Orlando* published by the Hogarth Press in 1928. In her spoof preface to *Orlando* Woolf thanked 'Mr C. P. Sanger, without whose knowledge of the law of real property this book could never have been written' (*Orlando*, 5). Woolf's mention of Sanger in the preface may though have been a satirical comment on the way in which the law as executed in the real world was applied to the fictional world of *Wuthering Heights* by Sanger.

IRENE COOPER WILLIS

The disputed authorship of *Wuthering Heights* is important because it obviously exercised Woolf's mind and provoked her strong denial of its attribution to Branwell Brontë. The authorship debate had been around since the 1860s and was still going strong in the 1920s. Woolf's reaction seemed to be more emotional than rational. In the mid-1930s Woolf would support a reasoned refutation of this claim by Irene Cooper Willis by publishing it by under the Hogarth Press imprint. Woolf either could not or would not write such a book herself, perhaps because she had stopped writing on the Brontës as novelists by the end of the 1920s. She had celebrated the Brontës as literary 'mothers' in her polemic *A Room of One's Own* (1929). If it was proved that Branwell Brontë had written *Wuthering Heights*, it left her arguments about female forebears in tatters. The views of partisans of Branwell Brontë's authorship upset Woolf for another reason as well. The Brontës were a link with both her Victorian past and with her father. The latter, memorably, had dismissed any idea that Emily Brontë had not written *Wuthering Heights* in his essay on Charlotte Brontë in the *Dictionary of National Biography*. Here Stephen had acknowledged that Leyland and Grundy claimed that Branwell Brontë had written at least a part of *Wuthering Heights*, but he concluded with devastating common sense, 'On the other hand, Charlotte Brontë, who was in daily communication with her sisters at every step, obviously had no doubt that it was written by her sister Emily. Her testimony is conclusive'. For all these reasons it is enlightening to trace Woolf's responses to such views about who wrote *Wuthering Heights.*

Irene Cooper Willis (1882–1970) was a British literary and history scholar and a barrister. She was educated at Girton College, Cambridge, and graduated in 1904. As a barrister she became a member of the Inner Temple and Lincoln's Inn, in London. Here, apparently, she met and worked with Sanger, who she assisted in editing the seventh edition of *A Treatise on Wills* by Thomas Jarman. It is likely that they also shared their mutual interest in the Brontë family, about whom they both wrote, although Willis did not do so until after Sanger's death.

Before writing *The Authorship of Wuthering Heights*, Willis had written a variety of books. Her first publications were an analysis of the First World War, which was originally published in three volumes which were amalgamated into one volume and published in 1928. Willis then turned to literary work, publishing books on two Victorian women, Elizabeth Barrett Browning (1928) and Florence Nightingale (1931). In 1933, Willis's first book on the Brontë family was published. It is significant that three of Willis's books focused on Victorian women; this appears to have been the literary age at which she felt most at home, in which she resembled Woolf whose ambivalent attachment to the past she shared.

It is worth pausing to note Willis's approached these three Victorian women as a study in a bygone era, which was clearly marked off from the twentieth century's 'modern' period. Here she adopted an intellectual approach to the modern, which again Woolf shared. Willis's opening chapter of *Elizabeth Barrett Browning* (henceforth *EBB*) is titled 'The Victorian Attitude'. In this chapter, Willis described the Victorians and offered explanations of why they were rejected by their descendants. Like Bloomsbury, Willis found the 'mid-Victorian era' was 'oppressively rigid and moral' and so it remained 'to those of us whose memories go back to any part of it, or who study it in literature, poetry or art' (*EBB*, 9). Willis elaborated on this argument: 'Morality was supreme. Even free thought in the sphere of religion was not allowed to undermine belief in immutable moral law. . . . A basic sanctity and fixity attached to [the Victorians'] conceptions, the most noticeable having to do with sex, property and filial duties' (*EBB*, 11–12). Willis contrasted the Victorian period with the modern world whose spirit is 'sceptical and profane' and whose morality is 'alert, flexible and self-determined. . . . It is a less serious but more workaday morality than of old' (*EBB*, 12).

According to Willis, these changes made it difficult to enjoy Elizabeth Barrett's poems, as she was very much a product of her age. Additionally, in Willis's view Edward Moulton Barrett 'overdid the part of Victorian father', even in that age (*EBB*, 17). Willis may also have been aware of Woolf's writings on the poet. In an early essay of 1906, Woolf had colourfully described Elizabeth Barrett as being 'a life-long prisoner' confined by her father who was a 'mad gaoler' (*E1*, 102). Over two decades later, Woolf made the same point about the tyranny of Barrett whose daughter's life she thought almost comparable to living in a convent (*E5*, 522). Most importantly, for Woolf, was that Barrett Browning's early life had damaged her poetry; she used the word 'seclusion' three times to describe the circumscribed existence of the poet (*E5*, 522–23). While Woolf's interest in Barrett Browning was as a writer, Willis approached her from a radical standpoint: that of slavery. Willis condemned Mr Barrett's imperialism and exploitation of slave labour in the colonies of the British Empire (*EBB*, 18). She also implicitly compared Barrett's treatment of his children to his treatment of slave labour (*EBB*, 22).

Willis's awareness of Woolf's writing was even more apparent in her biography of Florence Nightingale, since the opening sentence approvingly referred to Woolf's *A Room of One's Own*, which had highlighted 'that one of the greatest obstacles, in the past, to the success of women's work was the psychological atmosphere in which, or rather against which, that work was attempted' (*Florence Nightingale: A Biography*, 11). Willis continued to state the more subtle arguments that Woolf had deployed in describing the invisible handicaps of women wanting to work in the wider world. Willis contrasted the modern age with the Victorian world, as she had done in her biography of Elizabeth Barrett Browning: 'A hundred years ago, rational criticism had only just begun to nibble at the foundations of religious, political, legal, moral and social beliefs'; these had remained unquestioned by a majority of people long after 'some clear heads had exploded them' (*FN*, 21). Willis also showed her familiarity with Lytton Strachey's portrait of Florence Nightingale in *Eminent Victorians*.

Irene Cooper Willis's first book about the Brontës took the form of a biography; but while Law limited herself to Branwell, Willis wrote about the four Brontë children who survived to adulthood. Although the Hogarth Press did not publish her first general biography of the Brontës, there is a family connection with Virginia Woolf in that her half-brother George Duckworth's publishing firm published it in 1933, in Duckworth's 'Great Lives' series.

Willis touched on what would be the main theme of her next Brontë book—the authorship of *Wuthering Heights*. For whatever reason, Willis in her biography of the whole Brontë family did not devote herself to a serious and well-argued repudiation of the arguments for Branwell's nor put forward the case for Emily Brontë's authoring of *Wuthering Heights*. Having described Branwell Brontë's prolonged 'breakdown', Willis ends chapter VI with what she apparently thought to be a generally accepted view among her own contemporaries. She did not prevaricate, but simply stated: 'That Branwell wrote *Wuthering Heights*, or even had a hand in writing it, seems quite untenable. Apart from all external evidence, it is clear from the spirit, style and construction, both of the novel and the poems, that Emily wrote the book' (*The Brontës*, 105).

Yet, even for Willis the argument about the authorship cannot be entirely disregarded. She may not be as certain as she appears to be in the closing statement of chapter VI, for one of the sub-headings in the penultimate chapter is 'the confusion of authorships—*Wuthering Heights*'. Twenty pages later than her dismissal of Branwell Brontë's authorship, she cited Gaskell's description of the reception of *Wuthering Heights* as proof that Emily Brontë did write it:

> Those who doubt [Emily Brontë's] authorship of *Wuthering Heights* should refer to Charlotte's letters to Mr Williams and to a passage in the before-mentioned letter from Mrs Gaskell, quoted in Miss Haldane's book, where Mrs Gaskell says:

> "But Emily, poor Emily—the pangs of disappointment as review after review came out about *Wuthering Heights* were terrible. Miss Brontë said she had no recollection of pleasure or gladness about *Jane Eyre*: every such feeling was lost in seeing Emily's resolute endurance, yet knowing what she felt." (*The Brontës*, 125–26)

Two years later, Willis seemed to have decided that a fuller refutation of Branwell Brontë's authorship of *Wuthering Heights* was necessary; evidently, among Willis's contemporaries there was still strong doubt about this. Her second book was entirely devoted to this vexed question; its title was *The Authorship of Wuthering Heights*. It is divided into two parts: part I focuses on 'The Style of *Wuthering Heights*' and part II on 'Branwell Brontë's Writings'.

Howard J. Woolmer informs us that Irene Cooper Willis's second Brontë book, *The Authorship of Wuthering Heights,* was published by the Hogarth Press in March 1936. The print run was 1,200 copies. The book ran to ninety-four pages (138). A recent critic has written that it 'is a carefully researched and well-developed argument that rejects Branwell Brontë as the author of *Wuthering Heights*. Willis' text is a formal, academic and feminist attack upon critics who fail to believe that a woman could write a novel with the power and genius of *Wuthering Heights*, but she does so in a way that is easily accessible for the average reader' (Melissa Sullivan, endnote 13, 71].

In part I, Willis wrote that *Wuthering Heights* has been attributed to Branwell on the grounds of 'his much-talked-of conversational brilliancy, his literary ambitions and some hazy statements made by two or three people, years after the events they recalled, to the effect that Branwell had written a great portion, at any rate, of the book' (*Authorship*, 14). Willis doubted that there are sufficient grounds for taking this attribution of *Wuthering Heights* to Branwell seriously, as she believed that there is no resemblance between the novel and his other surviving writings (14).

Willis now identified Alice Law as 'Branwell's chief partisan' as one who believed that an '"unmistakable air of masculinity" hangs over every page' of *Wuthering Heights* (Willis, 14; Law, 156). This and the following quotation come from Law's *Patrick Branwell Brontë*. Alice Law had written that 'The very character of this terrible tale should convince any thoughtful or closely observant reader that no woman's hand ever penned *Wuthering Heights*. Such, indeed, was the universal opinion of the Press when it first appeared' (Willis, 14; *Patrick Branwell Brontë*, 156).

Willis pointed out that there was also some doubt about the authorship of *Jane Eyre*, including the rumour that the same person wrote both *Wuthering Heights* and *Jane Eyre*. It was thought that William Makepeace Thackeray might have written *Jane Eyre*. To explain this confusion, Willis appealed to recent psychological discoveries, viz., 'Nearly everyone, according to psychological authorities, is a mixture of masculinity and femininity in different proportions' (15). This is notable as it supports the theory of androgyny which Woolf advanced in *A Room of One's Own* and which we know Willis had read and admired. She also advanced an alternative argument: even if one accepted that it was written with 'unmistakeable masculinity' Branwell Brontë's authorship remained unproved.

Willis also alluded to E. F. Benson, whose *Charlotte Brontë* was referred to by Woolf (with disgust) in the same letter containing her view of Alice Law's contentious claims for Branwell's authorship of *Wuthering Heights*. Willis set out to discredit both Law and Benson—especially the former. She employed the recently invented technique of practical criticism to prove the consistency of style of *Wuthering Heights*. Willis found the style throughout the novel to be dramatic, direct, and primitive, with no casual digressions. In *Wuthering Heights,* she noted a consistent creation of sketches 'which flash into another scene. The scenes are lit by dialogue, verbatim or reported, but there is the same vivid, swift touch whether sketch or fuller picture is being drawn' (38).

This indicated to Willis that *Wuthering Heights* was produced by one mind. She, however, granted that to a critical reader, it did not prove that the mind was that of Emily and not Branwell.

Presumably, to surmount this obstacle, Part II moves from a consideration of the style of *Wuthering Heights* to an examination of Branwell's style in his surviving manuscripts. Alice Law had quoted from both Francis H. Grundy's *Pictures of the Past and Present* and Francis Leyland's quotation from William Dearden's article in the *Halifax Guardian* as evidence of Branwell's authorship. Willis's and Law's interpretations of these surviving documents from Branwell's contemporaries differ greatly. Willis observed that the recipient of Branwell's letter, Francis Leyland, 'no doubt . . . thought it all very brilliant, and evidently Miss Law thinks so too, for she has no hesitation in believing that the novel referred to in this letter was no other than *Wuthering Heights* (85–86). Willis's and Law's interpretations of these surviving documents from Branwell's contemporaries differ greatly. Willis cited the opinion of 'the authority on Brontë manuscripts', C. W. Hatfield, that the novel Branwell was actually writing was a surviving 25,000-word manuscript called 'And the Weary are at Rest' (49–50), which Willis considered 'pretentious drivel' and 'an illustration of [Branwell Brontë's] own drugged, inert state' (87). (This incomplete story had been privately printed in 1924 in a print-run of fifty copies by none other than Clement K. Shorter.)

After analysing this work, Willis's conclusions are scathing: 'the joins between the successive digressions are of the loosest kind; the pieces, as it were, are an odd assortment of clichés, words of concrete meaning, abstract expressions and heterogeneous verbiage. Grammar is lost sight of as much as the thread of the narrative. In short, the whole result, to use a slang word, is "bilge" (66–67). After examining other passages, Willis concluded: 'No wonder that the friends of Branwell Brontë thought him a brilliant talker! . . . But conversational brilliancy of this kind is one thing and story-telling is another.' Such a gift of the gab, Willis argued 'is indeed fatal to any impression except the impression of being dazzled' (75–76). The reader may be dazzled but in the long run was unable to 'get a clear impression of the characters and their situation and the development of the drama' (76).

Incidentally, eleven years after the publication of her book on the authorship of *Wuthering Heights*, Willis wrote an eleven-page article with the same title which was published in the *Trollopian*. Evidently, Willis thought that the battle of contested authorship had not been definitely won. Emily Brontë had not been acknowledged as the undisputed author of *Wuthering Heights*. In her full-length book for the Hogarth Press, *The Authorship of Wuthering Heights*, Willis had advanced positive stylistic arguments for assigning the authorship to Emily by contrasting the style of *Wuthering Heights* with a 25,000-word manuscript of Branwell's. In her article of the same title, Willis proceeds rather differently: her entire argument is devoted to discrediting the evidence put forward by, among others, Alice Law.

E. M. DELAFIELD

Claire Battershill has commented on the publications by the Hogarth Press in the 1930s that 'the debates and dialogues' of the previous decade resulted in 'more formalised and deliberately politicised engagements with biographical and autobiographical form'. The Woolfs created a series, which Battershill has described as 'a radical narrative experiment in which life stories are constructed entirely through quotation with no guiding narrative voice' which were 'designed to try out a new way of writing biography that did not tie a person's life story to a single biographical voice' (Battershill, 17) Indeed, the publisher's note to *Brontës: Their Lives Recorded by Their Contemporaries* confirms this conscious decision, reading: 'This is the second in a series of biographies which proceeds on a system different from the usual. The life of the person concerned is presented entirely through the eyes of his contemporaries: from contemporary descriptions by those who knew or saw him, and from contemporary documents'. The first one had been devoted to Charles Lamb. This, and the one on the Brontës, were the only ones produced in the proposed series of biographies, perhaps for commercial reasons.

The Brontës: Their Lives Recorded by Their Contemporaries, compiled and introduced by E. M. Delafield (1890–1943), was published in May 1936 at eight shillings and sixpence, with 2,000 copies printed of this publication. This was number 366 of the Hogarth Press's publications (Woolmer, 126). The frontispiece is the picture of the three surviving Brontë sisters by their brother, Branwell. What was, perhaps, surprising was that this volume's editor was far being a radical writer. It is possible that Woolf did not know of E. M. Delafield's rapid output of novels until Delafield's connection with the Hogarth Press. Indeed, Delafield is only once mentioned in her letters and twice in her diary. On 8 February 1935, Woolf perfunctorily noted in her diary that she had passed Delafield in the square; but she dismisses her as 'the Holtby type' (Winifred Holtby was also a middlebrow novelist. *DIV*, 8 February 1935, 278–79). Nearly two years later, Woolf just registered Delafield's attendance at the funeral of the manager of the Hogarth Press, Margaret West in four words (*DV*, 23 January 1937, 52). In her one letter concerning Delafield, Woolf was both more expansive and more sympathetic: 'I've been seeing E. M. Delafield, who writes the Provincial Lady; she is called Dashwood really; Elizabeth Dashwood; and lives in an old house like a character in Jane Austen; whom she adores. But she has to scribble and scribble to pay for it and her children' (*L5*, no. 3082: To Angelica Bell, 18 [17] November 1935, 445).

Nicola Humble included E. M. Delafield in her *The Feminine Middlebrow Novel 1920s to 1950s*. In this, Humble defined the middlebrow novel: it was:

> one that straddles the divide between the trashy romance or thriller on the one hand, and the philosophically or formally challenging novel on the other: offering narrative excitement without guilt, and intellectual stimulation without undue effort. It is an essentially parasitical form, dependent on the existence of both a high and a low brow for its identity, reworking their structures and aping their insights, while at the same time fastidiously holding its skirts away from lowbrow contamination, and gleefully mocking highbrow intellectual pretensions. It is also a predominantly middle-class form. (11–12)

Humble also observed that *The Brontës: Their Lives Recorded by Their Contemporaries* was one of the many contributions to the middlebrow Brontë 'obsession' during the 1930s (Humble, 67).

Delafield was certainly aware of Woolf and her literary experiments. Delafield's first-person narrator in the Provincial Ladies series presented herself as a writer who satirises modernist writing and its authors. As well as references to Woolf and Bloomsbury, the narrator in this series alluded to Charlotte Brontë. Bearing in mind that she would edit the book on the Brontës for the Hogarth Press, it is noteworthy that the actual books written by Woolf which are referred to in the series are the biographies *Orlando* and *Flush*. References to both Charlotte Brontë and Virginia Woolf begin early in *The Diary of a Provincial Lady*. The eponymous narrator records being asked for her opinion of Rebecca West's novel *Harriet Hume*, which she has not read: 'Have a depressed feeling that this is going to be another case of *Orlando* about which was perfectly able to talk most intelligently until I read it, and found myself unfortunately unable to understand any of it' (Provincial Lady Series, 6–7. Henceforth *PLS*). There is perhaps a sly allusion to *A Room of One's Own* when the Lady's husband inherits 'Five Hundred Pounds', a sum that will transform their lives (*PLS*, 77). In one of Delafield's sequels to *The Diary of a Provincial Lady*, the eponymous heroine recorded that she has been talking books with a literary woman called Ella Wheelwright and a Miss Paterson: 'I say that I have enjoyed nothing so much as *Flush*, but Miss Paterson again disconcerts me by muttering that to write a whole book about a dog is Simply Morbid' (*PLS*, 300).

The Lady satirised Bloomsbury and the modernist art its painters were producing. When she described the governess's supper, 'cheese, pickles, and slice of jam roly-poly, grouped on plate', she asked herself in parenthesis: '(Would not this suggest to the artistic mind a Still-life Study in Modern

Art?' (*PLS*, 85). In another sequel to *The Diary of a Provincial Lady*, the narrator again satirised modernist art. She had received a letter from her young daughter who is at boarding school which has a 'small drawing of an elephant, that I think distinctly clever and modernistic, until I read letter and learn that it is A Table, laid for Dinner' (*PLS*, 197).

The Lady satirised Bloomsbury more generally especially in its famous exclusiveness. Her friend has invited her to a Bloomsbury party, which is being given 'by distinguished novelist whose books are well known to me'—is this a reference to Woolf? The Lady accepts the offer if her friend Rose 'is sure it will be All Right. Rose replies Why not, and then adds—distinct after-thought—that I am myself a Literary Asset to society, nowadays. Pause that ensues in conversation makes it painfully evident that both of us know the last statement to be untrue'. Evidently, the Lady (and Delafield) know what reception of her middlebrow novels would receive in Bloomsbury circles (*PLS*, 185). Delafield also mocked the type of pretensions and literary gossip that she believed pervaded Bloomsbury. At this party, Rose pointed out a man who has 'written a book that will . . . undoubtedly be seized before publication and burnt'. Another guest added 'casually' that this writer is a 'genius' and is 'far in advance of his time'. This gossip was relayed to the Lady for a third time, by another guest. The writer in question varies. The Lady satirised her own social conformity: she disgusts herself by replying 'Oh really, in tone of intelligent astonishment'. She considers reporting the story herself as an acceptable opening gambit! (*PLS*, 186).

The Lady recorded that she and another country woman discussed the *Parish Magazine*'s possible contributors. They concluded that 'it would be hopeless to try and get a contribution to the Parish Magazine from anyone really good such as Shaw, Bennett, or Galsworthy' (*DPL*, 49). It is these very writers who were damned by Woolf as the Edwardian writers, from whom the Georgian writers should make a clean break. So, all in all, Delafield knew where she stood with Woolf as a novelist, although there is no evidence of Woolf having actually read any of the Provincial Lady series, or any other of Delafield's novels. It is safe to say that Delafield was far more knowledgeable about Woolf than Woolf was about her.

However, Melissa Sullivan offers an explanation for Delafield's Hogarth Press publication: 'Many middlebrow women writers published popular fiction both because they did not wish to write modernist fiction and because they could not support themselves through their academic non-fiction studies. Throughout the late 1920s and 1930s, however, the Hogarth Press increasingly published the work of middlebrow women writers who could not find an outlet for their academic interests in the mainstream literary public sphere'; one of these was E. M. Delafield. These changes parallel Leonard Woolf's growing involvement in politics and the evolution of Virginia Woolf's feminist principles on women and writing (Sullivan, 53).

E. M. Delafield's *The Brontës: Their Lives Recorded by Their Contemporaries* is divided into seven sections. Within each section the contemporaries' comments are arranged chronologically, beginning with the most distant in terms of dating and moving forwards in time. An exception to this general organization is the final section, 'Some Appreciations'. The period covered goes back as far as 1813 with the 'Announcement of the Rev. Patrick Brontë's Wedding' and extends to 1910 with 'Old Haworth Folk Who Knew the Brontës' by C. Holmes Cautley, which appeared in *The Cornhill*. Delafield had tracked down and included over two hundred separate items of information about the Brontës lives and their works. It is an impressive piece of selection and editing.

Delafield wrote a preface to *The Brontës: Their Lives Recorded by Their Contemporaries* in which she expressed the obligatory acknowledgement that every subsequent biographer of the Brontës owed a 'mighty debt' to Elizabeth Gaskell's *Life of Charlotte Brontë* (*The Brontës*, 13. Henceforth *TB*). At the same time biographers and critics of the Brontës increasingly objected to Gaskell's agenda of presenting Charlotte Brontë as an individual who had endured such exceptional suffering throughout her life that it elevated her into a perfect and heroic woman. Maintaining the critical trend, Delafield also proposed that Gaskell 'sacrificed more than she should have done to her novelist's sense of the becoming', and additionally Gaskell 'suppressed . . . with more skill than conscience, every aspect of Charlotte that might have revealed her as a faulty human being, as well as a high-minded sufferer' (*TB*, 13).

That Charlotte Brontë had been in love with her married teacher, M. Heger, in Brussels was well-known. Her letters to him had been published in *The Times* in 1913. There was an increasing indignation among Brontë scholars that although Gaskell had read and quoted parts of them, yet she 'omits everything that might give the impression that Charlotte loved a man already married' (*Brontë*, 14). As Woolf had done in her articles on the Brontës, Delafield shied away from this aspect of Charlotte Brontë's emotional life. Delafield considered why Gaskell suppressed these facts. Like E. F. Benson before her, Delafield stressed that Charlotte Brontë's husband and father were still alive and needed to be protected from this scandal. Delafield departed from Benson by advocating, somewhat tortuously and irrationally, that since the letters might have created a false atmosphere around Charlotte Brontë's memory, 'suppression actually became less dishonest than unexpurgated candour'. Nevertheless, Delafield conceded that the omission threw 'the whole portrait of Charlotte slightly out of focus.' She added that Gaskell was determined to see Charlotte Brontë—falsely—as 'the angel of the home' (*Brontë*, 14). This phrase is very close to Woolf's 'angel in the house': both Woolf and Delafield probably took the concept and phrase from the Victorian Coventry Patmore's poem, 'The Angel in the House'. In her 'Speech to the London and National Society for Women's Service', Woolf described how she had to murder this angel who preyed on women to make them conform to the masculine conventions and ideals of Victorian womanhood. She wrote that it was necessary for her to do this so as to free herself as a writer (*Essays 6*, 480–81).

Delafield repeated all biographers' descriptions of the closeness of the Brontë siblings. Like Benson (but more bluntly), Delafield asked: 'How far did Charlotte understand her sisters and her brother on the adult level? How far did they understand her?' (*Brontës*, 15). Delafield adopted (without acknowledgement) that there was a special relationship between Emily and Anne Brontë. Like Benson again, Delafield's view was that Emily and Charlotte Brontë would not have related well to each other as adults, as this Emily Brontë 'would neither have endured nor permitted'. Close contacts were impossible to Emily Brontë, since she was a 'genius', which she combined with mysticism. Delafield went further in her assessment of Emily Brontë's mind and again used a psychological term crudely (and inaccurately): had she not been a genius she would have been diagnosed as 'schizophrenic' (*Brontë*, 17–18). Even as she was dying, Delafield argued, she had to maintain her own sense of absolute freedom. This was part of her genius. Delafield differed from Benson who thought that Charlotte Brontë herself had provoked Emily Brontë's unyielding attitude by her own actions, which repeatedly roused Emily's resentment, and began with the ransacking of her desk by Charlotte and the discovery of her poems.

In any account of the three sisters as writers, stated Delafield, Branwell cannot be ignored. In Delafield's view, Charlotte Brontë 'openly displays scorn of his weakness'. Gaskell accepted her subject's view of her brother and was horrified at the vices 'that were held to be exclusively and mysteriously masculine' at that time (*Brontë*, 15–16). Delafield offered some simple common sense about Branwell: he should have been disciplined and sent to school. Delafield's single most important statement about Branwell Brontë was that his extant writings 'show no especial signs of talent'. This led into the contested territory of whether Branwell Brontë contributed to the writing of *Wuthering Heights*. She summarised the evidence for and against this proposition. Here she condensed Benson's arguments (over which he had taken several pages) to a couple of paragraphs. Delafield diverged from Benson. Her Provincial Lady Series had mocked and caricatured Freud, but she was, as a novelist, generally interested in exploring her characters' minds and had a penchant for contemporary psychology. Hence, she advanced an original view. The actual argument she used was a rather crude application of psychological theory as she understood it. It might not have appealed to Woolf, but they were agreed on dismissing Branwell Brontë as responsible for writing any part of *Wuthering Heights*: Delafield attempted to base her argument on the faulty character of Branwell Brontë.

Delafield had mostly commented on the life and works of Charlotte Brontë in her preface. In the final paragraph of her preface she remembered that her subject was all four Brontë siblings and made some general concluding remarks:

> Like some extraordinary astral phenomena, the Brontës flashed their course, and were gone. Gifted, warped, tragic creatures,—how little can ever be known of them, even when contemporary impressions are, as here, gathered together. They must always remain a source of inexhaustible research and enquiry, not only to the student of literature but to the student of human nature at its strangest. (*Brontë*, 20)

It appears to be Leonard Woolf who mainly dealt with E. M. Delafield when she was a Hogarth Press author. One cannot know if, or when, Virginia Woolf read Delafield's manuscript, and, if or when, she did, whether she approved of it. Woolf herself had ceased to write about the Brontë sisters' novels but she was still interested in Brontë scholarship.

Conclusion

Virginia Woolf's subject matter, both for her essays and her novels, was often derived from the nineteenth century. What has struck me, however, in the writing of this book is the difficulty of pinning Woolf down to any consistently held emotions or judgements. Frequently these qualities are reversed or contradicted. This complexity seems to be best caught by a conversation Virginia Woolf recorded she had had with her husband, Leonard Woolf, in 1920: 'L. at tea put me right: M[ary] H[utchinson] is one of the few people I dislike, I said. No: he replied: one of the many you dislike & like alternately' (*DII*, 8 September 1920, 63). This ambivalence in her personal relationships also applied to many other areas of her life, as, for example her attitudes towards the Victorian period and, within that, even to the Brontës themselves. Perhaps it is these persistence shifts, which she may have deliberately encompassed so as not to shut down debate which makes her books so relevant to the reader of the twenty-first century.

This strategy of constant shifts in perspective in terms of Woolf's attitudes was also reflected in the open-mindedness which she herself practised as a reader and which she endeavoured to instil in readers of her own essays and novels and in other literature. She did not ally herself with academic male critics who wanted to persuade the reader to their own particular viewpoint. Instead, she encouraged a method of reading through which the reader would reach his or her own evaluation of a text. Woolf strongly disapproved of the developing Cambridge department of English literature. Cambridge academics were at this time hostile to Woolf who returned their dislike. She wrote of their journal *Scrutiny* as that 'prigs manual' and declared that '[a]ll they can do is to schoolmaster' (*DIV*, 4 September 1935, 337). She disliked what she saw as their dictatorial approach to literary texts, which was the opposite of her own approach.

In her late feminist anti-war pamphlet, *Three Guineas*, Woolf turned back to the nineteenth century and the position of women in 1938, which she finally and firmly connected. She finds that the cloud which she had long viewed as hanging over the—and her—Victorian past had lifted. She concluded those nineteenth-century women who were 'the daughters of educated men' were pursuing 'the very same cause for which we are working now'. As an example, she singled out not a woman writer, but a social reformer, Josephine Butler, whose rallying cry 'Justice and Equality and Liberty' Woolf quotes several times in *Three Guineas*. These women (who had hated the term *feminist* and which Woolf had destroyed too) 'were in fact the advance guard of your own movement'. Nineteenth-century and modern women were fighting against 'the same enemy and for the same reasons'. Like Elizabeth Barrett Brown, Woolf now explicitly named acknowledged these women as 'grandmothers' as well as the 'mothers' of *A Room of One's Own*, writing: 'we are merely carrying on the same fight that our mothers and grandmothers fought; their words prove it; your words prove it' (*TG*, 228). The same thought is a dominant possibility of Woolf's last and posthumously published novel, *Between the Acts*. It is stated most clearly by Mrs Swithin: 'The Victorians . . . I don't believe . . . that there ever were such people. Only you and me and William dressed differently' (*BA*, 156). As early as 1919, Mrs Hilbery had said in Woolf's second novel: 'After all, what *is* the present? Half of it's the past, and the better half, too I should say' (*N&D*, 7).

Woolf was pulled between her emotional adherence to the Victorian period of her childhood and youth and her adult and intellectual engagement with Modernism. Her novels reflect this dichotomy: while she is constantly experimenting with novelistic techniques, she frequently used experiences and emotions from her Victorian past as her subject matter. In her critical essays, too, she repeatedly chose nineteenth-century authors and their texts. These for her were the great novelists; she wanted to write criticism of their works. By contrast, although she wrote on many contemporary authors, these were reviews rather than critical essays. Apparently, she found nothing to equal these Victorian authors. Primary among them were the Brontë sisters' novels. She began to be more preoccupied by the threatening future which was evolving through the 1930s. Even then, though, she encouraged other writers to contribute books upon the Brontës which reflected her own views of them.

Bibliography

Alexander, Christine. *The Early Writings of Charlotte Brontë*. Volume 1 (Oxford: Basil Blackwood Ltd, 1983).

——, *The Early Writings of Charlotte Brontë 1826–1832* (Oxford: Basil Blackwood Ltd, 1987).

——. 'Nineteenth-Century Juvenilia: A Survey.' In *The Child Writer from Austen to Woolf*, edited by Christine Alexander and Juliet McMaster (Cambridge: CUP, 2005).

Appignanesi, Lisa. *Mad, Bad and Sad: A History of Women and the Mind Doctors from 1800 to the Present Day* (London: Virago, 2008).

Bailin, Miriam. *The Sickroom in Victorian Fiction: The Art of Being Ill* (Cambridge: CUP, 1994).

Barker, Juliet. *The Brontës.* (London: Weidenfeld & Nicolson, 1994).

——. *The Brontës: Wild Genius on the Moors: The Story of a Literary Family* (New York: Pegasus Books, 2012).

Battershill, Claire. *Modernist Lives: Biography and Autobiography at Leonard and Virginia Woolf's Hogarth Press* (London: Bloomsbury Publishing Plc, 2018).

Bell, Anne Olivier, with Andrew McNeillie (eds). *The Diary of Virginia Woolf.* Five volumes (London: The Hogarth Press, 1977–1984).

Bell, Quentin. *Virginia Woolf: A Biography*. Vol 2: 1912–1941 (London: The Hogarth Press, 1972).

Bell, Vanessa. 'Notes on Virginia's Childhood.' In *Sketches in Pen and Ink: A Bloomsbury Notebook* (London: The Hogarth Press, 1985).

Bennett, Arnold. *Our Women: Chapters on the Sex-Discord* (New York: George H. Doran Company, 1920. Reprinted by Kessinger Legacy Reprints, n/d).

Benson, E. F. *Charlotte Brontë* (London: Longmans Green and Co., 1932).

Besnault, Anne. *Virginia Woolf's Unwritten Histories: Conversations with the Nineteenth Century* (New York and London: Routledge, 2022).

Bock, Carol. '"Our Plays": the Brontë Juvenilia.' In *The Cambridge Companion*, edited by Heather Glen (Cambridge: CUP, 2002).

Brontë, Anne. *Agnes Grey* (Oxford: OUP, 1991 [1847]).

Brontë, Charlotte. *Biographical Notice of Ellis and Acton Bell*. Appendix to *Wuthering Heights* (Oxford: OUP, 2009 [1847]).

————. *Jane Eyre* (Oxford: OUP, 2000 [1847]).

————. *Charlotte Brontë Juvenilia: 1829–1835.* (ed) Christine Alexander (London: Penguin Books, 1996).

————. *The Professor* (Oxford: OUP, 1991 [1857]).

————. *Villette* (Oxford: OUP, 2000 [1853]).

Brontë, Emily. *The Poems of Emily Brontë.* Edited by Edward Chitham and Derek Roper (Oxford: Clarendon Press, 1995).

————. *Wuthering Heights* (Oxford: OUP, 2009 [1847]).

Carlson, Susan Anne. 'The Impact of Clinical Depression on Charlotte Brontë's *Villette.*' *Brontë Studies* 45, no. 1 (2020): 13–26.

Cervetti, Nancy. *S. Weir Mitchell, 1829–1914.* (University Park, PA: The Pennsylvania State University Press, 2012).

Chapple, J. A. V., and Arthur Pollard (eds.). *The Letters of Mrs Gaskell.* (Manchester, UK: Manchester University Press, 1966).

Choe, Jian. '"Her pain [was] her suffering—her relief my hope": Illness, Empathy and the Ethics of Care in *Villette.*' *Brontë Studies* 46, no. 2 (2021):172–82.

Corbett, Mary Jean. *Behind the Times: Virginia Woolf in Late-Victorian Contexts* (Ithaca, NY, and London: Cornell University Press, 2020).

Courtney, W. L. *The Feminine Note in Fiction* (London: Chapman & Hall Ltd, 1904. Reprint from the University of California Libraries Collection, n/d).

Craig, Maurice. *Psychological Medicine: A Manual on Mental Diseases for Practitioners and Students* (London: J. A. Churchill, 1905. Reprinted by Forgotten Books, 2018).

De Gay, Jane. *Virginia Woolf's Novels and the Literary Past* (Edinburgh: Edinburgh University Press, 2006).

Delafield, E. M. *The Brontës: Their Lives Recorded by Their Contemporaries* (London: The Hogarth Press, 1935).

————. *The Diary of a Provincial Lady /The Provincial Lady Goes Further/The Provincial Lady in America/The Provincial Lady in Wartime* (London: Penguin, 2014).

Dell, Marion. *Virginia Woolf's Influential Forebears: Julia Margaret Cameron, Anny Thackeray Ritchie and Julia Prinsep Stephen.* (Houndmills, Basingstoke, Hampshire RG21 6XS: Palgrave Macmillan, 2015).

Dennison, Matthew. *Behind the Mask: The Life of Vita Sackville-West.* (London: William Collins, 2014).

Dinsdale Ann. 'Domestic Life at Haworth Parsonage.' In *The Brontës in Context*, edited by Marianne Thormählen (Cambridge: CUP, 2012).

Ellis, Steve. *Virginia Woolf and the Victorians* (Cambridge: Cambridge University Press, 2007).

Frank, Katherine. *Emily Brontë* (London: Penguin Books, 1992 [1990]).

Forsberg, Laura. 'The Miniature World of Charlotte Brontë's Glass Town.' In *Charlotte Brontë from the Beginnings: New Essays from the Juvenilia to the Major Works*, edited by Judith E. Pike and Lucy Morrison (London and New York: Routledge, 2017).

Gaskell, Elizabeth. *Life of Charlotte Brontë* (London: Smith, Elder & Co, 1909 [1857]).

——. *The Letters of Mrs Gaskell.* Edited by J. A. V. Chapple and Arthur Pollard. (Manchester, UK: Manchester University Press, 1966).

Gerin, Winifred. *Charlotte Brontë: The Evolution of Genius* (Oxford: OUP, 1967).

Gillard-Estrada, Anne-Florence, and Anne Besnault-Levita (eds). *Beyond the Victorian/Modernist Divide: Remapping the Turn-of-the-Century Break in Literature, Culture and the Visual Arts* (London and New York: Routledge, 2018.

Glendinning, Victoria. *Vita: The Life of Vita Sackville-West* (London: Wedenfeld and Nicolson, 1983).

Grundy, Francis H. *Pictures of the Past: Memories of Men I Have Met and Places I Have Been* (London: Griffith and Farrar, 1879. Reprinted by Scholar Select. (Milton Keynes UK: Lightning Source UK Ltd, n/d).

Harris, Maxine. *The Loss That Is Forever* (New York: Penguin Group, 1996).

Humble, Nicola. *The Feminine Middlebrow Novel, 1920s to 1950s: Class, Domesticity and Bohemianism* (Oxford: OUP, 2001).

Jackson, Kate. 'The Tit-Bits Phenomenon: George Newnes, New Journalism and the Periodical Texts.' In *Victorian Periodicals Review* 13 (Fall 1997): 201–226. Accessed online on 6 March 2023.

Jacobus, Mary. *Reading Women: Essays in Feminist Criticism* (New York: Columbia University Press, 1986).

Johnson, R. Brimley. *The Women Novelists* (London: W. Collins Sons & Co, 1918).

Kenyon Jones, Christine, and Anna Snaith. 'Tilting at Universities.' *Woolf Studies Annual,* volume 16, edited by Mark Hussey (New York: Pace University Press, 2010).

King, Julia, and Laila Miletic-Vejzovic. *The Library of Leonard and Virginia Woolf* (Pullman, WA: Washington State University Press, 2003).

Kitton, George. *The Dickens Country* (London: Adam and Charles Black, 1905. Reprinted by Forgotten Books, 2018).

Lamonica Arms, Drew. 'The Brontës' Sibling Bonds.' In *The Brontës in Context,* edited by Marianne Thormählen (Cambridge: CUP, 2012).

Law, Alice. *Emily Jane Brontë and the Authorship of 'Wuthering Heights'* (Altham, Accrington, UK: The Old Parsonage Press, 1928).

——. *Patrick Branwell Brontë* (London: A.M. Philpot Ltd, 1924. Reprinted as a Primary Source Edition, n/d).

Leaska, Mitchell A. (ed). *Virginia Woolf Pointz Hall: The Earlier and Later Typescripts of Between the Acts* (New York: University Publications, 1983).

Lee, Hermione. *Virginia Woolf* (London: Chatto & Windus, 1996).

Leyland, Francis A. *The Brontë Family: With Special Reference to Patrick Branwell Brontë.* Volume 2 (London: Hurst and Blackett, Publishers. Reprinted by Forgotten Books, 2015).

Logan, Deborah Anne. *The Collected Letters of Harriet Martineau.* Volumes 3 and 4. (London: Pickering & Chatto, 2007).

Long, Jean. '"The Awkward Break": Woolf's Reading of Brontë and Austen in *A Room of One's Own.*' In *Woolf Studies Annual*, edited by Mark Hussey. Volume 3 (New York: Pace University Press, 1997).

Maitland, Frederic William. *The Life and Letters of Leslie Stephe.* (Bristol, UK: Thoemmes Antiquarian Books Ltd, 1991 [1906]).

Mansfield, Katherine. 'A Ship Comes into the Harbour.' In *The Edinburgh Edition of the Collected Works of Katherine Mansfield.* Volume 3: *The Poetry and Critical Writings*, edited by Gerri Kimber and Angela Smith (Edinburgh: Edinburgh University Press, 2014).

Marcus, Jane. *Virginia Woolf and the Languages of Patriarchy* (Bloomington & Indianapolis: Indiana University Press, 1987).

Martineau, Harriet. *Harriet Martineau's Autobiography* (London: Smith Elder & Co, 1877. Reprinted by Forgotten Books, 2012).

———. *The Collected Letters of Harriet Martineau.* Volumes 3 (1845–1855) and 4 (1856–1862), edited by Deborah Anna Logan (London: Pickering & Chatto, 2007).

McLarren Caldwell, Janis. 'Mental Health.' In *The Brontës in Context* (Cambridge: CUP, 2012).

———. 'Physical Health.' In *The Brontës in Context* (Cambridge: CUP, 2012).

McNees, Eleanor. 'The Stephen Inheritance: Virginia Woolf and the Burden of the Arnoldian Critic.' In *The Cambridge Quarterly* 44, no. 2 (June 2015): 119–45.

——— (ed). *Virginia Woolf: Critical Assessments.* Volume II (The Banks, Mountfield, near Robertsbridge, East Sussex TN32 5JY: Helm Information Ltd, 1994).

Melville, Lewis. *The Thackeray Country* (London: Adam and Charles Black, 1905. Reprinted by Forgotten Books, 2018).

Mullan, John. *Anonymity: A Secret History of English Literature* (London: Faber and Faber, 2007).

Newman, Hilary. '*The Paston Letters* and "The Journal of Mistress Joan Martyn."' *Virginia Woolf Bulletin* 29 (September 2008).

Nicolson, Harold. *The Development of English Biography* (London: The Hogarth Press, 1968 [1928].

———. *Some People* (London: The Folio Society, 1951 [1927]).

Nicolson, Nigel, and Joanne Trautmann (eds.). *The Letters of Virginia Woolf.* 6 volumes (London: The Hogarth Press, 1975–1980).

Noble, Joan Russell (ed). *Recollections of Virginia Woolf by Her Contemporaries* (London: Peter Owen, 1972).

Paul, Janis M. *The Victorian Heritage of Virginia Woolf: The External World in Her Novels* (Norman, OK: Pilgrim Books, 1987).

The Poems of Emily Brontë, edited by Derek Roper with Edward Chitham (Oxford: Clarendon Press, 1995).

Punch. Historical Archive. Accessed online 6 March 2023.

Reid, T. Wemyss. *Charlotte Brontë: A Monograph* (London: Macmillan and Co., 1877. Reprinted by Leopold Classic Library, n/d).

Reus, Anne. *Virginia Woolf and Nineteenth-Century Women Writers: Victorian Legacies and Literary Afterlives* (Edinburgh: Edinburgh University Press, 2022).

Richardson, LeeAnne M. 'Currents of Art and Streams of Consciousness: Charting the Edwardian Novel.' In *Beyond the Turn-of-the-Century Break in Literature, Culture and the Visual Arts*, edited by Anne-Florence Gillard-Estrada and Anne Besnault-Levita (London and New York: Routledge, 2018).

Rosenberg, Beth C. 'The Essays.' In *The Oxford Handbook of Virginia Woolf*, edited by Anne Fernald (Oxford: OUP, 2021).

Rosenman, Ellen Bayuk. *'A Room of One's Own': Women Writers and the Politics of Creativity* (New York: Twayne Publishers, 1995).

Sanders, Valerie. *The Brother-Sister Culture in Nineteenth-Century Literature* (Basingstoke, Hampshire, UK: Palgrave, 2002).

Sanger, C. P. *The Structure of 'Wuthering Heights'* (London: The Hogarth Press, 1926).

Savage, George Henry. *Insanity and Allied Neuroses: Practical and Clinical* (Philadelphia: Henry C. Lea's Son & Co, 1881. Reprinted by Nabu Public Domain Reprints n/d).

Scull, Andrew. *Hysteria: The Disturbing History* (Oxford: OUP, 2009).

Senf, Carol A. 'Physical and Mental Health in the Brontë's Lives and Works.' In *A Companion to the Brontës*, edited by Diane Long Hoeveler and Deborah Denenholz Morse (Chichester, West Sussex, UK: John Wiley & Sons Ltd., 2016).

Shattock, Joanne. 'Newspapers and Magazines.' In *The Brontës in Context*, edited by Marianne Thormählen (Cambridge: CUP, 2012).

Shorter, Clement K. *The Brontës: Life and Letters*, 2 volumes (London: Hodder and Stoughton, 1980. Reprinted by Scholar Select, n/d).

———. *Charlotte Brontë and Her Circle* (Hodder and Stoughton, 1896. Reprinted by Forgotten Books, n/d).

Showalter, Elaine. *The Female Malady: Women, Madness and English Culture 1830–1980* (London: Virago Press, 1987).

Shuttleworth, Sally. *Charlotte Brontë and Victorian Psychology* (Cambridge: CUP, 1996).

Silver, Brenda R. '"Anon" and the "Reader."' *Twentieth Century Literature* (Fall/Winter 1979).

Smith, Margaret (ed.). *The Letters of Charlotte Brontë*. Volumes 1 to 3 (Clarendon Press: Oxford, 1995–2004).

Stape, J. H (ed). *Virginia Woolf: Interviews and Recollections* (Iowa City, IA: University of Iowa Press, 1995).

Stephen, Leslie. 'Biography.' In *Men, Books, and Mountains*, edited by S. O. A. Ullmann (London: The Hogarth Press, 1956).

———. 'Charlotte Brontë.' In *Hours in a Library*. Volume 3 (London: The Folio Society, 1991).

———. 'Charlotte Brontë.' In the *Dictionary of National Biography*.

———. 'The Essayists.' In *Men, Books, and Mountains,* edited by S. O. A. Ullmann (London: The Hogarth Press, 1956).

———. *Selected Letters of Leslie Stephen*. Vol 1: 1864–1882, edited by John W. Bicknell. (London: Macmillan Press, 1996).

———. *Some Early Impressions* (London: The Hogarth Press, 1924).

————. 'The Study of English Literature.' In *Men, Books, and Mountains*, edited by S. O. A. Ullmann (London: The Hogarth Press, 1956).

————. 'Thoughts on Criticism, by a Critic.' In *Men, Books, and Mountains*, edited by S. O. A. Ullmann (London: The Hogarth Press, 1956).

Sullivan, Melissa. 'The Middlebrows of the Hogarth Press.' In *Leonard and Virginia Woolf, the Hogarth Press and the Networks of Modernism*, edited by Helen Southworth (Edinburgh: Edinburgh University Press, 210).

Thomas, Edward. *A Literary Pilgrim in England* (New York: Dodd, Mead and Company, 1917. Reprinted by Forgotten Books, 2018).

Thormählen, Marianne. *The Brontës and Education* (Cambridge: CUP, 2007).

Trautmann, Joanna Banks. 'Some New Woolf Letters.' *Modern Fiction Studies* 30, no. 2 (Summer 1984): 175–202).

Tytler, Graeme. 'Heathcliff's Monomania: An Anachronism in *Wuthering Heights*.' *Brontë Society Transactions* 20, no. 6 (1992): 331–43.

Watson, Nicola. *The Literary Tourist* (Basingstoke, Hampshire: Palgrave Macmillan, 2006).

Willis, Irene Cooper. *The Authorship of 'Wuthering Heights'* (London: The Hogarth Press, 1936).

————. *The Brontës* (London: Gerald Duckworth & Co. Ltd, 1933. Reprinted London: Phototype Ltd n/d).

————. *Elizabeth Barrett Browning* (London: Gerald Hove Ltd, 1928).

————. *Florence Nightingale: A Biography* (London: George Unwin Ltd, 1931. Reprinted by Forgotten Books, 1931).

Winnifrith, Tom. 'The Background to Sir James Stephen's Letter.' *Brontë Society Transactions* 21, no. 4 (1994): 151–53.

————. Birstall Letters. *Brontë Society Transactions* 21, no. 5 (1994): 187–91.

————. Appendix A: 'The Birstall Letters.' In *The Brontës and Their Background: Romance and Reality* (London and Basingstoke: The Macmillan Press Ltd, 1973).

Wood, Butler. (ed.). *Charlotte Brontë 1816–1916: A Centenary Memorial* (London: T. Fisher Unwin, 1917).

Woolf, Leonard. *Beginning Again: An Autobiography of the Years 1911 to 1918* (London: The Hogarth Press, 1964).

————. *Downhill All the Way: An Autobiography of the Years 1919 to 1939* (London: The Hogarth Press: 1975).

Woolf Studies Annual, Volume 3 (New York: Pace University Press, 1997).

————. Volume 6. (New York: Pace University Press, 2000).

————. Volume 12. (New York: Pace University Press, 2006).

————. Volume 24. (New York: Pace University Press, 2018).

Woolf, Virginia. *The Cambridge Edition of 'The Years'* (Cambridge: CUP, 2012)

————. *The Complete Shorter Fiction*, edited by Susan Dick (Ithaca, UK, and London: Cornell University Press, 1985).

————. *The Essays of Virginia Woolf*, edited by Andrew McNeillie (volumes 1–4) and Stuart N. Clarke (volumes 5–6) (London: The Hogarth Press, 1897–2011).

————, Vanessa Bell with Thoby Stephen, *Hyde Park Gate News: The Stephen Family Newspaper*, foreword by Hermione Lee. Edited by Gill Lowe (London: Hesperus Press Limited, 2005).

————. *Jacob's Room*. The Cambridge Edition of *Jacob's Room*, edited by Stuart N. Clarke and Susan Sellers (Cambridge: CUP, 2020).

————. *Hyde Park Gate News: The Stephen Family Newspaper*. Virginia Woolf, Vanessa Bell, with Thoby Stephen (London: Hesperus Press Limited, 2005).

————. *To the Lighthouse* (Oxford: OUP, 2000 [1927]).

————. 'A Mark on the Wall.' In *The Complete Shorter Fiction of Virginia Woolf*, edited by Susan Dick (New York: A Harvest Book Harcourt Inc., 1989).

————. 'Memoirs of a Novelist.' In *The Complete Shorter Fiction of Virginia Woolf*, edited by Susan Dick (New York: A Harvest Book Harcourt Inc., 1989).

————. *Moments of Being: A Collection of Autobiographical Writing*, edited by Jeanne Schulkind (London: The Hogarth Press, 1985).

————. *Mrs Dalloway* (Oxford: OUP, 2000).

————. *Night and Day* (London: Penguin Group, 1992 [1919]).

————. 'Old Bloomsbury.' In *Moments of Being: A Collection of Autobiographical Writing*, edited by Jeanne Schulkind (London: The Hogarth Press, 1985).

————. *Orlando* (Oxford: OUP, 2000 [1928]).

————. *The Pargiters: The Novel-Essay Portion of The Years*, edited by Mitchell A. Leaska (London: The Hogarth Press, 1978).

————. *A Passionate Apprentice: The Early Journals 1897–1909*, edited by Mitchell A. Leaska (San Diego, CA; New York; London: Harcourt Brace Jovanovich, 1990).

————. 'Reminiscences.' In *Moments of Being: A Collection of Autobiographical Writing*, edited by Jeanne Schulkind (London: The Hogarth Press, 1985).

————. *A Room of One's Own* (St Albans, Herts, UK: Triad/Panther Books, 1977 [1929]).

————. 'A Sketch of the Past.' In *Moments of Being: A Collection of Autobiographical Writing*, edited by Jeanne Schulkind (London: The Hogarth Press, 1985).

————. 'A Society.' In *The Complete Shorter Fiction of Virginia Woolf*, edited by Susan Dick (New York: A Harvest Book Harcourt Inc., 1989).

————. *Three Guineas*. In *A Room of One's Own/Three Guineas* (London: Penguin Books, 2000).

————. *The Voyage Out* (Oxford: OUP, 2009 [1915]).

————. *The Widow and the Parrot*. Afterword by Quentin Bell (San Diego; New York; London: Harcourt Brace Jovanovich, 1988).

————. *The Years* (Oxford: OUP, 2000).

Women and Fiction: The Manuscripts of 'A Room of One's Own,' edited by S. P. Rosenbaum (Oxford: Blackwell Publishers, 1992).

"Women Must Weep—Or Unite Against War." *Atlantic Monthly* (June 1938).

Woolmer, J. Howard. *A Checklist of the Hogarth Press: 1917–1946* (Revere, PA: Woolmer Brotherson Ltd, 1986).

Wright, Sharon. *Mother of the Brontës* (Yorkshire - Philadelphia: Pen and Sword Books Ltd, 2019).

Index

About the Author

Hilary Newman is an independent scholar and was educated at Hollyfield School in Surbiton, Surrey, and at Goldsmiths' College, London University. She holds a first-class degree in English literature and an MPhil degree on Virginia Woolf. Over a period of several decades, Newman has published numerous articles on a variety of eighteenth- and nineteenth-century authors, including Frances Burney, Charles and Mary Lamb, and William Morris. She has been a life member of the Brontë Society since 1984 and has spent many annual holidays in Haworth and the surrounding area with her late husband. She has been a member of the Virginia Woolf Society of Great Britain since 1999 and has repeatedly published in the journals of both these societies.

Milton Keynes UK
Ingram Content Group UK Ltd.
UKHW020620140524
442502UK00002B/10

9 781666 940220